Truth and Tradition
in Chinese Buddhism

THE SLEEPING BUDDHA, WESTERN HILLS, PEIPING

Photo by White

Truth and Tradition in Chinese Buddhism
A Study of Chinese Mahayana Buddhism

Karl Ludvig Reichelt

Translated from the Norwegian by
Kathrina Van Wagenen Bugge

**Munshiram Manoharlal
Publishers Pvt. Ltd.**

ISBN 81-215-1000-7
This edition 2001
Originally published in 1928
Published with the permission of the original publisher
© 2001, Munshiram Manoharlal Publishers Pvt. Ltd., New Delhi

All rights reserved, including those of translation into foreign languages.
No part of this book may be reproduced, stored in a retrieval system, or transmitted in any form, or by any means, electronic, mechanical, photocopying, recording, or otherwise, without the written permission of the publisher.

Printed and published by
Munshiram Manoharlal Publishers Pvt. Ltd.,
Post Box 5715, 54 Rani Jhansi Road,
New Delhi 110 055.

"Fecisti nos ad te, Domine;
et inquietum est cor nostrum,
donec requiescat in te."
—*St. Augustine.*

To

ARCHBISHOP NATHAN SÖDERBLOM

IN GRATITUDE FOR HIS BRILLIANT
CONTRIBUTION TO THE STUDY OF
THE HISTORY OF RELIGION

TO

ARCHBISHOP NATHAN SÖDERBLOM

A TRAILBLAZER FOR BRILLIANT
CONTRIBUTIONS TO THE STUDY OF
THE HISTORY OF RELIGION

PREFACE

When the Jesuits first came into contact with Buddhism in Japan, in the sixteenth century they wrote of it as the work of the devil, who in it had cleverly imitated many things in the Roman ritual and was even deceiving men by adopting the Lutheran heresy of salvation by faith. Modern missionaries, on the other hand, have been inclined to account for apparently Christian elements in Buddhism by ascribing them to direct as well as indirect influences of Christianity itself. Others point to these similarities as evidence of tendencies not uncommonly found in the development of historic religions. In this book we have the work of neither the partisan adversary nor the partisan advocate, nor yet of a cold and scholarly but personally indifferent (and quite objective) student of the history of religions. The author has indeed supplemented his long and intimate personal observations and studies of Buddhism in China by scholarly and exacting study of original Buddhist texts and the published works of other Western students in this field; but his chief claim on our gratitude is his illuminating appreciation of what is best and even of much which at first sight seems hopelessly superstitious and corrupt in this ancient and prolific faith.

I believe the Christian church in China is ready to welcome this sympathetic presentation of the truth and traditions in Chinese Buddhism. Doubtless others will also give this work a warm welcome, for it abounds in fascinating descriptions of what many take to be meaningless ceremonies and brilliant suggestions as to the results of possible or actual contacts between Christianity and Buddhism during the twelve hundred years since they first met on Chinese soil. But its supreme service will be to Christian missionaries from the West. I write as one of these. We need just this kind of sympathetic and thorough presentation of the main points in Chinese Mahayana Buddhism, both as a background for understanding the great "culture land" of China to which we have

PREFACE

come, and also as an essential preparation in trying to meet the growing number of Chinese who feel the attraction and power of historic Buddhism in their own land. Such Chinese are to be found in the Christian church as well as outside. Intelligent sympathy and constructive thinking as well as unselfish devotion of life are necessary in any attempt to help build a spiritual home for the Chinese people of the present and the future.

In this book we find an impressive account of the long and rich history of Buddhism in China, and can hardly fail to see why thoughtful Buddhists, even those who are friendly to Christianity, while they concede the superiority of Christianity in practical good works, yet find Buddhism incomparable in its philosophy.

Again, we find here illuminating interpretations of everyday matters, temples, idols, names and phrases the real significance of which is so often overlaid by the squalor and neglect which spring from pitiful poverty, and by grossly ignorant superstitions. A flood of light is thrown into the darkness by the comment that "when a man is in earnest about the prayer," "Nan-mo O-mi-t'o Fu," it means that his conscience is in control of his life.

In particular, this book helps us to find a way through the tangled confusion which besets Buddhism by setting in relief the great ideas and heroisms which centre around the vows of Amida and the bodhisattvas for the "salvation of all living beings."

True it is, as an honest reader must agree with this book in affirming that if one wishes to understand China he must see it in the light of Buddhism. I think we can say yet more. We are learning that self-knowledge in the individual grows chiefly through intercourse with his fellows, and that the principle involved in this fact applies also to nations. I believe we can hardly fail to see from this study, even if we have not seen it before, that deeper knowledge of its own surpassing inheritance will come to Christianity from such intercourse as this book records and invites between itself and Buddhism.

LOGAN HERBERT ROOTS.

HANKOW.

AUTHOR'S PREFACE

The basis for this book is the series of addresses which the author delivered, by invitation, in the Scandinavian Universities during the spring of 1921.

In Uppsala the lectures were arranged for by the Olaus Petri Foundation, and it was further arranged that this honourable institution should be responsible for the publication of the lectures in book form.

This has been done, and the book has been issued in Sweden, published in Denmark, and presents itself in the garb of the Norwegian language. That we have in this way been able to put into practice "practical Scandinavianism" has given me no little pleasure, and I use this opportunity to present my hearty thanks to those men who have taken the lead in this matter. In the first rank of these stands Archbishop Söderblom.

At the time that the material was to be prepared in book form, it became immediately clear to me that I ought to treat the subject more fully. I felt that all that was essential must be included. I have therefore tried to give as complete a picture as possible of the different sides of Chinese Mahayana Buddhism.

This religion which, especially in later years, has manifested itself to be a living religion, and in a thousand ways exercises its influence over the life of the Orient, is pressing more and more into the foreground. It is therefore possible that this work, which is in a way the result of twenty years of study on the spot, may be considered of some interest.

In addition to a study of the sources in China and quite extensive travelling round about to the monasteries, the holy mountains, etc., I have also tried to consult all the better known works, both old and new, dealing with our subject, written in the various European languages.

Of the very greatest importance also has been the really intimate intercourse which I have had the privilege of enjoying with a number of the best and most learned monks and lay devotees in the various Buddhist centres in China. How I should like to be able to reach them also with my thanks,—the many noble and learned men, who, with illuminating tolerance and true religious zeal, have given me, through discussion and common study, unforgettable fleeting glimpses into the strange vasts of Mahayana's still undiscovered territory.

KARL LUDVIG REICHELT.

AUTHOR'S PREFACE TO THE ENGLISH EDITION

The Committee on Work among Buddhists appointed by the National Christian Council of China and many other Western students have made the request that this book should be translated into English.

The need of a reference book on Chinese Mahayana Buddhism, giving in a condensed form all the essential material and the most important technical terms in Chinese, has long been felt.

In the opinion of the committee mentioned above the book "Fra Östens Religiöse Liv," already used in Scandinavia for a few years, fairly well meets this need. So this book now appears in English dress, in places somewhat reduced, in others considerably enlarged, everywhere corrected according to the results of the latest investigations.

Hearty thanks are due to Mrs. Kathrina Van Wagenen Bugge, who took upon her the burdensome task of translating the book. This work she did very faithfully, and to the final result Mrs. H. T. Hodgkin contributed not a little by a careful revision of the manuscript.

Mrs. Hodgkin has also undertaken the onerous work of proof reading and the compilation of the index. For all this I extend to her my very hearty thanks.

I also feel very much indebted to my dear colleague, Mr. N. N. Thelle, for typing the manuscript.

KARL LUDVIG REICHELT.

CHING SHAN FENG, NANKING,
    JANUARY 31, 1927.

CONTENTS

CHAPTER		PAGE
	INTRODUCTION	1
I.	THE INTRODUCTION OF BUDDHISM INTO CHINA AND ITS HISTORY THERE	9
II.	THE INNER DEVELOPMENT OF CHINESE BUDDHISM DURING THE EARLY CENTURIES	26
III.	"THE JOURNEY TO THE WEST"	63
IV.	"THE ORIGIN AND DEVELOPMENT OF MASSES FOR THE DEAD"	77
V.	THE "PURE LAND" SCHOOL (CHINGT'U, 淨土)	127
VI.	THE BUDDHIST PANTHEON IN CHINA	171
VII.	BUDDHIST LITERATURE IN CHINA	203
VIII.	MONASTIC LIFE	228
IX.	PILGRIMAGES	284
X.	PRESENT-DAY BUDDHISM IN CHINA	298

LIST OF ILLUSTRATIONS

	FACING PAGE
THE SLEEPING BUDDHA	*Frontispiece*
BUDDHA'S FOOTPRINTS	11
GENERAL VIEW OF GOLDEN ISLAND	23
SAKYAMUNI	39
THE NESTORIAN TABLET	77
MI-LO FU	87
VAIROCANA	105
TI-TS'ANG	117
ENTRANCE TO CHAN-YUN MONASTERY	129
AN ANCIENT, FAMOUS PICTURE OF KWAN-YIN, BLESSING HER ACOLYTE (善財童子)	135
THE TYPICAL PICTURE OF AMITABHA	140
EAST WALL, YÜIN-KANG	143
GENERAL VIEW AROUND THE GREAT BUDDHA, YÜIN-KANG	155
BUDDHA PREACHING AT LING SHAN	169
MIAO-SHAN REFUSING TO MARRY	183
BUDDHIST TRINITY	193
LO-HAN T'ANG	209
ATTENDANT BODHISATTVA	221
GENERAL VIEW OF YUN-YEN MONASTERY	235
CHAI-T'AI MONASTERY	249
DODECAHEDRAL PAGODA, SUNG YU MONASTERY	261
FA-YU TEMPLE, P'UT'O	273
KUAN-YIN	287
LOCHANA	299
BODHIDHARMA	309

TRUTH AND TRADITION IN CHINESE BUDDHISM

INTRODUCTION

As the title of the book indicates, it will be our object to present the nature and history of Mahayana Buddhism as that history has been evolved on Chinese soil, and as it unfolds itself according to its own nature in the present-day life of this great culture-land of the Far East.

We have, therefore, taken as a motto for the entire book that great dominating saying which incontestably has become the principal thought of the Chinese Mahayana, "The salvation of all living things" (P'u chi chung shêng, 普濟衆生).

Mahayana Buddhism, or, in other words, the Buddhism of the Great Vehicle, has, in recent years, attracted to itself by its very massiveness the increasing attention of investigators. This interest is due not merely to its tremendous thought-structures and systems, and its highly developed apparatus of worship, which give it a special position in the life of the East, but also to the fact that it meets, in a most remarkable manner, many of the great religious cravings of life which men in all times and all places feel more or less consciously.

TRUTH AND TRADITION IN BUDDHISM

It is not without significance that it is Mahayana and Christianity which just at the present time gather to themselves the greater number of the religious "élite" of the East, for, as is well known, there are many points of similarity between these two religions. We should, therefore, fail in our purpose if we did not here take up this relationship for further investigation.

Hinayana, also the Buddhism of the Little Vehicle, (that is to say, the original Indian Buddhism) offers a great many points of likeness in form to Christianity; but one must say of these that, for the most part, they are of an accidental nature, have arisen under similar psychological conditions, or point back to a common possession from earlier periods in the history of the race.

It is quite otherwise with Mahayana (Ta Ch'êng, 大乘), with its striking cult of the trinity, its strong emphasis on faith as the saving fact, and on the great new birth which brings man into the "Western Paradise" (Hsi-fang Chi Lo Shih Chieh, 西方極樂世界) where the great merciful father of all reigns—he who has sent the "Mightiest One" (Ta-shih-chih, 大勢至) down to earth in human form, and who now with "his gracious spirit" (Kuan-yin, 觀音) draws men to himself.

We shall have opportunity to see all these and many other points of similarity as, little by little, we present the systems and ideas by means of quotations from literature and historical surveys. We mention the fact here merely to show how natural and

[2]

INTRODUCTION

explicable is the intense interest which in the last few decades has been seen among sinologues who have treated of thèse things. Occasionally, indeed, this interest has driven some investigators to too hasty conclusions, since they have proclaimed results before the lines of connection were entirely uncovered. The whole subject has, for this reason, come into considerable disrepute; but the dissatisfaction will vanish, and, indeed, is already beginning to vanish before the honest and laborious research work which is now being carried on according to the best scientific methods, and which has already produced significant results.

It is clear that specialists from the different countries of Asia must work together for this: sinologues who from China, Mahayana's second motherland in the Far East, can make comparisons with Buddhism's fresh spiritual advances in Japan; men who can explore the ancient monastic libraries of Korea, and push into the dim culture of Tibet and Mongolia; Indiologues who, from the ancient Pali and Sanskrit texts and the corrupt Mahayana systems of the boundary lands, can trace out the lines of thought and connections which point toward the West; Persiologues who can untangle the fine spiritual threads which knit ancient Iran, Persia, and Mesopotamia to Asia Minor and the kingdom of Greece on the west and to India on the east. But perhaps the greatest need is for men with large vision and a sane judgment, who can bind the whole together in a harmonious and scientifically justifiable manner.

TRUTH AND TRADITION IN BUDDHISM

As we shall see later, it has been proved beyond all doubt that certain of the countries here named very early received quite direct influences from Western Christianity, and this is evident in the moulding of the Mahayana doctrines. This is very probably the case with Nestorianism in China. On this we shall later have occasion to make a few remarks.

China must quite naturally play a leading rôle when the nature and activities of Mahayana Buddhism are to be investigated. From China Buddhism spread both to Korea and Japan. Here the great schools, or sects, were formed. Here, also, the new Tripitaka canon, which represents Mahayana, took shape. And finally here, in spite of all local shades of difference, one finds the purest form of Mahayana.

It is quite otherwise in Tibet and Nepal, where the coarsest demon worship and animism throw an almost impenetrable veil over Mahayana Buddhism's fine lines of thought.

No wonder that interest is more and more centred in China and Japan, and that students begin to take up the study of Mahayana in these lands as a separate religious form which deserves its own independent treatment. It is indeed high time that it were so. It has been long enough the case that to study Buddhism meant chiefly to immerse oneself in the original Indian Buddhism (Hinayana; Chinese: Hsiao Ch'êng, 小乘). In contrast to Mahayana this was called the "higher," or the genuine, while Mahayana was often looked upon as a corrupt variation, a less worthy religious form, which one could dismiss with a few general

INTRODUCTION

remarks. But times have changed. One has had to face the fact that the original Buddhism did not succeed in maintaining itself as a universal religion even within the boundaries of India. On the other hand, Mahayana, enriched and fructified by the deepest and highest currents of spiritual thought from the West and the East, has in quite a remarkable manner understood how to gather to itself not merely the indifferent masses in a more or less mechanical worship, but has also shown that it has been able to give to more deeply religious souls, the most highly cultured people of the East, some draughts from the universal springs of the life of God. It has become a living religion.

We have named especially China and Japan. Nowhere else has Mahayana so stirred the hearts of men or produced more beautiful flowers of thought. It is in these countries, too, that the title the "Higher Buddhism" has come to be used of Mahayana, a fact which may be somewhat bewildering to those who are accustomed to give that name to the original Indian Buddhism. But the name originated with the Chinese Buddhists themselves, who, in their ordination, first go through the "lower stage" (Hinayana) and afterwards are consecrated to the "higher stage" (Mahayana).[1]

One hears occasionally that Buddhism in the Far East is a decadent religion. This is not the case. On the contrary, a noticeable advance can be traced in

[1] Cf. Archbishop Söderblom's "Kompendium der Religions-geschichte," p. 265.

TRUTH AND TRADITION IN BUDDHISM

recent years. This advance has its deepest springs in the purest form of the higher Buddhism, that form which in so many ways reminds one of Christianity — the "Pure Land" School (Chingt'u, 淨土). We cannot, therefore, avoid devoting special attention to this particular form of Mahayana.

It is clear that a conscientious and serious consideration of these things will make necessary a new orientation towards the work of Christian missions. For some it may mean a complete revolution of thought with regard to missions and the attitude toward non-Christian peoples, especially those of higher culture. Nevertheless, the sooner this revolution comes the better for themselves and for God's world.

For others it will not mean a revolution, but only a clearer understanding of that which they have theoretically known and professed for many years. It will merely emphasize those profound words from our New Testament concerning God who "left not Himself without witness,"[1] "but in every nation he that feareth Him, and worketh righteousness, is accepted with Him";[2] the God who "made of one blood all nations of men for to dwell on all the face of the earth; . . . that they should seek the Lord, if haply they might feel after Him, and find Him."[3] These people will consider it an honour and a privilege to discover with St. Paul, the great foreign missionary, the "altar . . . to the unknown God,"[4] and, from among the great confusion of writings and systems, to seek out pearls of deep spiritual inspiration, such as the famous saying,

[1] Acts 14:17. [2] Acts 10:35. [3] Acts 17:26, 27. [4] Acts 17:23.

INTRODUCTION

"For we are also His offspring,"[1] quoted by St. Paul from one of the Greek poets.[2]

If one once surrenders oneself to this point of view about God's world and His marvellous leading of the races of men in order to gather them into the eternal kingdom of God through Christ, then it may happen that the new orientation of thought will be a source of the greatest blessing, that God Himself will become greater in one's thoughts, and that man's existence will be seen in a truer perspective. The whole will then work together as a positive missionary motive of the highest order.

A very special spiritual enrichment will be our portion if we enter upon a closer investigation of our present subject with this wider viewpoint. In numberless ways it will be shown how the innermost lines of thought in Chinese Mahayana Buddhism all lead out to that great thought about one universal saviour who is dimly perceived, and who, it is hoped, will offer the great response to all longings and ideals. If ever Justin Martyr's famous saying about Christ as "Logos Spermaticos" (the Word which, like the seed-germ, lies behind the religious systems of salvation) has had its application, it is surely here. But, if this is so, we are standing on holy ground. There will therefore be no question, either, of winning over Buddhism in China in any outward manner, but rather of winning Buddhists from within, so that they, in their own peculiar way, may move into Christ's great temple,

[1] Acts 17:28. [2] Aratus or Cleanthes.

and take their place there as gleaming jewels in His crown.

"Think not that I came to destroy the law, or the prophets: I came not to destroy, but to fulfil."[1]

[1] Matt. 5:17.

CHAPTER I

THE INTRODUCTION OF BUDDHISM INTO CHINA AND ITS HISTORY THERE

Buddhism began its propaganda in China openly about the year A.D. 61 after the Emperor Ming had had his famous dream; but, long before that, the ground had been prepared through fantastic legends and communications from China's neighbours on the west. There were many circumstances which worked together to pave the way for the new religion.

In the first place, the right religious conditions were present. Confucianism, with its clearly thought-out system of morals, had never succeeded in satisfying the deeper religious needs of the Chinese and, after that system became a state religion, it was felt more and more as a burdensome yoke. It gave no answer to the deepest questions of existence; it gave neither strength for the battle of life nor comfort in the hour of death.

On the other hand, Taoism had, to a high degree, awakened the desire for religious speculation. Hearts were turned to something undefined, something that could fill life and eternity with light and hope. By Taoism itself it was darkly hinted that this "something" was to come from the distant wonderlands of the West. Marvellous legends came from "T'ien-chu" (天竺, the old name for India), and lands lying still farther west.

TRUTH AND TRADITION IN BUDDHISM

In the second place, China acquired a real knowledge of India, of her strong and peculiar religious life, through the trade caravans that began to pass between the two countries.

During the reign of the Emperor Wu of the Han dynasty (140–86 B.C.), the Chinese traveller, Chang Chien, was sent to China's western and southern boundaries to deal with the tribes there. It seems that, on one of these journeys, he went as far as Parthia, where, at that time, Mithridates II was king. From that journey Chang Chien brought back with him to the Chinese court an account of Buddha's golden statue. This man, who had sat in prison for ten years among the Turks of eastern Asia, seems to have been among the first Chinese who knew the name of Buddha. Others, also, who were connected with the trade caravans little by little got hold of the strange legend of a mystical holy one in the neighbouring countries. Later on, Buddhist literature began imperceptibly to sift in over the borders, and, about the year A.D. 60, there was, among various circles in China, a certain acquaintance with Buddhism.[1]

---

[1] Of more doubtful nature is the account given by the old Buddhist monk, Tao-shih (道 世), in his historical work "Fa-yüan Chu Lin" (法 苑 珠 林), in the year A.D. 668. He recounts that, as early as 217 B.C., a monk from India, with the Chinese name of Li fang (利 防), came over to Sianfu with seventeen other "brothers." There they were imprisoned by the authorities, but later set free in a miraculous manner.

The same author believes that a great many writings had already been translated before the Ch in dynasty in China, but that these writings were burned. This last statement particularly makes the whole matter highly improbable, for, at that time, the Buddhist writings were scarcely completed and collected in India itself.

That which makes the question of China's first connection with Buddhism very difficult to decide is the fact that the greatest Chinese historian, Ssu-ma Chien, mentions nothing about these things, in spite of the fact that he lived

BUDDHA'S FOOTPRINTS

INTRODUCTION INTO CHINA

When, therefore, in the year A.D. 61, the Emperor Ming had his dream or vision, one of his ministers, Fu-yih, could immediately refer the emperor to the Indian deity, Buddha.

The dream was as follows: A huge golden figure came flying down from heaven. It halted in its course just over the emperor's palace. Here it swayed gently back and forth. The head was surrounded with a radiant light (hua-kuang, 華光), and the light of the moon and the sun fell upon its body. The emperor was greatly terrified, but, on Fu-yih's assurance that the whole thing was only a reflection of the radiant Buddha in India, he was quieted.

Prompted by his strange experience, the Emperor Ming sent a deputation to seek further information about this deity. The deputation consisted of eighteen men, who left the capital, Loyang (the present Honanfu), in the year A.D. 63, tracing their route across Central Asia. They finally reached Khotan, and from there travelled down to that part of north-east India which had shortly before been conquered by the "white Huns," Vagjis (Yüeh-chih, 月氏). Without great difficulty, they proceeded farther, and, within a short time, we find them in Magadha, south of the Ganges.

This place was a treasury of Buddhist relics and literature. The deputation succeeded in getting possession of a part of this treasure. Taking with them two Buddhist scholars (priests), they proceeded on the homeward journey. About the year A.D. 67, they

from 145 to 86 B.C. also that there is no hint found in the history of the Western Han dynasty written by the other great historian, Pan Ku.

[11]

reached China's capital city, Loyang. The relics and sacred writings had been loaded on white horses, and, for this reason, the first temple that was built in Loyang received the name of Pai-ma Ssŭ (白馬寺), the "White Horse Temple," a temple name adopted later all over China.

The two priests who had been brought from India were Kasyapa Matanga (Chinese: Shê-mo-têng, 攝摩騰) and Gobharana (Chinese: Chu-fa-lan, 竺法蘭). The former died quite soon after his arrival. The latter attained the age of sixty years in China, and did a very important work there.

Among the first books which these priests translated may be mentioned a freely remodelled and abbreviated text of Asvaghosha's work on the life of Buddha ("Buddha Charita Kavya"). There is an account, on the whole correct, given in five chapters, of Buddha's life as we know it from the Indian sources. Thus began the invading stream of Buddhist monks from India to China, which continued for over seven hundred years, and which became of such great significance to the "Middle Kingdom."

It is interesting to see how, during the first two hundred years, the immigrant monks held positions of leadership, and to note how the responsibility and administration little by little went entirely over into Chinese hands. Only when that took place did the great increase come. Then Buddhism became nationally established in China.

But China will never forget these first immigrant Buddhist missionaries, who so faithfully and ably went

INTRODUCTION INTO CHINA

forward with the difficult work of translation and organization, and who threw themselves into the work of propaganda so completely and whole-heartedly. When one now goes through the enormous mass of Buddhist writings translated and prepared by these pilgrims from India, and written in the highest and finest style by the old Chinese literati, one cannot but be filled with deep wonder and respect.

There is, however, another side which is, if possible, still more striking. Attention must be called to the *spiritual influence* which these representatives of the most intense religious life of the Aryan race have exercised upon the rather cold and calculating character of the Mongol people.

The Indian monks—who moved about in the first temples in China, sat in cells and carefully copied out sutras, went to their simple vegetarian meals and to the regular services—were deeply religious men, for whom the absorption into the absolute was life's main task. It came as a revelation; it was the "doctrine" or the "law," as it is called in the Buddhist phraseology, transposed into living human form. Little by little the cold hearts of the Mongols thawed, and, through this personal influence, that best type among the Chinese monks, that type of holy dignity combined with nobility of character which, since then, has stood before the Chinese Buddhists as the great ideal, and which, in individual cases, has been attained and put into effect in life by a very few, was created.

We shall come back to these Indian translators when we take up the subject of Buddhist literature in China.

[13]

TRUTH AND TRADITION IN BUDDHISM

The first three hundred years after the introduction of Buddhism into China are marked by rest and deep religious seeking. One therefore need not be surprised over the fact that the new religion, protected by the royal house, well prepared for by Taoism, and itself provided with all that splendid machinery of worship which only India's glowing spirituality could create, advanced along the whole line, steadily and surely, though not yet at double-quick pace.

Buddhism had especial success among the states which sprang up rapidly in the fourth and fifth centuries. Thus the people of Chihli and Shansi, under the later Chou dynasty in A.D. 333, received permission to take the vows and become monks. It was not long, then, before the country was swarming with monks and nuns. In the capital, Loyang, no less than forty-two monasteries, with their adjoining temples and pagodas, were built. In 381 A.D. nine-tenths of the people of north-west China were adherents of Buddhism. Both the "Eastern Chin dynasty" and the "Later Chin" (Hou Chin) supported the new faith most strongly. Indeed, the Emperor Hsiao Wu Ti (373–397) himself became a Buddhist.

After the fall of the Chin dynasty in 420, a period of affliction and persecution for Buddhism began. Both the Mongol dynasty of Wei in the north, and the Chinese Sung dynasty in the south were at one in their policy of persecution; for any religion favoured by the enemy is always suspect, and must be combated. This rule has consistently been carried out in China.

INTRODUCTION INTO CHINA

In A.D. 426 an edict was issued by the powers in the north to the effect that all Buddhist images and writings should be destroyed and the priests killed. Many Buddhist monks lost their lives, and much valuable literature was consumed by the flames. But with this it seemed as if the fury of the storm of opposition had spent itself. When it became evident that Buddhism had great power among the common people, the successor to the throne was diplomatic enough to revoke the edict in A.D. 451; and, in order to make amends, if possible, he later made a figure of Buddha in copper, fifty feet in height, and had it overlaid thickly with gold. It was also arranged that every city might build a monastery, and that fifty of the city's inhabitants should be allowed to "take the vows."

One of the later rulers, Hsiao Wu Ti, abdicated, in order to be free to study Buddhism. This was in A.D. 471. No wonder that, about the year A.D. 530, there were thirteen thousand temples in northern China alone.

Under the later emperors of the Sung dynasty in central and southern China, there was a more friendly attitude towards Buddhism. The literati, indeed, tried to keep up the opposition, but the people, who had already acquired a taste for the religious values which Buddhism brought with it, decided in favour of the new religion.

Among the best known of the emperors who, during this period, paid homage to Buddhism must be named Ming Ti (A.D. 465–473). He erected an enormously

TRUTH AND TRADITION IN BUDDHISM

expensive monastery in Hunan; this act gave rise to a sharp conflict with his ministers.

Still better known is Liang Wu Ti (502–550), who devoted himself with quite unprecedented zeal to the study of Buddhism. The most remarkable thing about him was that, besides this, he also sought in his government and in his private life to practise the best of Mahayana Buddhism's teachings. He is therefore called "China's Asoka." It was during his reign that the famous Bodhidharma (P'u-t'i-ta-mo, 菩提達摩), the twenty-eighth patriarch from Buddha in India and the first on Chinese soil, came to China (A.D. 527). He settled down in Nanking for a time; but, as Liang Wu Ti had not sufficient appreciation of the value of meditation, he left him and betook himself to Loyang, the capital of the northern dynasty. We shall speak later of his importance in the development of Chinese Buddhism.

Among Liang Wu Ti's building achievements may be mentioned the monastery of Ch'ang Ts'ien, in the neighbourhood of Nanking, where a shrine containing relics of Asoka was erected.

Among the later dynasties may be named the Ch'en dynasty, whose first emperor retired to a monastery after four years of rule in order to carry on a study of Buddhism. Under the Sui dynasty, a great deal of literary work was done among the Buddhists. During the years between A.D. 594 and 616, no less than three collections of Tripitaka were produced.

Finally, we have the period of the Tang dynasty. The first emperors were unfavourably disposed to

INTRODUCTION INTO CHINA

Buddhism to such an extent that severe persecution broke out during the reign of Kao Tsu. This persecution is connected with the name of Fu-yih, a minister, who sent in a complaint against the Buddhist society on the following grounds: the Buddhist monks and nuns, by their celibacy, consume the strength of society. They are unproductive individuals, who reduce the national wealth. This truly Confucian complaint found favour with the emperor, and strict rules were formulated to restrain access to the monasteries. It is said that under Hsüan Tsung, one of the later emperors, twelve thousand monks were forced back into civil life.

Later, a long period of prosperity had its beginning under this same emperor, who came to another way of thinking during his later years. Thus Tripitaka was once more issued under his auspices in the year A.D. 730. Now for a century and a half Buddhism had peace, broken only by a short period of persecution under Wu Tsung (844–847). The latter half of the eighth century was especially significant. The bulk of the common people devoted themselves with enthusiasm to the worship; the imperial house was filled with reverence for the tremendous system of thought and machinery of worship that stretched so wide and gave such hope for both the living and the dead.

The Emperor Su Tsung had a Buddhist temple in his palace, and permitted his eunuchs and his guard to dress in Buddhist costume; and his successor, Tai Tsung (763–780) was himself quite an able interpreter of the holy sutras. When his mother died, he selected

TRUTH AND TRADITION IN BUDDHISM

a thousand monks and nuns to say masses, not only at the time of the funeral but also every year, on the fifteenth of the seventh month. It is probable that the "Spirit Festival" (K'uei Chieh, 鬼 節) has a certain connection with this, though other things also may have had a bearing on it.

It was during this period, also, that one of Buddha's bones, which had been purchased in India, was brought into the capital with enormous pomp and splendour. This was under the Emperor Hsien Tsung (A.D. 819). It was on this occasion that the minister Han-yu sent in his famous protest, and, as a consequence, was degraded. He narrowly escaped with his life.

Persecution broke out again, however, and it was even worse than before. Just at this time there was great rivalry between the Buddhists and the Taoists. Several times it had come to the point of public disputations or wonder-working tests. As is usual in such cases, both parties claimed the victory.

The Taoists then had recourse to intrigue. They succeeded in convincing the Emperor Wu Tsung, a Taoist sympathizer, that Buddhism was dangerous to the imperial power, for it outshone even the "dragon throne" in its brilliance. As a consequence of this, he issued an edict in A.D. 845, by which "four thousand six hundred monasteries were razed to the ground, forty thousand temples destroyed, and two hundred and sixty thousand monks and nuns forced back into common society."

It is possible that this report is exaggerated; but it is certain that Buddhism never fully recovered from

INTRODUCTION INTO CHINA

this blow. History adds that, two years later, the emperor was taken ill because of all the Taoist "medicine of life" which he had drunk. He was so far through that he became dumb. In consequence, the edict was revoked, with the provision that only a limited number of monks might, by special permission, "take the vows."

In the succeeding centuries Buddhism was a *tolerated* religion; but, even under these conditions, it made its influence strongly felt. This is seen not least in the art of the time. The Buddhists were very clever in the art of printing. One can still go into monasteries in China where tremendous quantities of wood-blocks engraved with block-type are piled up. Under the Emperor Jên Tsung, fifty young monks were selected for special study of Sanskrit (1035).

The last great game of intrigue, set going by the Taoists under their protector, Hui Tsung, failed completely in its work.

Under Kublai Khan, Buddhism took a decided forward step; to such an extent was this true that statistics give the number of temples at that time as forty-two thousand, and the number of monks as two hundred and fifteen thousand.

In the years just following, we see that Buddhism was very strongly influenced by Lamaism from Tibet and Mongolia. This circumstance must account for the strong attempt which was repeatedly made to establish a secular order—a lower order of Buddhist clergy who could live in matrimony. This was, in fact, done, and one can find traces of it far down

TRUTH AND TRADITION IN BUDDHISM

through the years. Lamaism, both in its sculpture and its practice, has, indeed, often played upon this string. Not only in Tibet and Mongolia can one, at the present time, find pictures and statues which, for very good reasons, are covered with a curtain, but even in certain sections of China; and in the Lama temple in Peking, the same thing may be seen.

In order not to misjudge this, one must always remember that the motive is not to represent licentious art, but to make a quiet appeal to Buddhism's friends to remember that the reproduction of life is and will be one of the chief tasks for human society. Such an appeal might be needed in Tibet, where so large a percentage of the population go into the monasteries; but in China, with its abounding vitality, it is quite unnecessary.

The changing conditions for Buddhism continued also under the Ming dynasty; but, on the whole, the times were more favourable. One of the sovereigns, Wu Tsung by name (1308–1312), a great linguist, who was well acquainted with Sanskrit, did a great deal for the Buddhist church, so that, in his day, the number of monks increased enormously. Under his successor the literati sent in a long complaint asking that the society be suppressed. This, however, only resulted in the closing of the Buddhist chapel in the "Forbidden City." On the other hand, the monasteries on the island of P'ut'o (普陀) were established, and free copies of Tripitaka were distributed all over the empire.

During the later years of the Ming dynasty, Roman Catholic missionaries began their work in earnest in

INTRODUCTION INTO CHINA

China, and a stirring of fresh interest began about the year 1600, when these missionaries made their influence felt.

To begin with, it was noticed how strikingly the outward ritual of these two religions resembled each other. Later, when the "Pure Land" party began to expound more of their doctrinal system, it was seen that there were also points of remarkable similarity in the content of their teaching. This, instead of giving a point of contact, led to rivalry and disagreement, and, unfortunately, neither side was possessed of men so spiritually great that they could, with tact and wisdom, guide to a useful settlement. Thus again a great opportunity for the natural introduction of Christianity to China was missed.

A few Jesuit missionaries did, indeed, later try to make use of some of the points of contact with Buddhism; but this was often done so crudely that their more critical colleagues felt they must protest and dissociate themselves from such methods. This caused a strong reaction—a reaction from which the missionary propaganda of the Catholic Church in China is still suffering. The force of this reaction was partly due to another cause, namely, the unfortunate quarrel which, a little later, developed between the powerful emperor of the Manchu dynasty, K'ang Hsi, and the pope over the designation for God in Chinese. The Jesuits, with great appreciation of the importance of the matter, had adopted the mighty expression "Shang-ti" (上帝) for God, a term in which the loftiest thoughts of the Chinese

TRUTH AND TRADITION IN BUDDHISM

about a supreme god of heaven who grants power to all earthly authorities find their fullest and most majestic expression. The Dominican and the Franciscan monks, who came later, thought that this was inadmissible, and therefore referred the matter to the pope for decision. The Emperor K'ang Hsi, the great linguist, naturally considered that the right of decision should belong to him, and, as he did not get his way, he took revenge by gagging and persecuting the very flourishing Catholic mission — one of the saddest pages in missionary history.

This unfortunate occurrence, as can be understood, has, to a great degree, had an effect on the subject which we are here treating. For it was after that time that the paralyzing papal bull of 1742 was issued by Pope Benedict XIV, the bull which, under threat of the severest punishment, forbade the Catholic missionaries "to make any use whatever of the Chinese ritual." This decision, framed to prevent the wrong use of such ritual, prevents also the legitimate use of points of contact in worship and preaching. While the similarities between the two systems cannot be denied, all is explained by saying that this is another of "Satan's wiles for the seducing of souls."

In other respects, K'ang Hsi, like most of the emperors of the Manchu dynasty, was not merely passive but quite frankly inimical to the Buddhists. Therefore a series of severe edicts against them were drawn up under this dynasty, edicts which have greatly hampered the society and hindered its progress. The decree that each monk may have only one novice

[22]

GENERAL VIEW OF GOLDEN ISLAND, CHINKIANG

INTRODUCTION INTO CHINA

(pupil), that only a selected number of the larger monasteries in each province has the right of ordination, that officials have the right to inspect the monasteries, etc.—all this contributed largely to weaken the movement.

It was still worse when the Revolution broke out and China in 1911 was declared a Republic. In their zeal and eagerness, the Republican leaders, with Huang Hsin and Sun Yat-sen at their head, began to seize temples and monasteries, and to confiscate their property for school purposes, etc. Even the old and venerable Heavenly River Monastery on the Golden Island near Chinkiang, where all the abbots of the larger monasteries go through their severe course of meditation and asceticism—even this holy place was to be transformed into a school. It was not long, however, before public opinion put a stop to this vandalism. The oldest among the monks are also practised diplomatists who know how to make the best of affairs in difficult times. A number gave their lives in order to retain the old sanctuaries. Thus it happened that, while a number of local temples belonging to the other religious societies in China have gone for public use, the Buddhist society saved nearly all its possessions.

As religious freedom has, to some extent, been really established during these last years, it has quite naturally come about that this period has brought more favourable conditions for the Buddhist church. As we shall see later, this renaissance also has other causes of a more innate nature.

TRUTH AND TRADITION IN BUDDHISM

Here we shall merely mention the fact that throughout China, especially in the southern coast provinces, there is developing a feverish activity in the restoration of the old sanctuaries and the preparation of the material facilities for the reception of the great crowds which, during the unrest and disintegration of recent years, are pressing into the monasteries as aspirants for the dignity of monks, or coming as ordinary pilgrims.

In the years before the Revolution, this renaissance was also, in a way, stimulated by Japanese Buddhists. Without doubt there lay much real religious zeal behind this; but, as so often in the history of modern Japan, this was utilized by the leading politicians and militarists to promote the ends of national politics. On this account, it all came to nothing. When, during the war (1915), Japan openly brought forward the two notorious points regarding the work of Buddhist missionaries,[1] it served only to mark outwardly the breach. Nevertheless, no one must believe that this vigorous Buddhism from Japan, such as is represented especially in the Shinran School (Amida School) is hereby permanently cut off from all influence on Chinese Buddhism. When the political excitement

---

[1] The demands were to this effect:
1. Japanese hospitals, churches, and schools in the interior of China should have the right to purchase land on the same basis as Christian missionary institutions.
2. Japanese citizens should be granted the right to carry on Buddhist missionary work on the same basis as Christian missionaries from the West.

Both demands were refused.

INTRODUCTION INTO CHINA

has abated, we shall see that the "mother and daughter church" in the Buddhist world of the orient will find each other again, and undreamed-of results will ensue.

CHAPTER II

THE INNER DEVELOPMENT OF CHINESE BUDDHISM DURING THE EARLY CENTURIES

Having given in the preceding chapter a short account of the outward circumstances of Buddhism in China, we shall now turn to a still more interesting part of our subject, that which aims at disclosing the lines of inner development of this great system of salvation.

There are two things which will very quickly draw our attention: on the one hand, the faithfulness with which China has preserved and carried further the lines of thought which had the peculiar stamp of Indian Mahayana Buddhism; and, on the other hand, the artistic and harmonious manner in which the Buddhists of China have been able to introduce something of the specifically Chinese spiritual element into the system.

It lies beyond the scope of our subject to sketch in detail the radical transformation which took place in Hinayana, the original Indian Buddhism, when it came to China. Already, as early as the time of King Asoka, the narrow atheistic system had begun to break up, although the appellations "Mahayana" and "Hinayana" were first taken into common usage somewhat later.

We learn that, at this time (245 B.C.), a special conference (council) was held in Pataliputra, on the

INNER DEVELOPMENT

Ganges, in those days the capital of India, where only the stricter wing of the monastical orders was assembled. This council, therefore, is not recognized by the Chinese Buddhists. The latter accept only the great general councils: namely, the first, held in Bajagriha, 477 B.C., the year in which Buddha died; the second, in Vaisali, 377 B.C.; and the third, in Jullundur, under King Kanishka, about the year A.D. 100.

The same king, Asoka, identical with Piyadasi, whose name is engraved on the now famous Bairath stone, has, in a very striking manner, let his descendants know the causes which brought about his conversion to Buddhism. Chief of all was the feeling of guilt. (He had carried on bloody wars.) When he himself, through Buddhism, had attained deliverance, he exhorted all to consecrate themselves to "the three great values," Buddha, dharma, and sangha (Buddha, the doctrine, and the society). In this connection he also mentions some of the writings that should be read.

This inscription on the Bairath stone is of the greatest importance. In the first place, it gives a fixed chronological point. Moreover, it gives us information about certain writings which already, at that period, were looked upon as classics. The first Buddhist canon was in process of being compiled. But what interests us most in this connection is the fact that King Asoka acted openly as the mediating and reconciling element among the many schools which already, at that time, were so divergent in character. His words are stamped with the wider vision and the great devotion of Mahayana.

TRUTH AND TRADITION IN BUDDHISM

This school, little by little, gained the ascendancy in northern India, and held sway also over the Greco-Scythian people in the north-western part of the country. Thence, through Kashmir and Nepal, it travelled steadily northward and eastward as the "Buddhism of the Great Vehicle" (Mahayana), often gathering to itself the most heterogeneous religious conceptions. In Tibet we meet it weighed down with dark deviltry and fanaticism, until it becomes virtually unrecognizable.

Mahayana, however, had taken with it a large part, at least, of the principal classic writings of Buddhism, and these, in the main, were in Sanskrit. Sanskrit became, speaking generally, the religious language of North India, while Pali was that of South India, Ceylon, and Burma. When, therefore, we investigate the inner development of Mahayana, it will be largely the old Sanskrit texts from Kashmir and Nepal which will be the basis. In addition to this, however, we must remember the fact that Mahayana's development continued — indeed, first reached its bloom — on Chinese soil. Therefore the first Chinese writings which reflect this development must be treated as first-hand sources of the typical Mahayana Buddhism. Moreover, a number of the most genuine Mahayana writings from India were not included in the defective Sanskrit collection which the churches in Kashmir and Nepal adhere to. These writings are saved from oblivion and annihilation by the fact that they were later included in the Chinese translation. When, again, one calls to mind the fact that it was just during

INNER DEVELOPMENT

the reconstruction period, when Mahayana was being crystallized into its final form, that Buddhism came to China, one can understand what an important rôle it was which China played in this process. A number of Mahayanistic classical sutras were also written on Chinese soil.

There are two figures, especially, which emerge in the reconstruction period in India, two figures which in China also are well known and deeply respected. The one is the keen-witted and broad-minded Asvaghosha, who probably lived in the beginning of the second century after Christ: the other, the unswerving and spirit-filled Nagarjuna, who later, together with his disciple, Vasubandhu, gave Mahayana its distinctive form.

Asvaghosha (Chinese: Ma-ming, 馬鳴), in his whole development, stood in a peculiar position within the Buddhist society. He was originally a Brahmin. His religious studies and profound thinking brought him over, however, into the Buddhist flock, where, by virtue of his spiritual force, he very soon became a leader and pioneer. His conduct, on the one hand, is marked by deep reverence for Buddha. It is stated expressly that it was he who wrote the famous life of Buddha, "Buddha Charita Kavya." On the other hand, he seems to have had an eye for the flaws and weaknesses in the old system. As one follows his thinking, one gets a lively feeling that he not only brought with him some of the best ideas from the Brahmin doctrines, but that he also may have come into contact with the Western systems of salvation.

TRUTH AND TRADITION IN BUDDHISM

One cannot point out in detail how this has taken place; but, with the connection which was established at that time between Persia and India, one can easily imagine that Persian and other occidental trends of thought might have penetrated into India at that period.

It is also stated that this remarkable man wrote a book on "The Awakening of Faith" (Chinese: "Ch'i Hsin Lun," 起信論) (Sanskrit: Mahayana Sraddatpada), which contributed more than anything else towards giving Mahayana Buddhism its form, in one sense so concentrated, in another sense so all-inclusive. The book was first translated into Chinese in A.D. 550 by an immigrant Buddhist monk, an Indian named Paramartha (Chinese: Chên-ti, 眞諦). As we shall see later, it came to play a large rôle in China; and, at the

---

[1] Considerable light is cast upon this question by the most recent investigations of the great Indiologue, Dr. Farquhar. His book, "The Religious Literature of India," is especially significant.

Here it is asserted that the spiritual life which, just at that time, had developed in Turkestan and the north-western part of India, came to have a stimulating effect on the West as well as on the East. In other words, we stand here before one of the main sources of the spiritual life of the West as well as of the East.

On the possibility of Western influences in the formative period of Mahayana, Professor K. B. Westman points out that such a possibility cannot be denied, since in Kanishka's kingdom (i. e., Punjab and Afghanistan) at that time Hellenistic and Persian civilization was not unknown. In the religious art, there introduced into Mahayana, was essentially Hellenistic (Gandhara art). There may have been other influences as well from the Hellenistic mystical religions of the Near East. Such a hypothesis might explain the similarity in many of the customs and paraphernalia of worship between Mahayana and Greek and Roman Catholicism, since it is well known that the ancient church borrowed many of these things from these Hellenistic religions.

That the Indian Bhakti movement, which advocates an inward consecration to the deity, through prayer and meditation, has also been operative in connection with the later development of Mahayana on Indian ground, is now generally acknowledged, and that China, through its many pilgrims who went to India, took its share from this rich spring, is also certain.

INNER DEVELOPMENT

present time, there is probably no other book except "The Lotus Scripture" which is studied so eagerly by Mahayana's more enlightened adherents.

The Chinese account of the work done by Asvaghosha is somewhat bewildering. In fact, quite a number of persons by the same name are mentioned during the first centuries of the Buddhist propaganda in China. Chinese scholars, such as Mr. Liang Chi-chao, think that the work "Ch'i Hsin Lun" was written by another of the Chinese patriarchs.

Nagarjuna (Chinese: Lung-shu, 龍樹) carried Asvaghosha's thoughts further. Not only so, but he also bound these abstract ideas and instructions for worship to certain definite conceptions of Buddha, particularly to the idea of the great All-Father, Amitabha (Chinese: O-mi-t'o Fu, 阿彌陀佛), who later came to play such a dominating part in Mahayana's world of ideas. Since Amitabha's name is absolutely unknown in the history and literature of Buddhism in southern India, we must conclude that he was not of any importance in the consciousness of the monks in the early days of Buddhism.

Probably as early as under Vasubandhu (Chinese: Shih-ch'in, 世親), a disciple of Nagarjuna, another figure pushed its way to the fore, standing beside Amitabha, in the consciousness of the people. This was the famous and beloved Avalokitesvara (Chinese: Kuan-yin, 觀音), who later, together with the "Mightiest One" (Chinese: Ta-shih-chih, 大勢主) and Amitabha, came to form the trinity group in the "Pure Land" School.

TRUTH AND TRADITION IN BUDDHISM

When the first two Buddhist missionaries, Matanga and Gobharana, came to China, they do not seem to have emphasized any particular school. Their main object was to introduce *Buddhism*. The fermentation and schism in India could not, in the end, be kept out of the missionary work, however, and we therefore soon see China dragged into the discussion — indeed, before very long, it became the principal arena where the battle took place. If it cannot be said, therefore, that it was a pure Mahayana form of Buddhism which was introduced into China, at least it must be definitely asserted that it was a distinct Mahayana which was developed in the course of the first centuries.

We have preserved for us the names of some of the men who did the most towards giving Chinese Buddhism its peculiar stamp. As one might expect, it was not until after a couple of centuries that such leaders arose in China. In the beginning, the missionaries from India naturally took the lead. In the years A.D. 333–416, however, there arose a native Chinese who had a strong influence on future development. This was Hui-yüan (慧遠), born in Shansi in northern China, a remarkable Taoist, who afterwards founded the most pronounced of all Mahayana schools, the "Pure Land" School. The special dogmas of this school were found in China long before this time; but Hui-yüen put the doctrine of salvation by faith into strong relief by introducing some Taoist ideas and appellations. We shall speak of his disciples, T'an-Iuan, Tao-ch'o, and Hsan-tao, in a later chapter.

INNER DEVELOPMENT

It is remarkable to see how China, the new hopeful mission field for Buddhism, attracted to itself missionaries from various quarters, from the second century on. There were, for example, the Indian Lokaraksha, and that remarkable figure Anshikao, who seems to have come all the way from Parthia. There is much to indicate that he is identical with Prince Arsaces from that land. We hear, among other things, that he took part in the translation of the sutra about Amitabha into Chinese in the year A.D. 148. This opens the way for many interesting speculations. This man was evidently familiar with the lines of thought which, during that period, were attracting the religious minds of the West — Zoroaster's strong prophetic teaching, the worship of Mithras, etc.—but he himself had found satisfaction in Mahayana; and the first thing he did when he came over as a missionary into the story-land of China was to translate into Chinese the huge "Amitabha Sutra," now usually known by the name of "Wu-liang-shou Ching" (無 量 壽 經), "The Book of the Eternal in Time." With these two men, Mahayana first really began its great expansion in China.

The well-known Indian monk, Kumarajiva (Chinese: Chiu-mo-lo-shih, 鳩 摩 羅 什), also exercised a great influence. In A.D. 401 he was brought down as a prisoner from Tibet. Having arrived in China, he threw himself, heart and soul, into the work of translation, and it is almost unbelievable how much work he accomplished. His translation is still used in the monasteries all over China as the clearest and best in existence.

TRUTH AND TRADITION IN BUDDHISM

As we here begin our study of the inner development of Mahayana on Chinese soil, it is natural to look first at the word which has been used to express the name or conception of Buddha. It is very significant that neither a simple translation of the "Enlightened One" was found satisfactory, nor was recourse taken to the mere transliteration of the sound. The word "Buddha" had, at that time, under the spiritualizing influence of Mahayana Buddhism, become more than a mere name for the historic Gotama Buddha. It was used also as an appellation for the many "enlightened ones." The Chinese word for "Buddha" is "Fu-t'o" (佛陀), which, in sound as well as in meaning, corresponds fairly well to the Sanskrit word.

Ordinarily only the first part of the word is used, the word "fu" (佛), composed of the two characters for "man" (人) and "not" (弗). The deep meaning is evidently to have gone beyond the sphere of human life with its limitations, and entered into the absolute.

The Buddhists themselves in China usually explain the "fu" (佛) as "chio" (覺), to perceive, pointing to the deeper understanding of oneself and the universe.

It is, therefore, a metaphysical conception, which it is certainly quite impossible to express in a completely satisfactory manner in translation. It will not do simply to use the word "god," for the "gods" (shên, 神) in Mahayana Buddhism is the expression used for the highest category in the circle of transmigration, and, therefore, stands lower than "fu." For he who has become "fu" has passed beyond all

INNER DEVELOPMENT

mutations and changes, and no longer runs the risk of dropping back into any transmigratory existence. It would, therefore, be better, at least in certain connections, to express it by the monotheistic word "God," written with a capital letter — as, for example, in the often used and inexpressibly deep phrase "ch'êng fu" (成佛): "to be absorbed into the Godhead." On the other hand, however, this word does not contain that idea of majestic personality and absoluteness which is contained in our Christian conception of God. The worst mistake, however, is to express the word "Fu" everywhere by the name "Buddha," and think of the historical Buddha. As a matter of fact, the historical Buddha withdraws very decidedly into the background in real Mahayana, and, when he is mentioned, it is often as a new metaphysical figure, clad in the garb of spiritual glory. There is, therefore, no other way than to let the keen sinologues decide, in each case, which translation is nearest the meaning. In the quotations that we give in the following chapters, we shall try conscientiously to follow this rule. It will be of value, perhaps, to mention in this connection the fact that, when the first translators began the translation of the Bible into Mongolian, they adopted the name "Fu" as the appellation for God.

We said that the historic Buddha, from the very first days in China, was, for the most part, spoken of as the glorified, heavenly Buddha. As such, also, he is introduced in the oldest of the holy writings. He is enthroned in endless light and radiance, together with

TRUTH AND TRADITION IN BUDDHISM

myriads of other Buddhas and Buddha candidates (bodhisattvas) and the great and holy masters in the "heaven of the blessed," and is pictured always as the one who shall explain the "law" (the teaching, or way of salvation) to his mother or one of the troubled and questioning disciples. In this rôle, also, he is spoken of as belonging to the highest Buddha group—Tathagata. This old appellation from the Sanskrit "Tathagata" is designated quite correctly in Chinese by "He who is" or "who appears in this manner" (Ju-lai, 如來). It is evident, however, that Mahayana on Chinese soil has deepened its original conceptions, for "Ju-lai" means also the "norm which has appeared." That the Chinese understood it in this way is proved by the fact that they set down a parallel translation "Chên-ju" or the "true norm" (眞如). Nothing in the Sanskrit answering to this has been discovered. "Chên-ju," therefore, became the designation used for the mysterious latent divine power which lies behind of all existence, and "Ju-lai" was the expression used to signify that this divine power "had appeared," was personified, or, if one wishes, incarnated, in the highest Buddha group. That brilliant but often too audacious sinologue, Dr. Timothy Richard, here draws attention to the astonishing similarity in the thought of Isaiah[1] concerning "Immanuel," "God with us."

One thing is certain. This idea of a latent divine power, which lies behind existence, very soon received still clearer expression. This was in connection with the conception of the trinity which entered into

[1] Isa. 7:14; 8:10.

INNER DEVELOPMENT

Mahayana in such a remarkable manner during the early days, and which, down to the present time, plays such a tremendous part in the consciousness of Chinese Buddhists.

One first finds a theoretical allusion to the trinity in the great book "Hua-yen Ching" (華嚴經). It says that, as "Chên-ju," the true norm, develops, this latent power spreads itself in three directions. The first is "t'i" (體), or the body substance, which is the foundation for all things. The body here is, of course, conceived of spiritually. The next is phenomenal appearances, or "hsiang" (相). And the third is activity, or "yung" (用). Occasionally, these three attributes are designated by the better known names of "fa-shên" (法身), "pao-shên" (報身), and "hua-shên" (化身), or the personality of the law, the personality of the revealer, and the personality of activity. As can be seen, the first corresponds in many respects to our conception of "God" (Chên-ju), while the two other aspects remind one of the attributes of the Son and the Spirit (Ju-lai). We shall also see later how the rôles of the "Revealer" and the "Spirit" are merged together.[1]

This conception of the trinity comes again and again in endless variations in the Chinese Mahayana. This can be seen particularly in the different groups of large Buddha images in the temples. We shall see later how these groups show very clearly the different sides of the "absolute," and, therefore, how they are set up methodically and intentionally according as it is

[1] Cf. "The Awakening of Faith."

TRUTH AND TRADITION IN BUDDHISM

desired to emphasize one aspect or the other of the eternally latent divine power, the everlasting Buddha source (Yüan-fu, 原 佛).

With regard to the glorified heavenly Buddha (Gotama Buddha), it is said that, after he had become perfected in the various virtues (wisdom, holiness, mercy, etc.), he entered into the Tathagata group and became "Hsi-fang Ju-lai Fu" (西方如來佛), or the "Tathagata of the West." Moreover, it is clearly asserted in the Chinese Mahayana that the number of Buddhas is countless, and that, long before Gotama Buddha came into the world, there were many appearances of the Buddha. Indeed, Gotama himself, according to the legend, was originally a heavenly Buddha who, in merciful love, took upon himself the form of a man in order to teach the children of men the way of redemption. We shall look into this more closely in the chapter "The Buddhist Pantheon in China."

As the character of Mahayana unfolded, another Buddha type, Amitabha (Chinese: O-mi-t'o Fu, 阿彌陀佛) came to occupy the chief place in worship as well as in thought. His image very soon acquired one of the principal positions in the temples, being placed either as the central figure, or being set up on the side of honor (left side) of Sakyamuni Buddha.

It is very difficult to trace out the sources from which the conception of Amitabha arose. A large number of guesses and conjectures on this question are given by the Chinese. Hinayana Buddhism does not

SAKYAMUNI

INNER DEVELOPMENT

once mention the name, and in the Indian Veda literature there is not a hint of it. Some assert that he is the ninth son of the Buddha of Wisdom. The larger number hold to the explanation that he is the son of one of the prehistoric Buddhas named the "Freely Existing King." After having gone through all the steps to Buddhahood, and taking his famous forty-eight vows, he was born for the last time into the land of bliss, the "Western Paradise" (西方極樂世界), as the Chinese call it (Sukhavati). Here he was united with the two others in the Tathagata group Kuan-yin (觀音) and Ta-shih-chih (大勢主). From that moment, he could not become incarnate again, and for this reason he works through his two powerful assistants above mentioned. These two, as bodhisattvas, can "fên shên" (分身), divide their bodies, and thus come to the help of the created world. This is especially the case with Kuan-yin or Kuan-shih-yin (觀世音) (Avalokitesvara), "The one who hears the cry."

It is also very common to depict Amitabha as the great heavenly Buddha, who stands three generations removed in age from Sakyamuni Buddha. Some assert further that Sakyamuni Buddha was merely one of Amitabha's last incarnations. Still others maintain that Amitabha is a collective expression which takes in all Buddhas and all the Absolute. Therefore when one prays the commonly used short prayer "Nan-mo O-mi-t'o Fu (南無阿彌陀佛) ("I honour thee and resort to thee, Amitabha"), one has prayed to and called upon all the Buddhas. Others say that the syllables in the name stand for the most important

TRUTH AND TRADITION IN BUDDHISM

virtues which are necessary for attaining the honour of Buddhahood: O = goodness, mi = moral conduct, t'o = contemplation, fu = knowledge. (Cf. the famous book "Hsüan Fu P'u," 選佛譜, "Suggestions for the Attainment of the Dignity of Buddhahood.") There is assuredly no other name in the whole Buddhist terminology in China which so strongly holds the interest of those given to meditation and speculation, and provides so fruitful a field for religious mysticism and profound reflection.

According to the Chinese Buddhists, the "historical" foundation for the understanding of Amitabha is to be found in the classics strictly adopted by the "Pure Land" School. Here in the great and small "Sukhavati Vyuha Sutra" ("Wu-liang-shou Ching," 無量壽經, and "O-mi-t'o Ching," 阿彌陀經), Gotama Buddha introduces the merciful All-Father Amitabha. We are told that, before becoming a Buddha, Amitabha was a pious and good monk by the name Dharmakara, who subsequently became a powerful bodhisattva. As a bodhisattva he made forty-eight great vows to rescue all living beings in all the different spheres of life. Having in this way stored up boundless merit and saving power for "innumerable lost souls," he became the "Buddha of boundless age and light" (Wu-liang shou, Wu-liang kuang, 無量壽, 無量光).

On one point all, even the greatest rationalists among the monks (and there are a remarkable number), seem to agree, and that is that, when one follows the Amitabha idea to its uttermost limit, one ends finally with one's own heart. For it is there that Amitabha

INNER DEVELOPMENT

ultimately reveals himself—and that not as something from without, but at the very centre of one's own human existence, as one's real and best *ego*. Thus one meets expressions among the deepest thinkers within the Buddhist world in China which, in holy exaltation, reach their climax in the confession: "Amitabha is myself!" I have heard it personally in a few great moments when I have been with monks in their cells and had a chance to talk things out with them, and it has struck me that this confession was always accompanied by a certain gesture. The hand was laid on the heart. The striking likeness to the mystics among the Persian Sufists, the spiritual branch of Mohammedans, will here instantly impress itself on all who are at all acquainted with the history of religion.

As we shall see later, the name "Amitabha" has in time taken on a more monotheistic tone. This was especially true during the period when Nestorianism made itself most felt.

What has been said here of Amitabha will be sufficient to give an impression of the tremendous significance his name acquired in China, and will show how all the threads in the web of Mahayana lead back to him. We shall postpone the further treatment of his nature and functions to the point when we can concentrate on the purer and more refined form of Mahayana, that which is comprised in the "Ching-t'u" (淨土), or "Pure Land" School. We must at this point proceed to look at the more historical aspects of Mahayana's inner development in China.

[41]

TRUTH AND TRADITION IN BUDDHISM

It has already been mentioned that China became more and more the stage for the great breaking up of forces within the Buddhist society. This is due to the fact that the centre of gravity for the life of Buddhism had been transferred to China. The reaction against Buddhism grew stronger in its native land, India, and finally it was actually pushed out of its cradle. The split between Hinayana and Mahayana also grew steadily deeper, until the former found a sure resting-place for itself in Ceylon, Burma, and Siam.

While this withdrawal was in progress, however, a new factor had already begun to make itself felt, a factor which served more especially to increase the confusion in China also, namely the practice of pilgrimages.

Lokaraksha and Anshikao (Arsaces), the zealous missionaries of Mahayana in China, had, with great success, proclaimed the principal doctrines of the "Great Vehicle," and, in that way, had led the rather colourless form of Buddhism, which first had entrance into China, into more definite lines. Later, a great many other Buddhist monks of various schools and sects came over from India into China. Little by little, it became quite common also for the Chinese Buddhist monks to travel westward on pilgrimages, and many and varied were the sacred writings and relics which they brought back with them to China.

Some of these pilgrims travelled all the way down to South India, even to Ceylon, and quite naturally they received strong impressions of Hinayana Buddhism also. So the confusion increased with every new

[42]

INNER DEVELOPMENT

pilgrimage that was undertaken. Here without doubt we find the chief cause of the tangled and overweighted condition which stamps the Chinese Mahayana down to the present day.

This situation is all the more strange as it is constantly said in the books of travel of that period that "now that this pilgrimage has been brought to a happy conclusion, we have finally succeeded in completing that which was lacking in the scriptures and securing the desired clearness in the formerly contradictory systems." China was positively flooded with scriptures, and it is with apparent impatience that the patrons of Buddhism among the emperors appointed one "commission" after another to give Mahayana's Tripitaka on Chinese soil its final form. The great internal contradictions between Mahayana and Hinayana scriptures which continually emerged filled the air with excitement, and the most amazing theories were propounded by which to explain the whole. We shall go into this matter in greater detail in the treatment of the Chinese Tripitaka and Buddhist literature as a whole.

Among the famous pilgrims, we must mention Fa-hsien (法現), A.D. 399; Sung-yün (宋雲), 518; I-ch'ing (義青), 634–713; and Hsüan-chuang (玄奘), 629–645.[1]

Of these men, the first and the last are especially worthy of attention. Professor Legge's translation, "Fa-Hsien's Record of Buddhistic Kingdoms," gives

---

[1] Our sources for an understanding of these pilgrims are, besides their own records of their travels which are still partially preserved, the two books: "Memoirs of Famous Monks" (from 519) and "Memoirs of Remarkable Monks" (from 1415).

TRUTH AND TRADITION IN BUDDHISM

a good view of that remarkable pilgrim's life and thought. Through his books of travel, we can follow him across Gobi's dangerous desert sands,. where "only the bleached bones along the way showed the path." We can see how the tribes on the borders of the Chinese Empire were already influenced by the "law," or, in other words, the "way of salvation" as Buddhism had outlined it. It is also interesting to notice that it was Mahayana that was especially cultivated.

Among the many remarkable experiences which the monk had in northern India, we may mention especially the sight of the immense "Maitreya statue," eighty ells high and eight ells at the base from knee to knee. (Here the position of meditation is clearly indicated.) It was in the "kingdom of To-lieh" that Fa-hsien saw this imposing image. He tells also enthusiastically of how the neighbouring princes vied with one another in bringing homage to the Maitreya statue.[1]

Then comes a description of the various holy places in northern India, where legends of Sakyamuni Buddha were particularly numerous, and where immense pagodas were built over relics of his bones. In general, one sees unrolled before one's eyes, through Fa-hsien's accounts of his travels, the great traits in the life of Sakyamuni. This is done in so living a way that one feels none but a religiously inspired soul could have given such an interpretation, while his local descriptions of the landscape give a vivid setting to the whole.

[1] Maitreya resides in the Tushita heaven, and, in obedience to Sakyamuni's special commission, will, after a period of five thousand years, descend to the earth as Buddha to establish the great period of peace in the world. He is, therefore, in a special sense called "Buddhism's Messiah."

[44]

INNER DEVELOPMENT

For fifteen long years Fa-hsien was away on his journey. No wonder that he was a famous man when he returned to his fatherland, and that his book, in Chinese, Korean, and Japanese, has since become a favourite with all yearning Buddhists of the East.

Still deeper mystery and romance lie over the written notes of the last-named pilgrim, the famous Hsüanchuang, who, between the years A.D. 629 and 645 undertook his long and dangerous journey, partly through the same regions, but also going still farther West. In his day, Mahayana had attained its full flower, but other systems also, such as the so-called "mystical mantras" (a system of conjuring and magic), and strange animistic, spiritistic system from Tibet had had a confusing influence on Mahayana.

A tremendous impression was made by Hsüanchuang's descriptions on his spiritually minded contemporaries and successors in China, as can be seen especially in a book which was written at a later date, the famous "Hsi Yu Chi" (西遊記) ("An Account of the Journey to the West"), a rather fantastic copy of the original writings of the pilgrim. As this book takes us, in a remarkable manner, into the thought of the times, and shows in the clearest possible way how Mahayana was considered to be the highest of all known religious forms, we have thought it best to give a résumé in a separate chapter.

With the coming to China of the Indian monk Bodhidharma in the year A.D. 520, the centre of gravity was moved not merely actually but formally from India to China.

Bodhidharma was the twenty-eighth patriarch in direct line from Sakyamuni Buddha, and was India's last patriarch. He then became China's first patriarch, founding that honourable line of "fathers" (Chinese: Tsu-shih, 祖師), who have, for all time, in the opinion of Buddhists, cast a light of glory over the Yangtze valley, where they settled.

Bodhidharma is known in China by the name of P'u-t'i-ta-mo (菩提達摩), or, in abbreviated form, Ta-mo (達摩). On the ancient scrolls he is recorded as Ch'a-ti-li (剎帝利), and is said to have been an offshoot of Brahma's (Chinese: P'o-lo-mên, 婆羅門) stock. From a religious point of view he belonged to the so-called Dhyani School in India, and transplanted it to Chinese soil under the name of Ch'an Tsung (禪宗), the Meditation School. This man's work had tremendous significance for Chinese Buddhism. Indeed, even Korean and Japanese Buddhism count him as one of the most important patriarchs. His Japanese name is "Daruma."

Bodhidharma stayed most of the time at Loyang in North China, the first home of Buddhism in China; but he also visited the region of the Yangtze. At that time the Emperor Liang Wu Ti lived in Nanking. He had furthered the progress of Buddhism as few others had done. By erecting buildings and encouraging literary work, he had sought to secure a sure foothold for the doctrine among the common people. He mentioned all this in his conversation with Bodhidharma when the latter came to Nanking. The patriarch's reply was: "These are all outward things which are of no benefit. The truly valuable things are attained only by that inner purification and enlightenment which come through quiet pondering and meditation." These words are very significant of this man's life principles. In the midst of a confused and unsettled time, when the most varied literature and the most diverse systems of salvation set men's thoughts fermenting, he stood forth with his strong and simple demand, "Seek meditation, for there you will find that clearness and peace which the study of the scriptures alone can never give." That which gave his words greater power was the fact that he himself carefully carried out this practice of meditation. To begin with, he sat "uninterruptedly for nine years with his face turned towards a wall in order not to be distracted," and, in addition, through his busy life, he continued a habit of regular daily meditation up to his last days. Here is his declaration in brief: "Buddhism is too deep and inclusive to be translated into writing, and even less can it be completely understood merely by the study of the scriptures. That which is necessary in addition is persistent and systematic meditation. By means of meditation one can also implant this deeper understanding in a spiritual manner in others. The source of all doctrine is one's own heart. From it can be brought forth unutterable treasures."

Bodhidharma had many disciples. Not only so, but he established a school, in the true meaning of the word; and this school, which afterwards developed into one of the principal sects of Buddhism, is the most widespread and influential in China down to the present day. Ch'an Tsung (禪宗), the Meditation School, has succeeded in welding together some of the later schools into one large sect. We shall return to this in a later chapter.

Not all, however, were pleased with this solution of the difficulties. There were many highly educated monks with special ability to adjust everything in a rational way, who quite naturally looked about for other means of getting out of the impasse. This was especially the case with the Abhidharma sect, which had been transplanted from India, and which placed so much value on narrow and careful definitions, and wanted to turn back the wheels of development to the "Golden Age" of Buddhism.

Just at the period when the tides of confusion flowed highest, there arose one of China's own monks with a word of authority and a definite solution — a solution which, down to the present time, has served as a firm foundation for the men of more reflection among China's Buddhists. This was the monk Chih-i (智顗), or Chih-k'ai, from Anhwei province, who lived in the latter half of the sixth century. He was first attached to the monasteries in Nanking, but came to spend most of his life in the coast province of Chekiang, where he died in 597. Here, in the T'ien-t'ai (天台) Mountains, afterwards so famous, where, at that time, there was a strongly developed monastic life, he

INNER DEVELOPMENT

founded his school and ordained over four thousand priests. The school or sect has ever since borne the name T'ien-t'ai Tsung (天台宗), the T'ien-t'ai School.

In contrast to Bodhidharma, whom he followed in the beginning, Chih-k'ai laid stress on the value of the study of the scriptures, but not to such a degree that he failed to recognize the value of meditation. Chih-k'ai believed that, by means of persevering study and reflection, not only would the apparently strong contradictions within the Mahayana scriptures disappear, but the truth-seeking soul would, by this very act, gain enlightenment and attain deep peace. As an assistance to other seekers, he set forth the result to which he himself had come after many years of reflection and study. As this conclusion has been widely acknowledged, and has found almost universal recognition among the Buddhists of China, Korea, and Japan, we shall give a brief account of it here.

It is nothing less than a system of classification which, in a sense, gives a key to the understanding of the immense and extremely heterogeneous mass of Mahayana literature. It is, perhaps, not necessary to add that the system is by no means satisfactory to present-day sinologues, who demand accurate research, for there are, as we shall see, so many postulates and astonishing jumps to conclusions that one becomes quite dazed. In addition, the historical foundation on which the whole system is built is altogether too shaky. Nevertheless, the solution is ingenious and interesting, and, if one is to understand the scholarly monks in their explanations, and the higher meaning of the Buddhist worship, one must always keep the T'ien-t'ai School system in mind.

Chih-k'ai's main principle was that the speeches and utterances of Sakyamuni Buddha point to five great periods in his life, and, therefore, Mahayana's original writings must be classified in the same manner. Each of these scriptures belongs, in fact, to one of these five periods, and Chih-k'ai believed that it was his reward that, after diligent study, he had reached the point of understanding the place that each scripture should take, organically and historically. Not only so, but, by investigating the lines of development in these five periods of Sakyamuni's life, it became clear that the various systems of salvation, far from contradicting one another, rather completed one another.

The five periods, therefore, are to be interpreted as follows:

1. The first period covers the first three weeks of Buddha's life after he had received enlightenment. At that time he gathered about him the bodhisattvas and heavenly beings, and discoursed to them on the subject of his great and all-embracing teaching. This is to be found in the voluminous work "Hua-yen Ching" (華 嚴 經) (Sanskrit: "Buddhava-tamsaka-mahavaipulya Sutra").

2. When Buddha realized that his lofty teachings could not be understood by ordinary persons, he began to simplify his system, and proclaimed the "four truths about suffering, and salvation from suffering, together with the truths of the eightfold way." If one follows these directions, one can achieve the dignity of

INNER DEVELOPMENT

an arhat.[1] This period covers the next twelve years of Buddha's life, and its teaching has found its literary expression in the Hinayana scriptures.

3. When the master perceived that his disciples fell into the mistake of thinking that the whole truth was contained in the above-named Hinayana scriptures, he hastened to declare to them that he still had immeasurably more about which to enlighten them. What they had already heard was but an introduction to the truth. Now they should enter into that great enlightenment which would not only make them personally saints (Chinese: lo-han, 羅漢), but would make them co-workers in the great labour of salvation for the world. They should become bodhisattvas (Chinese: p'u-t'i-sa-to, 菩提薩多, abbreviated form p'u-sa, 菩薩). This period extends over the next eight years, and corresponds to the writings which are peculiar to Mahayana.

4. When Buddha's disciples heard these lofty and spiritual truths being developed, they very soon came to the realization that the common man could not possibly be able to grasp them, and, therefore, for him there remained, after all, only one way of salvation open, that which was presented by Hinayana. Buddha was obliged, therefore, to use the next twenty-two years of his life in clearing away this misunderstanding. During this time he proved that Hinayana was merely a preparatory stage, a first vehicle, which could convey all who truly believed upward into the higher realm of thought, i. e., into Mahayana. The principal work in

[1] The arhat is especially prominent in Hinayana.

which these teachings of Buddha appear, and where, consequently, we find the teachings of Mahayana crystallized and simplified to the extreme, is called "Ta Pan Jo Ching" (大般若經): "Mahapragnaparamita Sutra").

5. Finally, when Buddha had reached old age (seventy-two), he began to preach the loftiest and deepest doctrine, asserting that every individual may attain to Nirvana. Indeed, he himself had come down to earth for this very purpose, and had taken upon himself the repeated pangs of birth in order to preach this universal salvation (the salvation of all living things). The teachings connected with this are collected in the famous "Lotus" scripture, " Fa-hua Ching" (法華經) (Sanskrit: "Saddharma Pundarika Sutra"), the book which, according to the views of the T'ien-t'ai School, is the keystone, the universal book of salvation, and, therefore, the principal scripture for the whole of Buddhism.

Later, other writings were introduced into this fifth section, works which are considered the natural fruit of the universal gospel of "The Lotus Scripture." First of all is "The Nirvana Scripture," "Nieh-p'an Ching" (涅槃經) (Sanskrit: "Mahaparinirvana Sutra.") In this book it is maintained that all creatures have within them the seed-germ that may become a Buddha, and can, therefore, be certain of reaching the eternal bliss of Nirvana.[1] Quite naturally the most developed form of Mahayana, which we know in the "Pure Land" scriptures, has been placed in this

[1] Here the conception of Nirvana is filled with a new content.

INNER DEVELOPMENT

fifth period. Here, therefore, belong the typical "Pure Land" scriptures, the great and the little Amitabha scriptures (Sanskrit: "Sukhavati Vyuha Sutra")—the "Wu-liang-shou Ching" (無量壽經) and the "O-mi-t'o Ching" (阿彌陀經)—and the "Kuan-wu-liang-shou Ching" (觀無量壽經) (Sanskrit: "Amita Yurdhyana Sutra").

It is difficult to describe what significance this ingenious classification, and the views connected with it, received in China, Korea, and Japan. For many hundreds of years Chih-k'ai's solution stood as the only right and unassailable one. It was on this account, also, that the remarkable spirit of toleration spread over the Buddhist society, which, before this, had been so stirred up. There was no system so strange that it could not find a place in this great harmony. Indeed, it was only a sign of Amitabha's endless grace that he had so many different kinds of "vehicles" for suffering and struggling humanity, suited for each country and each individual's need.

It is no wonder, therefore, that from the T'ien-t'ai School there went forth a number of great men who each founded a school of his own, which, however, did not come into conflict with the parent school. This was the case both in China and in Japan.[1] The founders both of the Meditation School and of the "Pure Land" School in Japan came from this school.

The emphasis which this school laid on literary studies could not fail to have a most beneficial influence on the lives of the monks; but, in this case,

[1] Cf. Professor A. K. Reischauer's work: "Studies in Japanese Buddhism."

TRUTH AND TRADITION IN BUDDHISM

as always, certain extravagances appeared. The fact that, in their zeal for copying the sutras and showing their earnestness, men sometimes opened a vein and wrote the holy books with their blood was a comparatively innocent practice. More serious was the fact that certain ingenious brains began to make short cuts into the treasure-house of literature in a perfectly external and mechanical way. For example, a man would, at certain intervals, go up to the library hall to "fan ching" (翻經). The object of this was to get the books "dusted through" in the simple meaning of the word. The monks sat with duster in hand and carefully dusted off the books, at the same time glancing at the writings here and there, as they turned the pages. This practice has continued down to the present day in certain places. Without really getting into the deeper thoughts, the monks gained a slight acquaintance with the great treasures of the libraries, and were, as the Germans would say, "*ein Bischen literärisch angehaucht.*"

The process became still more mechanical when the airing and dusting of the books was done by placing the whole of the Mahayana literature in an enormous cylindrical closet which revolved upon its own axis. The work of merit then consisted in keeping this in motion by means of a huge handle. In China at the present time one sees very little of this practice; but it continues in Japan up to our own day.

Just as "The Lotus Scripture" was the favourite work of the T'ien-t'ai School, the image of the typical

[54]

INNER DEVELOPMENT

Buddha representing the doctrine became quite naturally its most popular "Fu." The representative of the "doctrine" (dharma) is Vairocana (Chinese: P'i-lu-chê-na, 毘盧遮那), and we meet this interesting Buddha-form constantly in the treatises and the ritual of the T'ien-t'ai School.

One must not, however, judge the influence of this school by the number of monasteries and monks who take their name directly from T'ien-t'ai, for their number is small. The same is the case as with the "Pure Land" School. The real power is seen in the tremendous influence which the T'ien-t'ai School has exercised on the thought and practice of the earlier schools. One finds everywhere, both in ritual and in rules for living, a deep dependence on the teaching of the T'ien-t'ai School. Indeed, even Ch'an Tsung (the Meditation School), which should represent the very opposite standpoint from T'ien-t'ai, proved not to be entirely able to withstand its influence. From the T'ien-t'ai School have come forth not only deeply spiritual men, but also many rationalistic scholars. Some of their writings are considered by the older monks as positively dangerous.

In Japan in recent years there have been formed groups who more or less openly oppose Chih-k'ai's five periods. They maintain that Sakyamuni Buddha can, at the most, be said to have merely hinted at Mahayana, while the original and certain way of salvation is given in Hinayana. It is, therefore, quite noteworthy that, in recent years, two fairly distinct schools of Hinayana have grown up in Japan. We

[55]

TRUTH AND TRADITION IN BUDDHISM

have nothing quite equivalent to this in China, although here, also, we see a few attempts in the same direction. One thing is certain. We shall very soon see a new critical school appear in China, also—a school from which we may hope to get specialists who can help the sinologues in the great and difficult work of sifting which the investigation of Mahayana requires. The most outstanding representative of this new movement is the very learned, religious, and energetic monk, T'ai-hsü (太 虛), at present president of the Buddhist academy in Wuchang, and editor of the great magazine *Hai Ch'ao Yin* (海潮音).

In closing this chapter, we may be permitted to give a Taoist-Buddhist story of Christ recently discovered by us at the Christian Mission to Buddhists at Ching-fêng Shan (景風山), Nanking. It will undoubtedly shed a little more light upon some of the problems now baffling us in our study of China's religions.

"Travelling westward from China for three years, covering a distance of ninety-seven thousand li, one arrives at the western border of the 'Land of the Western Tribes' (西羌界). From that land has been handed down an account of a virgin named Maria, who, during the time of the right (first) Han in the year 'Hsin Yu yüan shih yüan nien' (辛酉元始元年), reverently received the following message from the Heavenly Spirit (天神), Chia-pei-o-êrh (嘉俾阿爾), 'God (天主) has in a special way selected thee to become a mother.' She instantly conceived and later gave birth to a child which she most reverently and

[56]

INNER DEVELOPMENT

joyfully wrapped in ordinary clothes and placed in a manger. All the heavenly spirits (angels) filled the air with music. After forty days the mother brought the child with her up to the holy master, Pa-tê-lei. (罷德肋), who gave him the name Jesus (耶穌). When twelve years old he followed his mother up to the holy temple. When returning, they were separated, and the mother suffered pain and sorrow in her heart for three days and three nights. After that time she went back to the temple, and there she found Jesus sitting in one of the upper seats discussing God's work and plans with old, wise and venerable masters. When he saw his mother, he became very happy. He followed her back to their home, and fulfilled his filial duties, honouring and serving her.

"When thirty years old, he left his mother and his master, and travelled around in Judea (如德亞), preaching religion and purifying the people (傳教淑人). He also performed numerous miracles.

"In the meantime, many of the higher families and some of the leading men, led by their evil and proud hearts, began to envy and hate him because they saw the heart of the people turning to him. Consequently they began to think out a way by which they could put him to death. Among the twelve disciples of Jesus there was a man named Judas (茹答斯), already for a long time given over to covetousness. He cleverly apprehended the trend of thinking then prevailing in his native country. In order to attain an insignificant gain, he led a crowd of men at midnight, who took hold of Jesus, bound him with ropes, and brought him to the courts of Caiaphas (亞納斯在) and Pilate (比剌多). There they stripped him, fixed him to the stone pillars, and flogged him, giving him more than five thousand lashes, so that his whole body was scourged. During this whole proceeding he was quiet, not uttering a single word in self-defence—just like a lamb. The evil crowd took thorn-bushes, and made a crown of thorns which was pressed down round his temples. They also threw a scarlet robe over his body, and kneeling down and feigning reverence adored him as a king. Then they made a huge cross which he was compelled to carry. Pressed under this heavy burden, he fainted on the way most pitiably. His hands and feet were fixed to the cross with nails. When thirsting they gave him gall to drink. As he passed away the heavens darkened, the earth trembled, and stones tumbled down one against the other. At that time he was thirty-three years old. On the third day after his death he rose from the dead, and his body appeared in radiant splendour. He showed himself first to the mother, whose grief in this way was assuaged. After forty days he decided to ascend to heaven. At that time he stood face to face with his disciples, numbering one hundred and twenty men, giving them the command to scatter through the world and complete the work of preaching. According to this, whosoever received holy baptism was cleansed from sin and could enter his church. Having laid down these principles, a host of saints from the old times gathered round him and escorted him up to the heavenly kingdom.

INNER DEVELOPMENT

"After ten days the heavenly spirits (angels) descended to earth and received the mother. They brought her with them up to heaven, where she was placed over the ninth 'p'in' (立於九品之上) (the supreme rank according to the 'Pure Land' doctrine. It is shown in the picture of the opening of the lotus. The ninth 'p'in' shows us a person sitting on a purple-gold terrace, like a great lotus which has opened during one night. After seven days such a person attains to that supreme wisdom which can never again be lost). In this way she was made the Heavenly Mother Empress who rules the whole world. She especially defends the disciples, so that they may go into all the world in their great mission of proclaiming the doctrine."

The account given above is found in the great Taoist-Buddhist work "Shên-hsien Kang-chien" (神仙綱鑑), as well known among the Buddhists as among Taoists. The work as we have it in this institute is composed of twenty-two volumes, the eighteenth volume being bound as two separate books. There is also a special volume attached giving the pictures of the most important saints and deities. Here interesting pictures of Maria, and Jesus blessing a young worshipper, are found. The scope of the book is very broad, aiming at a somewhat full presentation of the saints and gods known to the Chinese and included in the Taoist and Buddhist pantheon as worthy of worship.

TRUTH AND TRADITION IN BUDDHISM

The text translated above occurs in the ninth volume.[1] It is followed by a very interesting account of Mohammedanism.

It is clearly stated in the preface that the Taoist monk, Hsü Yu-ch'i (徐有期) or Hsü-tao (徐道), is the real author. He lived on Pao Shan (包山), at the present time known as Fu-yu Shan in Kiangsi province. There he stayed in the temple Ling Wu Fu Leo. A man, probably belonging to the Moslem community, helped Hsü-tao complete the work, which took three years to finish. The name of the helper is given as Li Li (李理), and he is said to come from Junan (汝南). He is styled a man of Ch'ing-chên (清眞), which probably indicates some connection with Mohammedanism. Hsü-tao kept the manuscript secret for a time, but later, when his nephew, Chang Chi-tsung (張繼宗), was appointed chief priest of Lung-hu Shan (龍虎山), in Kiangsi, the stronghold of Taoism, the manuscript was published at that place, and is now found in many Taoist libraries. A learned hermit by the name of Huang Chang-lun (黃掌綸) assisted Hsü-tao with the publication, and two of the best-known Buddhist monks of that time, Ping-hsüeh (冰雪) and Hsin-ming (心明), wrote brilliant prefaces to the book.

The date of the publication of the book is given as "K'ang Hsi Kêng Ch'ên Ch'ang-chih Jih." (康熙庚辰長至日), that is to say, in the thirty-ninth year of K'ang Hsi's reign, corresponding to the year A.D. 1701.

[1] Vol. IX, pp. 26-28.

INNER DEVELOPMENT

The traditions and written or printed materials on which the various descriptions of the saints and deities are based must, of course, be of a far earlier date. Especially does this seem to be the case with the traditions in connection with the story of Jesus and Mary.

The whole chapter, which contains many other legends, has as its heading, "The Virgin Maria Gives Birth to Jesus," and is stamped with the perfect heavenly trigram (乾卦). The importance of this chapter is consequently obvious.

The author introduces the record of Jesus in connection with the mighty men taking part in the strifes and struggles under the Emperor Kuang Wu Ti (A.D. 25–58) in this way: "During the winter-time the western tribes rushed in, but Ma Yüan (馬援) (one of the great generals of Kuang Wu Ti) dispersed them and drove them away. People from those western countries give the following account." Here follows the text given above. The author therefore manifestly means that the story about the wonderful birth and life of Jesus was brought to China by those invading western tribes in the first century after Christ. A glimpse at the text given above will soon tell us that certain influences from Buddhism can also be traced. As was to be expected, the style and wording of the record correspond to the Roman Catholic mode of thought and expressions in vogue during the time of K'ang Hsi (T'ien-chu, 天主, is used for God; T'ien-shên, 天神, for angels, etc.); but this does not contradict the assumption that we really have here an old Christian tradition.

TRUTH AND TRADITION IN BUDDHISM

As will be seen, the text gives a fairly accurate and very touching presentation of the life and death of our Saviour. It is, however, significant that any reference to Joseph is completely omitted. A new, strange personality, Pa-tê-lei, takes his place as the master. The characters for Pa-tê-lei are most probably a transliteration of the Latin word *pater*.

Of great interest is the closing part, dealing with the ascension of the holy mother. The text here is very clear, so that there is no doubt as to Maria taking the high place of the Buddhist Madonna, Kuan-yin, sitting on the purple-gold lotus, and from the heavenly places reigning over the world with boundless wisdom and mercy. Whoever has studied the scriptures of the "Pure Land" School (Chingt'u) will at once apprehend what it means that Maria "was placed over the ninth p'in" (立於九品之上). After the discovery of this document, the assumption that the Buddhist Kuan-yin idea was essentially influenced by the Roman Catholic thought of the merciful Madonna is very much strengthened.

CHAPTER III

"THE JOURNEY TO THE WEST"

Among the many literary treasures of China of special interest to us, is the book "Hsi Yu Chi" (西遊記) ("An Account of the Journey to the West"), dating from the late Middle Ages. This book, from the Taoist and Buddhist points of view, is in many respects comparable to "Pilgrim's Progress," so well known in Western lands. Like its Western counterpart, it, too, has exercised a strong influence during times when spiritual life was at a low ebb. At the same time, because of its humourous style, it has been regarded as light reading and has been frequently played as drama in the Chinese theatre. In its dramatic form it bears the name "Ch'ü T'ang Ching" (取唐經) ("The Writings Fetched During the Tang Dynasty"). One cannot say with certainty who the author was. Some have thought it was Kublai Khan's advisor, Ch'iu Ch'u-chi (邱處機). One thing is sure: the historical background is the official mission of the monk Hsüan-chuang (玄奘) to the fairyland of India in 629–645, his purpose being to secure several Mahayana scriptures. The hero of the book is, therefore, called Hsüan-ch'uang. The scene is laid partly in the heavenly regions, partly in the kingdom of death, and partly on earth.

The author has in a very clever way personified the various aspects of human nature, the passionate, and

[63]

the sensuous, but he reveals, too, the longing of the human heart after God and redemption. Most of the well-known Confucian, Taoist, and Buddhist gods take part. The author shows, with sure hand, the interrelation of these religious systems, how they interlock, how they supplement one another, and how at that time they had come to their most beautiful fruitage in the Mahayana school, or higher Buddhism. It is probable that the author had some knowledge of Christianity gained, it may be, from the Nestorian movement in its latter days.

The object of the book is to show what help the different religious systems can give to the poor human being in his struggle for redemption. In this connection the author sets forth what he considers to be the most primitive type of human nature, a human type that stands no higher than an ape.

One of the chief characters in the drama, therefore, is an ape, who in untamable wildness makes his way into human society and takes a human name. He takes as surname the character "sun" (孫). Later, when his more spiritual longings begin to awaken, he uses the characters "wu" (悟) and "kung" (空)—meaning "he who ponders on the mysterious." When he becomes resourceful and practical, he takes an additional name "Hsing-chê" (行者), the practical.

Sun (孫), who was originally born of a block of stone, and had, therefore, like his brothers, much of the rock nature in him, soon began to stand out among his fellow-apes. There was a beautiful river which flowed close by the place where they all lived. One time

THE JOURNEY TO THE WEST

they thought they would like to explore and find the source of the river. So they followed it back till they came to a place where it fell in a cascade from the mouth of a cave. Determined not to be baffled in their search for the source of the stream they agreed that he should be king who could leap through the waterfall into the cave and come back unscathed. This was done by our hero, who thus became ruler in the kingdom of the apes. Hidden by the waterfall, he discovered an iron bridge which led to a spacious hall, comfortable and well lighted. Over this he led the ape colony and here they settled and lived for a long time in joy and comfort. The place was called 'The Heavenly Cave Veiled with Curtains of Water, the Happy Flower and Fruit Garden."

One day, however, the apes noticed that their king was strangely silent, and soon he began to weep. They crowded round him in consternation, to hear what was the matter. Sun explained: "In spite of the fact that I am happy now, I am afraid when I think of the future." The apes assured him that there was no cause for fear. Sun continued: "Although we, as long as we do not come into conflict with the laws and customs of human society, need not fear wild animals, a time will come when we are old and feeble and will begin to fear the great judge of death, who will drag us out of the land of the living." When the apes heard this, they also covered their faces in sorrow, for they, too, feared death.

After a time one of them had a revelation, and he stood forth in their midst and said: "Great King, this sorrow of thine is an opportunity to attain the endless life. Of all the wonders of this world, the three greatest are these: the Buddhas, the immortal Taoists, and the Confucian gods. These have gone beyond all changes and will never be born again to another death, but will live as long as heaven and earth exist." The king asked if he knew where they lived, and the answer came: "They live beyond death, in the ancient valley between the mountains of the spirits."

When Sun Wu-kung heard this, his immediate decision was to travel abroad and meet these three wonderful groups. The next day his subjects prepared a great farewell banquet where peaches, precious herbs, and costly wines raised the spirit of festivity to the highest point, and the following day Sun Wu-kung started off on his long journey. He made himself a little boat, took a bamboo pole in his hand, and let himself be carried down with the current. A south-east wind drove him into the country of Shenpu. From there he continued his journey by land until he met a company of fishers and salt-burners. Sun transformed himself into a tiger, which rushed fiercely upon the workmen. Most of them took flight; one, however, took to his heels so late that Sun caught him. As it was necessary for him to have some clothing, he stripped his victim and dressed himself as a man.

He now began to walk as a human being, and when, after a time, he entered a city, he had acquired a good carriage and a proper gait. He stayed long enough in the city to learn human speech and customs, and contrary to his previous practice, he began to take his meals in the daytime and to sleep at night.

During this time he searched continually for the dwelling-place of the three groups of immortals, but nowhere did he find any who could help him to find them; none sought eternal life, all were striving after riches, comfort, and fame. After nine years of vain search, Sun came to the borders of the great western ocean; here he secured a boat and sailed across to the land of the unicorns. On his arrival there, he saw rising majestically before him a high mountain, thickly wooded and very beautiful. He climbed it, till he reached the summit. While he stood and looked about him, he heard a voice singing. Following the sound he came upon a man chopping wood, and from the words of the song, Sun surmised that he was in the presence of a holy man.

He was directed by the pious wood-cutter to the house of a wise and holy teacher who lived in the neighbourhood. This was no other than Hsü-p'u-t'i (須菩提), one of Buddha's most valued disciples. He was the Indian Subhuti, to whom, according to "The Diamond Sutra," Buddha himself expounded many deep and weighty truths.

The ape king succeeded in gaining an audience with this exalted one, just as he began his daily lectures to his thirty disciples, and after a short examination Sun was admitted into the group of pupils, receiving at the same time the special name, Wu-kung.

After many years of study he attained to the higher understanding of both the physical and psychical worlds, but the crowning achievement was his mastery of the secret arts of magic. With the help of seventy-two different formulæ and motions, he was prepared to make himself invisible, assume various bodily forms, and ride on the clouds through the heavens with the speed of lightning. His proficiency was such that he became a menace to the security of the school, so he was banished by the master. Returning to his old friends in "The Heavenly Cave Veiled with Curtains of Water," he was received with great joy. His return was opportune, for just at that time his kingdom was threatened by powerful enemies. Sun immediately exercised his magical powers and destroyed them all. The apes felt themselves safer than ever under their learned and powerful king.

After this victory he became intolerably arrogant and ambitious. He established his fame and his kingdom by means of several successful expeditions out into the world; to the deep caves of the dragons, where he appropriated multitudes of swords and an immense club; and later down to the borders of the sea, where he took for himself that mysterious spear which later was such a great help to him. While he was in Hades he took the opportunity of questioning the ten kings who punish the ungodly spirits and keep the death records of all living things. In the register he found his own name, and the span of his life was given as three hundred and forty-two years. Sun seized a pencil and struck out all that concerned him and his nearest ones. Now he had really become an immortal (hsien, 仙).

THE JOURNEY TO THE WEST

The following day representatives from the caves of the abyss and from the kingdom of death came up to the throne of God[1] with the prayer that heaven would lay hold upon Sun Wu-kung, the frightful monster who was everywhere causing the greatest confusion. The Eternal One upon the throne, Yü-ti (玉帝), at first decided to send out some of the heavenly legions to arrest Sun, but yielding to the prayer of the angel Venus (Tai-pai chin-hsing, 太白金星), he changed this decision and determined to try by establishing Sun in the heavenly world to get him if possible to mend his ways. The "angel of the literary star" received an order to draw up an edict which should be presented to Sun, giving him the supervision of a certain stable in heaven.

He accepted the appointment, and thus began his first career in the heavenly regions. The angel Jupiter conducted Sun to his new arena of work, one division of heaven's stables. There he was to have the supervision of the wild horses! When Sun realized that he had been appointed to the lowest office, he rebelled and left all the grandeur of heaven to take up his position again in the apes' camp. He planned in the course of time to arm them and all the evil spirits for war against heaven. At this time Sun's unbridled licence and haughty arrogance completely dominated him.

Once more heaven sent a punitive expedition against him, but he drove all back with his magic powers. Then heaven agreed to try him in that high position

[1] Here the Taoist god Yü-ti.

TRUTH AND TRADITION IN BUDDHISM

which he himself had long boasted that he would reach "the holy and mighty one, equal with heaven."

Sun took his place in the heavenly regions and all went well for a time. As he had no special work to do, the gods were rather fearful lest the whole experiment should again fail. Later, therefore, he was appointed to keep watch over the heavenly peach orchard of the gods. He was immensely delighted with the sight of the enormous garden with fruit-trees planted in three long rows. This delight was naturally increased when he heard that the greatest wisdom and limitless immortality were to be attained by eating of the fruits.

Sun immediately felt a great desire to taste the fruit of immortality, but as servants and workmen accompanied him everywhere it was difficult to get at it. One day he commanded them to go out of the garden, as he wanted to rest. When they had gone, he took off his human clothing and began to climb the trees, after the fashion of apes. He was soon sitting in the branches eating to his heart's content of the delicious fruit.

It happened, however, that the queen of heaven, Hsi-wang-mu (西 王 母), was celebrating her birthday that day. This occasion was celebrated by the gods every year as a great peach festival. When her servants came into the garden to gather the fruit they found very little was ripe, for Sun had eaten it all.

When he heard of the festival and realized that he alone among the heavenly dignitaries had not been invited, he was furious. He betook himself instantly to the banquet-hall and reached there before any of the invited guests. The table stood ready, loaded with all kinds of delicate fruits and delicious wines. Sun wished to consume some of the dainties at once, but as the waiters were constantly in and out, this was not an easy matter. Sun was not without a plan, however. By means of his incantations, he called forth a great swarm of insects which settled on the waiters and by their sting caused a drowsiness that was absolutely irresistible. While the servants slept in their several corners, Sun sat himself down and gave himself up to tasting everything. He was especially interested in the wine. After a time he rose staggering from the table and went off, but mistaking his road arrived at the castle of "Tou-shuai" (兜率) where Lao-tse (老子) lived. Here he found the jars in which the "pills of immortality" lay hidden. Naturally he laid hands on these and with a guilty conscience hastened back to earth to the kingdom of apes.

Once more heaven had to send out a punitive expedition. After many vain attempts they finally succeeded, with the help of Kuan-yin, in binding and fastening the frightful monster. He was placed under a high mountain, and there under the hundredweight load, he had time to repent. While the centuries went by, Sun steadily emitted groans, sighing after release.

There was one who had not forgotten him, however; this was Kuan-yin. When his term of punishment was almost completed, she came past the mountain where he lay and from beneath which only his strong claws struck out. She spoke to him tenderly and offered him deliverance. But the way of salvation is

[71]

TRUTH AND TRADITION IN BUDDHISM

narrow: he had to pledge himself to accompany the holy monk, Hsüan-chuang, who was just being sent out by the imperial court to begin his long and toilsome journey to the Western lands to secure the holy Mahayana scriptures.

At this point we come to the real "pilgrimage" which we shall merely sketch in outline. This journey to the Western regions is described with marvellous imagery full of colour and movement.

In all the dangers and difficulties to which they were now exposed, Sun Wu-kung was faithful and true to his master and his beautiful white horse, and used for them all his supernatural powers and all his magic. At the same time he was often wild, cruel, and impetuous, testing the master's patience many a time, so that it often seemed as if the whole undertaking would fail. Meanwhile, through his numberless trials, through Hsüan-chuang's constant reminders, and through the faithful help of Kuan-yin, he advanced step by step until at last this wild ape-man became a sanctified bodhisattva. One thing which Kuan-yin used to tame him was the famous cap with nails in it; this he had to wear continually. Every time his refractory nature began to get the upper hand, the thorns grew out sharp as nails on the inside of the cap. These pierced into his temples and caused intolerable pain.

On the journey westward, the pilgrims met all the terrors and intrigues of hell. No sooner was one army of devils overcome, than another came on. Now they were enticed by deceptive will-o'-the-wisps, now met by the most terrible monsters. It was fortunate, therefore, that two additional members joined their company. One was an abortive human being, who, through a lamentable mistake, was born of a sow, and therefore had to go through life not only with a pig's name, Chu-pa-chieh (猪八戒) (the pig who observes the eight commandments), but also in appearance reminding one strongly of the pig breed, with his big snout and flapping ears. The other was an unsuccessful Buddhist monk, the "Sand Monk" (Sha-ho-shang, 沙和尚). He had been left behind in the desert and had become a robber. Both, inspired by Kuan-yin, accepted the call and joined the pilgrimage to the Western paradise, and both were sanctified and renewed during the journey.

The last three sections of the book are especially impressive—the journey over the river of death, the arrival at the mountain of the spirits, and the return and final metamorphosis.

As they stopped before the dark river after the thousand dangers were at last happily passed, the great question arose: "How shall we cross over here?" An exceedingly rotten bridge could be seen, but as none of them dare try it, there was nothing left but to try the equally poor ferry which was close by. In the greatest terror the master and his companions climbed down into the boat, and it was carried out into the deep rushing stream. They had a feeling that the waters were closing over them, but immediately after there came a wonderful sense of security. The reason was not far to seek. Quite near to the boat several corpses were floating. These they perceived to be

TRUTH AND TRADITION IN BUDDHISM

their own bodies. They had become disembodied spirits, and an undreamed-of joy and strength filled them. They sped on their journey up the river-bank and across the bright meadows toward the great mountain. They had reached Ling Shan (靈山), the mountain of spirits, and become part of the heavenly world. The climax is reached as they stand before Ju-lai (如來), the highest Buddha, and in company with the holy spirits kneel in worship and praise before his throne.[1]

Finally, after making a speech to the pilgrims, Ju-lai directed his two disciples, Ananda and Kasyapa, to give them a complete collection of the Buddhist scriptures. These disciples, thinking the pilgrims more advanced spiritually than was the case, gave them a collection of books with blank pages, books which only the most enlightened spirits could read. The mistake was discovered in the course of time and the pilgrims received an edition of the books written in the ordinary way.

When they were about to leave on the return journey, Kuan-yin approached the throne of Ju-lai and said: "These pilgrims have taken fourteen years to get here; on the way they were constantly beset by dangers and were often near the point of destruction. I beseech thee to give me the authority to ensure that they and their books reach home within the course of

---

[1] The heaven which is here pictured is the Mahayana heaven where Amitabha rules. In comparison with the Taoist heaven where Sun Wu-kung played so many tricks on Yü-ti (玉帝) one notices a much greater sublimity and dignity.

THE JOURNEY TO THE WEST

eight days." To this Ju-lai agreed, and borne by eight strong cherubs (chin-kang, 金剛), after eight days' flight they arrrived again at Hsianfu, the ancient capital of the emperor of the Tang dynasty.

There the people had long been waiting the return of the pilgrims. During their absence preparations went forward for the housing of the books they were to bring home. A library was built and finished the third year after their departure. As each anniversary of Hsüan-chuang's departure came round the emperor himself went to this building to pray and make offerings. On one of these occasions, while the emperor and a great crowd of worshippers were again assembled for solemn worship, they saw in the distance the master coming on his white horse. Their joy was indescribable and on the pilgrims' arrival there was endless feasting and thanksgiving. The emperor declaring that neither silver nor gold could remunerate their benefactors, promised that he would himself write an introduction to the books, telling what Hsüan-chuang had done for his people, the story thus told to be handed down to all ages. With the help of his "Hanlin" (scholars of the highest degree) he then wrote the famous introduction.

The people all rejoiced that the master could now begin to read and explain the scriptures to them. They assembled in the great lecture-room, excited and attentive, but just as he was about to open his lips, the sound of the beating of cherubs' wings was heard, and the master and his three disciples were carried away in the spirit to the "Western Paradise."

TRUTH AND TRADITION IN BUDDHISM

The emperor and his people were seized with holy fear. Under the influence of what had happened, they decided that day to found the great association for the rescue of all lost souls in Hades, the "Land and Sea Association," also popularly called the "Yü Lan Hui" (孟蘭會). After their return to paradise the master was canonized as the "Buddha of Sweet Incense," Sun Wu-kung as the "Conquering Buddha," Chu-pa-chieh as the "Angel of the Golden Altar," and Sha-ho-shang became the "Golden Lo-han." All the hosts of heaven were present at the ceremony, and all sang together the "Pure Land Song."

THE NESTORIAN TABLET, CH'UNG-SHEN MONASTERY, SIANFU, SHANSI

CHAPTER IV

"THE ORIGIN AND DEVELOPMENT OF MASSES FOR THE DEAD"

If we were to take up the general subject of masses for the dead a lengthy treatise on the history of religion would have to be written; we therefore content ourselves with treating of masses for the dead in relation to Buddhism only.

In no other religion do masses for the dead play so large a part as in Buddhism. Even in Hinayana there are vague hints and dim intimations that through special forms of oblation one can get into touch with the needy souls in the lower regions, but it was only with the rise of Mahayana that these masses reached that degree of importance which they now hold in the religious life and worship of the East.

The ingenious technique and deeply religious foundation of these masses were not immediately brought to perfection. On the contrary, centuries went by before the system was fully developed, and this fuller development seems to have had some connection with the influence of the Nestorian Church.[1]

In order to understand our subject it will first be necessary to give a brief review of the cycles of transmigration and the theory of hell peculiar to Buddhism. We shall observe that in regard to these matters Mahayana has in general taken over the

[1] Cf. Professor P. Y. Saeki's book, "The Nestorian Monument in China."

TRUTH AND TRADITION IN BUDDHISM

position which Hinayana held, and which it in turn had taken from the Indian Vedas.

In Chinese Buddhism, these things are interpreted in the following manner:

In the continuous cycle of birth and death, always renewed by man's inherent desire to create, there are six great divisions or orders. The cycle is called in Chinese "lun-huei" (the wheel, with turns, or returns, the "wheel of life"). The highest order in the cycle is "heaven" and in this the "gods" (shên, 神) collectively are resident. This is called "t'ien-tao" (天道), the heavenly way. It is as the name signifies, a good place, and those who live there are also good. They are "t'ien-jen" (天人), heavenly men or good spirits. But they are not perfect; that is, they have not reached the ultimate goal of existence, the absolutely sure and safe place from which falling away and backsliding are excluded. To gain this, they must enter completely into Buddhahood, "ch'êng fu" (成佛), attain the absolute, and be absorbed in God. Then, and only then, have they reached the place where time is not, where all is peaceful and absolutely clear and bright, where all secrets of the universe are comprehended—the state of "chih-kuan" (止觀); the resting-place from which one perceives all things. Other words for this final goal are "Ch'an-ting" (禪定), the fixed state of meditation, or "Nieh-p'an" (涅槃), Nirvana.

Heaven, therefore, or rather the "heavens" are inhabited by Buddha candidates, "who after a longer or shorter time will attain the absolute" (Nirvana).

MASSES FOR THE DEAD

Their reason for delay in entering into final Buddhahood is usually that they have made a promise to come to the help of the rest of creation, which lies deep down in the lowest orders of the cycle, where the terrors of darkness, sorrow, sin, and perdition torture the souls.

He who has gone so far as to become a Buddha candidate or bodhisattva (Chinese: p'u-t'i-sa-to, 菩提薩多, or p'u-sa, 菩薩), has as one of his distinctive characteristics, not only all-seeing wisdom and great peace, but also absolutely boundless (Wu-liang, 無量) mercy. He has p'u-t'i hsin (菩提心), a compassionate heart for all who live and suffer—and he does not desire to enter into full blessedness before he knows that all creation is redeemed. Therefore, each of these bodhisattvas has his own chosen sphere of activity in those orders of the cycle, deepest down, where creation languishes in endless torment and pain. In the various writings where these merciful Buddhas and bodhisattvas are invoked and worshipped, this "sworn promise" plays a great part. The Buddhas are entreated, nay even adjured to help, on the basis of the solemn promise of mercy which they have given. Just here we stand before the objective facts in the Buddhist idea of redemption and atonement.

Theoretically this interpretation of the highest order of the cycle is quite distinct and clear. In the Chinese form, however, this definition is somewhat obscured by the fact that certain Buddhas are said to dwell in this or that "heaven" for certain periods. Thus it is often said in the Mahayana scriptures that Sakyamuni reveals himself, for example, in the so-called "Tao-li heaven"

(Tao-li T'ien, 忉利天), where he proclaims his "law" or gives an interpretation of some obscure point before all the powers of the universe. "Tao-li T'ien" is a collective term used for the thirty-three heavens, eight heavens for each of the four points of the compass, and one central heaven where Ti-shih (帝釋— Indra) rules in majesty.

The process of ascending upwards through all the "heavens" described in detail in the famous sutra "Leng-yen Ching" (thirty-three heavens and twenty-eight subsidiary heavens), is also thought of as an overcoming of the three great spheres or "chieh" (界). The first is the "Yü-chieh (欲界), the sphere where lust holds sway. The second is "Shê-chieh" (邑界), a better type of life, but one still dependent upon and attracted by the external appearance of things and all that appeals to the senses. In this sphere, there still exists a difference between sexes, consequently matrimony is also included. The third sphere is the "Wu-shê-chieh" (無色界), the state where all that has to do with the "lust of the eye" and the affections has been disposed of, the sphere where the "heavenly man" can ascend to the arhat and bodhisattva world, where they "neither marry, nor are given in marriage, but are as the angels of God in heaven."[1]

The next group is the human order, or "Jen-tao" (人道). Here men and women journey together in motley variety and yet alike in the one great fact that they have a human existence. Their destiny as human beings — man or woman, rich or poor, stupid or clever,

[1] Matthew 22:30.

MASSES FOR THE DEAD

beautiful or ugly, happy or unhappy—is determined by "acts" (Karma) done in an earlier existence. Retribution, reward, punishment, take their unalterable, law-abiding course. This decides all social differences and destinies in life.

Nothing is stated more clearly in Chinese Buddhism than this doctrine of "Yin-kuo" (因果), the law of retribution. It comes again and again in the sutras; it is the key-note for the whole doctrine of transmigration, the foundation of the whole complicated system of the Buddhist hell.

The best types in this order are those "who have a good root strongly developed in their hearts," "shan-kên" (善根), and who themselves foster its further growth through a dutiful and gentle human life. Such a person can in this life attain not only to the position of an arhat (lo-han, 羅漢), a saint, but he can become a bodhisattva (p'u-sa, 菩薩) for whom the entrance to the "Western Paradise" stands open when he leaves his tenement of clay. Many, very many, however, spoil their chances by an unholy and sensual life, so on the cessation of this mortal life they are born into one of the lower more evil orders.

Next in order comes the demon group, which in Chinese is called O-hsiu-lo-tao, 阿修羅道 (i. e., the way of demons). It is a transliteration of the Sanskrit word "Asuras." The demons are half good, half bad. Just because their nature is thus divided, they are constantly at strife with him who is absolute goodness, holiness, and justice, namely God. It is remarkable that Chinese Buddhism has here taken as the term for

[81]

TRUTH AND TRADITION IN BUDDHISM

the supreme God, the name which corresponds to the Indian Indra: namely, the god Ti-shih (帝釋). Among the demons the men are ugly and the women beautiful. The chief of the demons, who is also called O-hsiu-lo (阿修羅), is thought to dwell in the depths of the sea, where all is gloomy and unpleasant. This third order is nevertheless included among the "three good orders."

The poor creatures who have sunk down into the next three orders of torment and punishment, the so-called "san wu tao" (三惡道), the three evil ways, are very much worse off. First among these comes hades, the Buddhist hell ("ti-yü," 地獄), where punishment is carried out through long æons (kalpas), Chinese: chieh (劫). Buddhism believes in a horrible and ingeniously cruel hell. In many respects it resembles the hells of Hinduism, but in China a note of more abject terror coupled with a refinement of torture have been introduced.

Eighteen hells, situated at the "T'ieh-wei Shan," the "Iron-Encircled Mountain" (鐵圍山), ranging from the most scorching heat down to the most icy cold, come first. Of these, ten are especially notorious, being ruled by the ten famous "kings" or hangmen-chieftains. All these hells belong to the "Wu-chien Ti-yü" (無間地獄), or the hells where everything is boundless. At the head of these ten hells with their hangmen stands the overlord, whose nature is stamped by the most inflexible severity and justice. His name is Tung-yü (東嶽) and he lives on the famous mountain T'ai Shan (泰山) in Shantung province. He rules through his head chieftain Yen-lo (閻羅). The latter figure is particularly feared. A recollection of Yen-lo will cause the most hardened Asiatic to blanch with terror. It is the Yama of Hinduism which is represented in him. Among other parallels, the Minos of Plato's system comes nearest to this sinister figure.

In popular thought and speech these two overlords are often coupled with the ten "hangmen-chiefs." Then it is said that the "ten kings in hades" mete out the penalties and execute the punishments either directly or through the numerous assistants who surround them, i. e., the host of devils.

The names of these ten mighty kings, divided into the above-mentioned two groups, are as follows:

Tung-yü (東 嶽), Overlord

1. Ch'in-kuang (秦 廣)
2. Ch'u-chiang (初 江)
3. Sung-ti (宋 帝)
4. Wu-kuan (伍 官)
5. Yen-lo (閻 羅), chieftain
6. Pi'en-chêng (變 成)
7. T'ai-shan (泰 山)
8. Ping-têng (平 等)
9. Tu-shih (都 市)
10. Chuan-lun (轉 輪)

The close connection between supervision and punishments has gradually come to be regarded as taking place in the following way. On earth there have always been greater and lesser spiritual princes and officers, who keep careful records of all men's good and evil deeds. These report to the officials of both heaven and hades, and punishment or reward then follows in due time.

If there is one thing that is made clear to the Chinese, it is that

> "Good is recompensed with good,
> Evil is recompensed with evil
> And if payment is slow in coming,
> It is because its hour has not yet arrived."

[83]

TRUTH AND TRADITION IN BUDDHISM

The idea of an officer who supervises and keeps a register on earth, is quite in keeping with the legal system of the whole orient in ancient days. The system is worked in the following method. The whole surface of the earth is divided into sections (ti-fang, 地方), each with its local superintendent. He is usually called "t'u-ti" (土地), and images of him and his family made of wood, clay, or metal, are placed in small temples or covered altars. Such "earth altars" and small local temples are seen in city and country all over China (t'u-ti miao, 土地廟).

The local superintendents are then ranged under a greater "official" (all-spiritual beings). In the cities these are called ch'êng-huang (城隍), city gods; in country districts ti-huang (地隍), district gods. These "gods" are enthroned among consorts, children, and servants in stately temples (ch'êng-huang miao, 城隍廟, and ti-huang miao, 地隍廟), and great festivals with street processions are arranged annually in their honour.

Buddhism has allied itself with these ancient local deities, and by that very fact has secured a tremendous hold on the common people in China. For it is clear that just here the Buddhist priesthood with their masses and holy ceremonies can serve humanity burdened by sin and guilt, by pleading their cause with these dispensers of justice and retribution.

In these same local temples one often sees portrayed the ten hangmen-chiefs with their two overlords, divided into two groups, in the act of torturing or tormenting their victims. One feels a special horror

MASSES FOR THE DEAD

about these temples, a horror which recalls acutely the feeling one has on going into an ancient Chinese yamen, whence so many are led to the execution ground. A common name for the tortured, hungry, and thirsty spirits in hades is ê-hun (餓魂), hungry ghosts. We shall return later to these gloomy places, when we quote extracts from the curious literature which is connected with the masses for the dead.

There are, in addition, five hundred small and one thousand very small hells, through which lost souls have to go.

In the fifth order in the cycle come ê-kuei (餓鬼), the hungry spirits or order of devils. These are the creatures who have sunk so deep that they rejoice in evil, and who therefore gladly allow themselves to be used as assistants and co-laborers in all kinds of destructive enterprises by the more "professional devil princes." They enter gladly into the service of the "hangmen" and torture to their hearts' content the lost in hades. Among them, too, there are many grades. Most numerous are the so-called "hungry devils" who constantly rove about, restless and unblest, in the boundless spheres of the kingdom of hades. There are tremendous numbers of these, for the greater part of the wicked people in the world are recruits for this restless and hungry horde when their thread of life is broken off. Special efforts must be made to reach these hungering spirits, as we shall see, otherwise they will irretrievably go over into that professional devil group which becomes hardened in evil and disfigured by ugliness (yeh-ch'a, 夜叉, or lo-ch'a, 羅利).

[85]

Finally, we have the "ch'u-shêng" (畜生), or the animal order. This lies the deepest down of the "evil ways" and is recruited from the worst criminals and malefactors on the earth. According to the nature of their sins, they go, at death, into various animal forms, from the horse, cow, wolf, and tiger, down to snakes and crawling things. Numerous books and pictures in China treat of this horrible transformation. One sees how the animal skin stretches slowly out over the human body, how the character of the eye is changed and the animal look appears. For the creatures of this order, there is also a feeble glimmer of hope in the interminable darkness. Buddhism does not hold the conception of an everlasting hell, which the peoples of the West have become familiar with. Countless æons, kalpas after kalpas, may pass, in number so great and in duration so long as to be uncountable, but the final result is still the "salvation of all living things."

Buddhism in general deals with such vast dimensions and conceptions that one feels oneself cast out into the endless spaces of the universe, and yet along its own lines of thinking, it comes back to something not unlike Professor Einstein's position in our modern Western thought: space and time flow together, and the thought that is projected into the mysterious universe returns finally to its own starting-point.

In connection with transmigration, there has been a deep and ingenious development of this thought. The stream of life moves in three great periods, which again form a cycle for further movement. The first period began with Sakyamuni Buddha and ended five

MI-LO FU, LAMA TEMPLE, PEIPING

MASSES FOR THE DEAD

hundred years after his death. It is called "Chêng-fa" (正法), here translated as the first right model period. The second period lasts from the end of Chêng-fa for another five hundred years and is called "Hsiang-fa" (像法), the period in which pictures must be used. In this period men must work their way to the truth through pictures and books. From the end of the second period and lasting for a further two thousand years comes "Mo-fa" (末法), the final period. Then sin and need are increased to such a degree that Buddhism itself apparently goes to pieces. At this point, Maitreya (Mi-lo Fu, 彌勒佛) appears with his millennial kingdom. A new cycle of life begins, with hope and redemption for all living things. Thus one cycle follows another until all living things are redeemed.

It can be more easily understood against this background what tremendous significance masses for the dead must naturally have in Mahayana Buddhism. Without doubt we stand here before one of the most central beliefs of this whole religious system. One can also begin to have some understanding of the feeling of sympathy which so strongly characterizes Mahayana.

When masses for the soul were first instituted, it was naturally thought important that they should have a firm objective foundation in the traditions of Sakyamuni Buddha. Such was found in the old legend of Ananda, told in the "Yü-chia Yen-k'ou" (瑜伽燄口). Ananda saw the hungry spirits in hades (*pretas*) and in his pity asked Sakyamuni Buddha if there were not some way of satisfying their hunger. He then received

[87]

TRUTH AND TRADITION IN BUDDHISM

directions regarding a method by which food could be sent over into the other world through the special prayers of monks before the statue of Buddha, in the "assembly of the congregation." Upon this, from a historical point of view, very slender foundation, has been built up the immense fabric of masses and offerings for the dead which we shall now examine more closely.

It is of course well known that from the most ancient times the Chinese have been brought up to reverence deeply their ancestors. This had to be taken into account, and some arrangement made to meet this need. Anything that could help dutiful sons in their obligation to the dead, was as a matter of course welcomed by the Chinese. There was much in Buddhism that tore the individual away from society and from kith and kin, so it really was necessary to have something positively constructive to mollify and conciliate the more critical Chinese and those who were Confucian sympathizers.

It had not escaped the notice of the Buddhists that the Nestorian Church, largely because of its solemn masses "seven times a day for both the living and the dead," had obtained a strong hold on the people. They had also seen with wonder the "seven times seven" days' festival with the closing fiftieth day of feasting, which gathered together the Nestorian monks and priests in prayer for the dead and the living, annually. When one adds to this the fact that during the seventh and eighth centuries, new mystical mantra writings filled with magic formulæ and incantations

MASSES FOR THE DEAD

found their way from India to China, it can be understood just why this period should see such a rise and development of masses for the dead, as had not been marked before.

There is one man especially in this period, whose name is inseparably connected with the rapid development of masses for the dead. This is Amogha Vajra, (Chinese: Pu-k'ung Chin-kang, 不空金剛). He was a monk, who came over from northern India to China in the year 719, with his great teacher Vajra Bidhi (Chinese: Chin-kang Chih, 金剛智). In 732 he succeeded his master as patriarch of the Yogacharya School. Between 741 and 746 he was sent to India by the Emperor Hsüan Tsung, to get more Buddhist writings. The two succeeding emperors also held him in high esteem and when he died in 772, after a long and active life, he received the hitherto unheard-of posthumous title of "Minister of State for the Kingdoms of the East." He stood so high that all three emperors, at their coronations, had their crowns sprinkled with holy water by his hand. As a matter of fact, leaders of the Nestorian Church also had this honour on several occasions.

With statesman-like understanding, Amogha quickly saw that it was important to outshine the Nestorians, if possible, in the arrangements for the masses for the dead.[1] When one examines more closely the ritual which he issued, there can be no doubt that he and his helpers copied the rituals of the Nestorian Church

[1] He lived side by side with the Nestorians in Sian, where it is a well-established fact that the Buddhist monk Prajna himself, translated one of the Buddhist scriptures, in collaboration with the Nestorian priest Adam.

TRUTH AND TRADITION IN BUDDHISM

in many places. We can see this by a careful comparison of the Nestorian "Song of the Saints" and the "Baptismal Hymn," so beautifully translated in Professor Saeki's book.

They had, however, much more material than this at their disposal. There was the whole of Mahayna's vast store-house to draw upon, and in addition to this the translation of the rather obscure mantra literature which had newly arrived from India, with its fantastic magic formulæ and incantations. Further, they had no scruples about the kind of ideas and beliefs they introduced.

It was no wonder that Mahayana's masses for the dead went beyond any that had ever been heard of before, not only in the pomp of their externals, but also in the extravagant and fantastic nature of their content.

After fifty years of work in China, Amogha had got so far that he was able to arrange his "opening night" for the great drama which has since become so well known in the East—the "Feast for the Wandering Spirits"—that ceremony which later under the name of "Yü-lan-p'ên" (盂蘭盆), or "Yü-lan-p'ên Hui" (盂蘭盆會) (Sanskrit: Ullambana), has gone its way down through the centuries and has gathered together so many millions in religious ecstacy.

Before we describe this ceremony in detail, we shall cite an example of the way in which the rather slender historical foundation for these masses which has said to have been discovered in the first primitive Buddhism, was further built upon.

[90]

MASSES FOR THE DEAD

The story of how Maudgalyayana (Chinese: Mo-ho-mu-chien-lien, 摩訶目犍連, or Mu-lien, 目連), one of Sakyamuni's disciples, the pious son, saved his mother, is now popularly told in China as follows:

A pious mother, who had always been the most scrupulous vegetarian, fell sick, probably the result of excessive asceticism. She tried all kinds of cures, but all were in vain. Then one of her sons came to her and said that he could help her, if she would be willing to eat meat. The mother refused most vehemently. In spite of this the son prepared a dish which resembled vegetarian food but contained a little meat. She ate it and was soon quite well again.

One of the slaves in the house told the truth of the matter to another son, Mu-lien, and he, fearing lest his mother had thereby lost all hope of salvation, told her. She, secure in her innocence, denied it, calling upon all the gods to bear witness to the fact that she had not eaten meat.

In the dramatic presentation of the story which is most often given (it is one of the loveliest dramas on the Chinese stage), the mother is represented as saying, "If I have eaten meat, I pray that all the gods may cast me down into the deepest hell!" Immediately blood streams from her nose, mouth, and eyes, and the devil-hangmen draw her away to hades.

Mu-lien does everything in his power to rescue her. He lays upon himself all kinds of tortures in order to expiate her sin, but everything seems in vain. One night he sees her in his dream; her clothes are in tatters and her countenance bears traces of the greatest suffering. He sees how the hangmen in hades steal the money and the food that he has burned for her support. He hears her suppliant cry, "Come and help me." Thereupon he determines to go to hades (die). He wanders through the various zones in the kingdom of death, and after a long and persistent search finds her. She has been placed in a great cauldron where she is to be dismembered and cooked. He casts himself down before the devil-executioner and beseeches him to be allowed to take the torture upon himself. This is permitted, at least for a time.

In the dramatic presentation, one sees Mu-lien, appearing in the various torture scenes, always strong and firm. But when his need is the greatest, Buddha reveals himself in light and glory, and makes known the happy news that his mother can be saved if a body of monks will come together, and perform a mass for her soul. So after a while, one sees a row of monks drawn up solemnly before the figure of Buddha, and after the chanting and the musical instruments have sounded for some time, the gates of hell spring open, releasing the happy son with his redeemed mother. The scene closes with a high-pitched song of praise.

"*The Feast for the Wandering Souls*"

As we now attempt to give a description of the ceremonies which down through the years have been performed for the release of the wandering and lost spirits, it is natural to take first the "Feast for the Wandering Souls," or "Yü-lan-p'ên Hui" (盂蘭盆會), which has already been mentioned.

MASSES FOR THE DEAD

The main object of this ceremony is to conduct the souls as rapidly and safely as possible over the vast sea of want, hunger, thirst, and torment, which they got into when death overtook them, because of their sins. This has given rise to the expression "tu chung-shêng tʻo-li kʻu-hai" (度眾生脫離苦海), "to help all creation across the sea of pain," used in China again and again in speech and writing.

When a man dies, if there are any rich relations, pious and conscientious sons and daughters, widows or younger brothers, who can start the machinery, the whole matter can be arranged quite quickly. They simply order so many masses to be said in some temple or monastery, or allow the chief room or courtyard in their homes to be temporarily made over into a prayer hall ("taochʻang," 道場), where monks can chant their masses by the day, or even by the week. Often, however, there are no relatives to come to the help of the dead, or their poverty is such that nothing sufficient to meet the case can be done. If this happens, the monks, together with pious and philanthropic people, step in and help. Ever since the time of Amogha, it has been looked upon as a particularly meritorious act to contribute towards making the great "feast for the wandering souls" as splendid as possible.

Without doubt, much true sympathy and religious fervor is expressed in these acts. On the other hand, this feast is frequently used in a quite shameless way for personal gain or self-aggrandizement, money is coined out of it, and the whole business takes on such a noisy and theatrical tone that its religious significance almost completely vanishes.

The observance of this festival is regulated partly by the calendar, as it goes by the ten-, twelve-, or fifteen-year periods in the old Chinese cycle of years. In addition, there may be special cases of necessity which call for extra observances. Occasionally there may be one or more earnest and pious people who see that a performance of the ceremony is arranged for. The date for the feast is announced in plenty of time by the posting up of big yellow placards. People are urged to send in lists of all who may have died by drowning, murder, or other accident. Likewise, a request is sent out for money or other gifts.

Great preparations are made for the feast. The city's butcher-shops are often officially ordered to stop all slaughter and sale of meat. People are urged to fast (i. e., to refrain from partaking of all kinds of animal food). Along the river-banks great figures made of paper are set up, representing the gracious bodhisattvas of the lower world, Ti-ts'ang, Kuan-yin, the "earth gods" of the place, and so on. Terrifying images of animals, whole rows of devil-hangmen from the lower world, with Tung-yü and Yen-lo at their head, as well as scenes of horror from the torture-chambers of hell are all represented, made of coloured paper, stretched ingeniously on bamboo sticks.

The chief preparations are made on some open place, usually near a pond or a river. There terrace-like altars are set up, filled with incense burners, jars with flowers, inscribed pennants which flutter in the breeze,

MASSES FOR THE DEAD

etc. Near the altar is placed a large house of paper, divided into five rooms. In the centre room stand two paper figures of the famous Yin-yang Ssu (陰陽司), who conducts souls from this world into the other. He is represented with one side of his face white, the other black, for he is supposed to have access both to the land of the living and of the dead. The side rooms are supposed to be waiting-rooms for men and women, respectively, who are on their way to deliverance.

In smaller paper houses stand figures which give out food and clothes to the hungry and freezing spirits. There are also thirty-six shops, where the spirits can provide themselves with all necessities. Money, consisting of stamped paper notes and imitation silver and gold bars, is sent over to the dead in immense quantities; this is burned.

The other world is then notified that the ceremony is about to begin, by the burning of a large paper pennant. At the same time a paper horseman and horse are burned. This is the herald, who hurries off with the inscription to the land of the dead.

Then begins the mass. Long sutras are read, often accompanied by the most ear-splitting music. Offerings of food, rice, tea, small cakes, etc., are set out. This is a very important part of the performance, really a sacramental act. Only monks with long practice can perform in a perfect way all the finger manipulations, the gracious sprinkling of water, and the throwing out of rice grains, etc., in connection with this ceremony. If there is a pond in the neighbourhood

TRUTH AND TRADITION IN BUDDHISM

a small bridge is built over it. A priest stands with papers in his hand, and deals them out liberally to all the "poor people" who are thought to be passing over the bridge of death. The papers are handed to the priest on the other side, who then burns them.

Up on the central stage (the three-storey altar) stand a whole staff of Buddhist monks, who in long-drawn-out and high-pitched tones, chant the scripture and play musical instruments. The leading monk stands between two others on the central platform, holding an ivory staff in his hand. On the lowest platform stand five monks, who are especially occupied with the chanting. By the tones of the music, one who is initiated into the mystery will understand how far they have got in the advancing process of redemption. He will know when that great moment comes when they have "broken into hades" (p'o-liao ti-yü, 破了地獄), and when the way has been opened to the great pool of blood where the deeply sunk souls of women are specially tortured (p'o-liao hsüeh-hu, 破了血湖). He will be able to follow the further development, as the saving procession presses in through the barred torture-chambers, and be present when the burst of triumph at the end announces the great victory. It is midnight when these notes of victory are sounded. Then everything ceases at one stroke, for from that moment all things begin to move forward towards the dawn and daylight!

The book which is especially connected with this ceremony is "The Ullambana Scripture" (Chinese:

MASSES FOR THE DEAD

"Yü-lan-p'ên Ching," 盂蘭盆經), which we shall come back to later. It is said to have been translated into Chinese by Dharmarakcha (265–316).

The ordinary Kuei Chieh, "Feast of the Spirits" is held more regularly on the fifteenth of the seventh month. Then in the warm, late summer evenings one often sees a beautiful sight along the river-banks. A similar display of paper houses and figures, altars, and incense burners is set out, only smaller in size. Quite characteristic, also, is the setting afloat of small "candle boats" on the river. A candle is cleverly fastened on a piece of wood, and surrounded by coloured paper. As these hundreds and thousands of twinkling "candle boats" drift down the stream in the still summer night, they turn one's thoughts into solemn religious channels. One cannot but think of the many unfortunates who every year are drowned or killed in some other way along China's many rivers and highways.

Buddhism has made a remarkable impression upon the religious life of China, by means of these annual "spirit festivals," and the realistic presentation of the horrors of perdition and the certainty of retribution; but perhaps most of all by means of the great masses for the dead. Through these things it causes this people, naturally a rather materialistic race, to stop for a time in their restless chase after the things of this life, and think of that life which is to come, and of their sacred duty towards the needy.

In contrast to the other festivals, there is much greater solemnity about the feasts on the birthdays of the great bodhisattvas. It is not common at that time to allow theatrical performances.

We have already briefly described the masses for the dead where one, three, five, or ten monks take part. It remains now to describe the special performances which take place in the large temples and monasteries, for the release and redemption of more or less definite groups of the departed. These performances may be on behalf of one family or one individual, of some especially afflicted section of the country, of the whole land, or of all lost souls "within the four seas."

In order to set this cumbersome machinery in motion, the monasteries often make an appeal to the sympathies of well-to-do men and women, and these benefactors are memorialized with laudatory phrases written on decorative scrolls and tablets. If, however, the monastery is a rich one with large resources in land, they arrange the whole thing at their own expense.

One cannot get away from the fact that in spite of all the "commercial spirit" and greed, in spite of the very stilted form and outward fuss of the performance, there are nevertheless many of the monks and their lay helpers who are fired by real spiritual zeal. A spirit of deep sympathy and fellowship in suffering is felt by them, both during the time of preparation and during the conduct of the mass itself. This was evidenced during the last terrible war which laid waste Europe and made itself felt to the uttermost parts of the earth. When the Buddhist monks in China read the newspapers and saw day after day telegrams giving news of the most terrible death rolls on all fronts, they

MASSES FOR THE DEAD

decided on their own accord to hold special masses for the souls of those who had fallen in Europe. "For," they said, "we see the kingdom of the dead filled with harried spirits from the field of battle, and something extra must be done for them."

The common form for these great performances in the temples is the well-known "Shui-lu tao-chang" (水陸道場), that is to say, "masses for the souls on sea and land." It is reckoned in the temples that at least a thousand Chinese dollars is necessary to hold even a very modest "sea and land mass." Enormous quantities of dishes with fruits and vegetables must be prepared. Rolls of silk and paper and other materials must be made ready. Immense quantities of paper objects, great heaps of paper money, etc., are required.

At these times, one finds a number of the rooms in the second storey of the temple, which ordinarily stand empty, transformed into the most wonderful outfitting shops. Wall scrolls and banners inscribed with the finest quotations from the holy writings are found on all sides, and a great host of monks, often under the personal leadership of the abbot, take part in the masses.

Part of the mass takes the form of a procession, when the monks pass in long rows from room to room. The mass goes on from sunset till midnight. Then suddenly everything is silent and still. The performance continues for a week, and sometimes even longer, especially in the "Pure Land" School, where every year they hold a "seven times seven" mass forty-nine days and one closing day of solemn feasting.

TRUTH AND TRADITION IN BUDDHISM

The most beautiful and really also the most affecting form of this labour of love for the redemption of lost souls in hades, is, however, associated with a simpler ceremony. This goes on in certain temples and monasteries quite regularly, in others ceaselessly, night and day. It is the reading of those portions of the scriptures which are especially connected with the "saviour of the lower world," the great and radiant bodhisattva Ti-ts'ang (地藏). As there is much of special interest connected with him, we must accord him special attention. In the larger monasteries one often finds a special hall in his honour. Where they have not this, usually a small enclosure is partitioned off the main hall, where his image with an altar and an uncommonly big bell are placed. Occasionally this arrangement is found up in the tower, which then becomes a prayer tower. Often a little image of Ti-ts'ang is placed just under the bell.

Monks take it in turn to sit before this image and read the scriptures in a low voice, at certain intervals pulling a cord. This cord is connected with a wooden ram and every time the cord is pulled the ram strikes the bell with great force (Yu-ming chung, 幽冥鐘, the bell before the gloomy valley) and a deep long boom resounds through the rooms and out into the night.

Many of these bells are exceedingly old. It is a mystery how the ancients were able to cast these colossal things, and get such deep, strong tones, so indescribably full of feeling and beauty. Only one who has lain awake and listened to the regular boom in a monastery in the small hours of the night can

MASSES FOR THE DEAD

form any conception of the weirdly solemn, and yet indescribably reverent feeling which these simple "night masses" before the image of Ti-ts'ang give one. It is no wonder that in Buddhist verse and poetry, the "sound of the bell, which quaveringly rings out in the darkness of night" has become one of the most commonly used symbols for the deeper connection between human life and the "land of shadows." The long, deep tone, lasting for one minute or more, is certainly well adapted to carry the thought of prayer and sympathy over to the other world.

We have already mentioned the "mystical mantra scriptures," which in the time of Amogha entered into the fabric of the masses for the dead. Later they developed on Chinese soil in a still wilder and more fantastic manner and the more serious-minded and careful monks have therefore a certain hesitancy about using them. Many of these serious Buddhist monks will have nothing whatever to do with official masses. Some of them on principle will not take part in any of these things, especially if there is an element of "business" or financial speculation in it. They prefer to live in great poverty and devote themselves to meditation and the study of the scriptures, for they feel that it is difficult to preserve a "clean escutcheon" if they are mixed up with the questionable practices connected with the masses for the dead.

The greater number of the monks, however, take part, and a few with particularly good voices and with a special inclination towards the melancholy, can carry the business to great lengths.

TRUTH AND TRADITION IN BUDDHISM

The topmost point is reached by those who are really artists, in the special "ceremony of redemption," which the Chinese call "fang yen-k'ou (放餸口); filling the hungry mouths. It is here that the "mystic mantras" have reached their climax in China. We shall therefore give a description of this ceremony. The technique and theory of this system has not yet been thoroughly investigated by any sinologue. We hope to come back to it later in a special detailed treatment.[1]

This ceremony can also be "ordered" by grief-stricken people who wish to help their dear departed ones. There are often, too, philanthropic people or those who wish to acquire special merit, who hire a little band of especially trained monks to perform this mass which usually takes three evenings or more.

This may take place in the temple hall, or preferably in one of the side rooms. On an improvised platform sit the three leading monks before a large table. They are placed on specially constructed seats, and sit with their legs crossed under them, like living Buddha images. It is an important point that these three shall represent the triune Buddha: Sakyamuni, the Buddhist doctrine, and the society. Naturally the central figure is the most important, as he represents Buddha himself. These three men must have a good ear, good singing voices, and must possess great

[1] There is much which reminds one of the holy pantomimes in the ancient church, in which the victims in purgatory were led forth to paradise.

MASSES FOR THE DEAD

dexterity of fingers, for, as we shall see, the fingers and hand movements play an important part.

In front of these three, but lower down, sit the assistants. These are monks who join in the mass, with verses of song, and with musical instruments. There are, as a rule, four on each side of the oblong table. If they are well-trained monks they can recite the enormously long text of the mass, page after page, from memory. In case they are uncertain of the text, they have the book on the table before them.

The scene begins with a fanfare of musical instruments. A little bell is rung, and then the "living Buddha" begins to sing the first verses of the mass in an endlessly long chant. Dressed in an especially beautiful costume with an arrangement resembling a halo round his head, he sings his verses with solemn and impressive expression. It is a high-pitched lament of woe over the hungering, thirsting, and freezing souls, which flit about the gloomy chambers of the underworld, but it contains also a happy promise of redemption to be obtained through the compassionate Buddhas. Here the instrumental music strikes in. There is a perfect storm of tumultuous shouting and violent music, which is intended to burst open the doors of hell. One can see by the expressions of the three leaders that it is a serious business. Their countenances stiffen into a grim and iron-hard expression, and their hands, which now come into action, are clenched as if for a blow. With a loud knock on the table with

TRUTH AND TRADITION IN BUDDHISM

a thick wooden implement, the "living Buddha" announces that the doors are opened.

The second act is introduced by the ringing of a bell. One hears in the tones of the chant that the first shadowy vales of hades are passed. What is of special interest in the succeeding acts is the hand and finger movements. Long and careful practice lies behind these manipulations and genuflections. Handbooks with illustrations of these movements are studied by generation after generation. Several of these books are before me as I write these lines and I recognize the positions of the fingers, etc., as I have seen them many times while standing by, watching the monks during the conduct of this strange service.

There is something hypnotic about the whole affair and one has a peculiarly unpleasant sensation as the performance proceeds, for in a remarkable way the practised monks bring out the various torments and terrors of hell through these movements of the hands: one sees the bound, the savage, the tortured; the glimmering tongues of fire and ice-cold showers of rain, the brutal scorn and dull self-abandonment of the lost souls.

But in the midst of all these woes the presiding monks will begin the sacramental act of filling the burning (hungry and thirsty) mouths of the wandering spirits: the sprinkling of the water from the jar of the merciful Kuan-yin, the distribution of rice from the blessed bowl of Sakyamuni, the waving motion of the blessed lotus in the hand of Ta-shih-chih, the consoling sight of the golden tower in the hand of O-mi-t'o Fu.

VAIROCANA

MASSES FOR THE DEAD

By these functions rays of hope steal in. One sees in the position of the fingers a pagoda rising up, one feels that one is led in through open temple doors, where incense and light, music and the harmonious tones of the chant, bear one up to loftier spheres. A lotus blossom is laid in the hand, and the three "Buddhas" acquire something of exalted repose and the light of great pity in their expressions. After the many scenes of frenzied despair which brought the paleness of fright into their faces to such a degree that drops of sweat ran from their foreheads, it is a great relief to come to these quiet and peaceful parts of the ceremony.

There is, indeed, art and solemn earnestness in this ceremony, but it escapes into black magic and animistic exorcism. It is therefore quire natural that the more spiritual monks and the profound thinkers within the Buddhist society keep out of it, but for the many who have sunk so low as to take the whole business more or less as a means of making a living, this ceremony for "filling the hungry mouths" is a splendid source of income.

Before we go on to further description of the central bodhisattva of these masses for the dead, Ti-ts'ang (地藏), we shall very briefly describe another Buddha figure who has left his mark on the historical development of the masses for the dead. This is the famous Vairocana (Chinese: P'i-lu-chê-na, 毘盧遮那, or merely P'i-lu, 毘盧). According to the classic account, he belongs to the threefold incarnation of Buddha

[105]

(Trikaya). As is well known, there are several explanations of this.

We confine ourselves to that explanation which has quite finally been adopted by the great "interpreters of the law" (Fa-shih, 法師) in the Buddhist society in China, namely, that Vairocana is the incarnation of Buddha's law or doctrine (dharma; Chinese; fa, 法). His image, therefore, is always found in the places where the law is to be proclaimed. Corresponding to Vairocana, one has also the other Buddha type which represents the society or the association of monks grouped in a monastery (sangha; Chinese: sêng, 僧). He is called Lochana (Chinese: Lu-shê-na, 盧舍那; or simply Lu-shê, 盧舍). The central figure in this group of three is Sakyamuni Buddha.

It is without doubt owing to Chih-k'ai's famous literary school (T'ien-t'ai School) that the worship of Vairocana came into favour so early, and was later cultivated as a separate religion. Chih-k'ai was most interested in the "doctrine." The fundamental scriptures for him was "The Lotus Scripture" ("Fa-hua Ching," 法華經). It was not before A.D. 725, however, that this "religion" got its own name. It was called the "Great Sun Religion" after one of the principal writings "Ta-jih Ching" (大日經), "The Great Sun Scripture" (Sanskrit: "Maha Vairocana Sutra").

This took place just at the time of the great expansion of the Nestorian Church when its name "shining" was first used. There are many things which point to the fact that there was considerable co-operation and connection between these two forms of teaching. This is also plainly shown in the final form of the name of the Nestorian Church in China: Ching Chiao (景 教), the "Shining Religion." With great forethought the old Nestorians chose the adjective "ching" (景) which, analyzed into its simple elements, 京 and 日, means "great and shining" or "great" and "sun," a term which undoubtedly for the people of that time must have led their thoughts to the "Great Sun Religion" centering in Vairocana.

On the other hand, however, the Nestorian Church has certainly exercised no small influence in shaping the content of the idea of the "Great Sun" and its religious school. Unmistakable traces of Christian ideas meet one everywhere in this doctrine—the idea of God as the "father of light," of Christ as the great "light of the world" who by his work of salvation burst the "bonds of death" so that he could himself descend in triumph into the depths of the kingdom of death and proclaim his "law" to the rebellious spirits.

It is no wonder that Amogha, the great promoter of masses for the dead, gave himself, life and soul, to the "Great Sun Religion," and that Vairocana came to be not only the shining representative for the light of learning, but also the incarnation of the idea of great compassion, an idea which had taken its most beautiful and richest form in Amitabha. A few sinologues believe, for this reason, that the two forms blended together for a while during the flourishing period of the "Great Sun Religion."

The close connection between the Nestorian Church and the "Great Sun Religion," appears also in the

[107]

many common terms for the various "servants in the church." The "Catholicos" of the Nestorians became "Fa-chu" (法主). Their "Episcopos" became "Ta-tê" (大德); their monks took the same name as the Buddhist monks "sêng" (僧); their archdeacon was called "ssŭ-chu" (寺主), or superintendent of the monastery, etc.

Just as these two doctrines had their flowering at about the same time, so also they were companions in times of persecution and decline. It is perhaps no mere chance that the apparent disappearance of the "Great Sun Religion" and the "Shining Religion" took place at about the same time. The Vairocana School was merged with the other Buddhist schools, and for many years now it has been difficult to find any traces of its special forms and expressions. Indeed, one must hunt long even in the best monastery libraries before one finds the old "Ta-jih Ching" (大日經) ("The Great Sun Scripture"). The most learned amongst the monks have a dim idea that the "Great Sun Religion" was one of the names of the now extinct "Mi Chiao" (密教) (the "mysterious school of religion").

According to the statement of the learned monk T'ai-hsü (太虛) most of "The Great Sun Scripture" is to be found in the voluminous "Hua-yen Ching" (華嚴經), more particularly in the portion called Yü-chia-shih ti Lun (瑜伽師地論), the scripture for the "Mi-tsung" (密宗) or "Yü-chia-tsung" (瑜伽宗), the old secret school in Buddhism (Yoga-caryabhumi-shastra). A careful study of this scripture by able sinologues will have to be made in order to get full light upon the

[108]

MASSES FOR THE DEAD

question of the relationship between the old Mahayana and the Nestorian Church.

The consequence of all this was that it became necessary to get another central figure for the machinery of the masses for the dead. Such a figure was found in the great and compassionate bodhisattva Ti-ts'ang (地藏). His Indian name is Kshitigarbha (the treasure-chamber of the world); the meaning of the name in Chinese also corresponds to this. He does not seem to have played any great rôle in Indian Buddhism, but in China, Korea, and Japan he is enormously popular. In the last-mentioned country he bears the name Jizo. A parallel in the religious system of Zoroaster is Srosh.

In China the following legend has arisen regarding his life:

Ti-ts'ang was in reality a prince, the son of a king. His surname was Chin (金) (gold) and his given name Ch'iao-chio (喬覺). In the reign of the Emperor Chih Tê of the Tang dynasty (A.D. 754) he abandoned the empty life of this world and became a monk. As such he wandered to China.

There are two opinions as to where Chin Ch'iao-chio's native country was. The Chinese themselves and many foreigners with them think that he came from Siam. In the scriptures and stone tablets preserved in the mountain monasteries at Chiu-hua Shan (九華山), the name of Chin's native country is sometimes given as Hsin-lo (新羅), sometimes as Hsien-lo (暹邏). If the last-mentioned characters are the original, then there can be no doubt that the supposition

[109]

mentioned above is the right one, because Hsien-lo is manifestly used for Siam. But so far it has not been conclusively proved that these characters are the original ones. There are, on the other hand, strong historical grounds for the assumption that Hsin-lo must be the original. If this is so, then Chin came from Korea. The strongest argument for this assumption is the fact that there reigned just at that time in the little kingdom of Hsin-lo, or Silla, in Korea some kings by the name of Chin. A real kingdom of Siam was first established much later, as is clearly brought out by R. T. Johnston in his "Buddhist China."

When Chin was ascending the Yangtze River by boat and saw the nine wonderfully beautiful mountain peaks near the city of Tat'ung (Chiu-hua Shan, 九華山, the "Nine-Flower Mountains") he decided to disembark there, having first received from the magistrate of the place "as much ground as his prayer-mat could cover." As he sat himself down there to meditate, people became aware of a holy radiance which seemed to surround the place. Upon this his divinity was established and his existence secured. For seventy-five years he sat upon that spot in deep meditation, and in the seventy-sixth year in the seventh month and the thirtieth day of the month of that year which was called "K'ai-yüan" (開元) he attained to the great enlightenment and passed away. At that time he was ninety-nine years old. Several well-known lay devotees from the neighbouring places came to visit Chin and provided for his needs.

MASSES FOR THE DEAD

A minister named Min (閔公), who was an ardent devotee of Buddhism, heard about this pious recluse and his white dog, who was always by his side. Min greatly longed to see the holy man. Once a year, therefore, when he had one hundred monks with him as guests, he always left one place vacant. At a later meeting between these two, Ti-ts'ang begged that he might have "a place for his monk's cap in China" after death. Min therefore brought it about that the whole mountain region with the nine peaks was given over to Ti-ts'ang.

After death Chin's body was wonderfully preserved for a long time, and tongues of fire flickered over his grave, making it perfectly clear that the pious recluse was no other than Ti-ts'ang, who by dying had descended to hades in order to rescue the hungry and miserable spirits.

The tomb, over which the famous pagoda was later built, is still shown and the millions of pilgrims who yearly visit the famous mountains, are able, after special preparations, to catch a glimpse of the underworld through a mountain crevice. For it was thither that Ti-ts'ang, in his boundless pity and love for the lost, went when he disappeared.

After the death of Ti-ts'ang, Min and his son entered the Buddhist society as monks. Their images are often seen set up beside that of Ti-ts'ang. The figure of the son, Tao-ming (道明), stands on the left, and the father on the right side, for "the son introduced the father to the learning of Buddhism."

TRUTH AND TRADITION IN BUDDHISM

As might be expected, many of the most spiritual of the Chinese hymns of supplication have come to centre around Ti-ts'ang. The wonderfully impressive title "Yu-ming Chiao-chu" (幽冥教主), the "Master of the Kingdom of Death," referred to his person. The conception was that Amitabha, as the great All-Father, he who is the great and true "Saviour from the West," in his boundless grace and mercy, decided to show his compassion to the lost souls in hell, through the meditation of Ti-ts'ang. For this reason, there is a trace of Amitabha's compassionate expression in the image of Ti-ts'ang. Indeed, one must look far to find another image which comes up to that of Ti-ts'ang in beauty and grace. Beaming with light and peace, with a countenance which discloses the most incorruptible justice and compassion, his image often stands surrounded by the most grim and horrible devil-hangmen. Here there is a double line of thought. On the one hand is the unbreakable law of compensation, which Ti-ts'ang also must accept, but which is administered by other powers in the universe (divine powers) and therefore does not lie within his sphere of action. On the other hand is the law of grace, which has its foundation in the compassionate Buddhas and bodhisattvas, those beings who always represent wisdom, holiness, and the tenderest pity.

Here we are faced with the fundamental difference between Buddhism and Christianity. Buddhism lacks the majestic conception of a complete unity, which we have in God, who is the source and administrator of

[112]

MASSES FOR THE DEAD

justice and the law of life, as well as the eternal source of love and mercy.

How, then, is Ti-ts'ang able to achieve the redemption of the lost? At this point enters in the doctrine of propitiation as it is known in Mahayana. He has made promises on oath, and these oaths assert that he himself will not leave the gloomy chambers of the underworld and rise up into the Buddha existence before the last of the inhabitants of hades has been redeemed. It is clear that there lies a supreme self-sacrifice in this act, indeed *a kind of vicarious atonement*.

The other bodhisattvas, in their own spheres of activity, have taken the same action and made the same promises to help mankind. And not only they, but holy persons on earth, persons with something of the "good root" (shan kên, 善根) in them, can share in this great work of atonement and salvation. For them, too, it will entail such sacrifice as abstaining from all animal food, setting apart regular times to meditate and to pray for the lost, reading the holy scriptures on their behalf. Through such acts as these, they can assist Ti-ts'ang in his overwhelming task of redeeming the countless multitudes in the kingdom of death. By means of this united effort it is as if a new power were stored up, an atoning and remedial power, which with the inexorability of a law of nature will allay the agonies of the lost, and so stir their souls that they can begin to long for purity and godliness, and thus rise towards holiness. Compare St. Paul's pregnant words: "Now I rejoice in my sufferings for your sake, and fill up on my part that which

TRUTH AND TRADITION IN BUDDHISM

is lacking of the afflictions of Christ in my flesh for His body's sake, which is the church."[1]

Under these conditions, it becomes clear that masses for the dead performed in this world must be of the greatest significance, and a new meaning is felt in the long, booming strokes of the bronze bell which, in indescribably deep and ringing tones, in the stillness of the night, carry the tributes of men into the gloomy land of the shadow of death. On this account, also, we can understand the enormous attraction Ti-ts'ang's mountains (Chiu-hua Shan in Anhwei province) has for pilgrims year by year.

The story of Mu-lien's search for his lost mother, given before in this chapter, is also included in the "Yü-lan-p'ên Ching" (孟蘭盆經).

Below is given a summarized translation from the Chinese of the mass-book "The Scripture of the Dish" ("Yü-lan-p'ên Ching," 孟蘭盆經) (Sanskrit: "The Ullambana Sutra"). It was translated into Chinese in the year 315 by Dharmarakcha:

"It has been told us that Buddha once met with his disciples in his usual way in the garden, Ch'i-shu-chi-ku-tu Yüan (祇樹給孤獨園) in the kingdom of She-wei. At that time Ta-mu-chien-lien (abbreviated to Mu-lien) had advanced so far towards the gates of perception that he could nearly understand the great principles of life. He had an earnest desire to save his parents, and so repay their care and trouble.

"With his awakened eye of wisdom, he saw clearly that his dead mother had sunk down among the

[1] Col. 1:24.

MASSES FOR THE DEAD

hungry spirits. He saw how starved she was, to such a degree indeed that skin and bones had grown together.

"At this vision, Mu-lien felt unutterable pangs, and he therefore took his bowl, filled it with food and sent it over to her. His mother took the cup, covered it with her left hand, so that the devils should not grab it from her, and with her right hand took some of the food. It had not reached her mouth, however, before it was changed into glowing coals of fire, so that she could not eat it.

"Then Mu-lien cried out in the deepest anguish, and the tears rolled down his cheeks. In wild haste he ran back to Buddha and laid the story before him.

"Buddha said to him: 'The roots of your mother's sin are many and deep. You alone will therefore never be able to save her, in spite of the fact that the report of your obedient and filial spirit has stirred both heaven and earth. For neither heaven nor earth, neither any of the gods of nature, nor demons nor devils, neither the four kings of heaven, nor the wise teachers, can save her alone. It will be necessary in this case to call together the Buddhist society, that is to say, the Buddhist monks from the four corners of the earth—only then can she be saved from perdition. I will also tell you now how salvation from all need and sorrow can ordinarily be accomplished.

"'On the fifteenth day of every seventh month, the Buddhist monks from all the corners of the earth must come together, for it has been reckoned out that that time is the most favourable to pray for the ancestors up to the seventh generation, as well as for the parents

[115]

TRUTH AND TRADITION IN BUDDHISM

who are still alive and sit bowed under sorrow and grief. That is the time to give them plentifully all kinds of dishes and herbs, all offered in a bowl with water. Beside this, incense bowls, paper, candles, beds with blankets and other appurtenances, together with all sorts of refreshments, shall be set out for them.

"On the appointed day, all the holy ones—whether those who live as hermits and practice meditation or those who have attained to full sanctity, or those who wander in meditation among the trees, or those who through their six gates of apprehension have reached the full understanding; or those who still stand at the fork of the road between good and evil (Shêng-wên Yüan-chio 聲聞緣覺) or the ten great bodhisattvas from the ten great places, or those who have just become "pi-ch'iu" (比丘), all who have the same longing and who have heard the pure commandment in their souls and live according to the teaching of the saints, the virtuous and meek, all these, together with the company of Buddhist monks, shall bear forward the offerings of food, in a reverent manner, on behalf of the many parents and ancestors who are in torment down in the three evil orders of transmigration. By making the same offering for living parents, the length of their life may be increased up to one hundred years of age.'

"At that time Buddha gave orders to all Buddhist monks to read first the sections of the holy writings which deal with all true adherents of the Buddhist faith, and in addition at every meal, to carry out the work of meditation for ancestors up to the seventh

TI-TS'ANG

MASSES FOR THE DEAD

generation. Offerings of food shall be placed before the images of Buddha that stand in the temple halls or in pagodas. When the chanting of the masses is over and the monks have made their vows, the meal may begin.

"In this way Mu-lien's mother was saved from the torments of the hungering spirits. Mu-lien then said to Buddha: 'Thy disciple's mother has now attained to blessedness by means of "the three great values" (san-pao, 三寶, Buddha, the doctrine, and the society); by means, too, of the divine power which goes out from the Buddhist monks. Now, with regard to the future, if all disciples of Buddha, in a similar manner, will "set forth the dish" for the salvation of parents and forefathers up to the seventh generation, will that be possible?'

"Buddha answered: 'There you ask an uncommonly good question. I was just about to say it; but since you put the question first yourself, nothing could be better! Good people such as "pi-ch'iu" (比丘) (those who have reached the second degree in consecration), nuns, kings, princes, the highest officials and ministers, lords and the various ranks of magistrates, citizens and common people, who desire with earnestness to carry out their vows of obedience to parents and ancestors up to the seventh generation, ought all to do it in the following way: On Buddha's day of rejoicing, which falls on the same day as the date reckoned out by the monks, the fifteenth of the seventh month, a meal should be arranged, consisting of all sorts of dishes which shall be offered on a tray, for all the

TRUTH AND TRADITION IN BUDDHISM

Buddhist monks of the heavenly regions. These, then, shall make the vows and give the great promises of an old age without sickness or need for the living, and of redemption for ancestors up to the seventh generation, from the spheres of the hungering spirits, so that they may be born into that human and heavenly existence where limitless joy abounds.

"'For this reason every dutiful son and disciple of Buddha ought always to remember his parents and ancestors up to the seventh generation, and every year on the fifteenth of the seventh month give expression to his desire to prove his filial piety by offering the "large dish" (p'ên, 盆) before Buddha's statue and the monks, in order to repay his parents in this way for their care.'

"All the Buddhist disciples took this vow with joy."

A synopsis of "The Scripture Concerning Ti-ts'ang's Fundamental Promises." Chinese: "Ti-ts'ang Pên-yüan Ching" (地藏本願經).

This great, and in its own way remarkable, book, gives a very complete account of the anguish of perdition and hades, as well as of the process of salvation as it is accomplished through endless kalpas, by Ti-ts'ang, the compassionate bodhisattva of the lower world.

There is much internal evidence to sustain the supposition that the book dates among the latest sutras in the Chinese Tripitaka. This can be seen not least in the true Chinese colouring and the greatly developed

[118]

MASSES FOR THE DEAD

hell-apparatus which is portrayed. Moreover, each section closes with a strong appeal to all good men and women to take part in building pagodas, images of Buddha, and temples, and to bring their offerings thither in the form of incense, paper money, etc. In brief, the "business atmosphere" appears very strongly.

There are also parts of great beauty, however; as, for example, the description of the great scene when Buddha calls together all the dignitaries of heaven, together with the officials of the world and the lower regions, myriads of princely spirits and shining Buddha forms, gleaming white as the "snows of the Himalayas," countless in number as "flying dust motes," together with the multitudinous lost souls of hell. The different qualities are portrayed in the different tones of light and shade, and there is laid bare a panorama of the most fantastic character.

Ti-ts'ang's great mission to hades gets its solemn authorization from Buddha himself in the following manner:

It is recorded as a dialogue with Wên-shu (文殊) (Sanskrit: Manjusri), the bodhisattva of wisdom. Buddha gives his friend a glimpse into the future, and the latter asks, "Who are all this great multitude?"

Buddha answers: "This is the assembly of all those whom Ti-ts'ang, the great bodhisattva has, through endless kalpas, brought to redemption (i-tu, 巳度), those who are now in the process of salvation (tang-tu, 當度), and those who shall be saved in the future (wei-tu, 未度)."

[119]

TRUTH AND TRADITION IN BUDDHISM

Further on in the book an account is given of how Ti-ts'ang happened to hit upon the idea of offering himself for the redemption of the Universe. He saw before him, in a vision the "all-embracing master," who in a moment had acquired full knowledge of both the present and the future. Looking upon the noble and shining countenance of this Buddha, he was seized with an earnest desire to be like him. On asking what he should do to reach this point, the "all-embracing master" answered: "If you wish to reach this state of enlightenment you must through endlessly long periods of time help the many unfortunate creatures in hell to attain salvation." Then it was that Ti-ts'ang took the great vow: "In all the future days, through uncounted kalpas, I will apply myself to practising the various methods of salvation on behalf of all the unfortunate creatures who are in the different stages of transmigration of wandering spirits. Until I have freed them all, I will not myself enter into the dignity of Buddhahood."

Under various names and characters Ti-ts'ang now appears throughout the book as one who "exemplifies the most varied methods of saving the perishing." One very common method is by preaching. It can be said, in a way, that he "established a work of preaching" down in hades. He takes over the rôle of Vairocana. There seems to be unmistakable influence here from the teaching and rites of the Nestorian Church.[1]

[1] Cf. the clause in our creed "He descended into hell," found in 1 Peter 3:19, 20 and 4:6.

[120]

MASSES FOR THE DEAD

In several of the later sections of the book, Ti-ts'ang appears also as teacher. There is, for example, the scene where the "holy mother" (Buddha's mother, Mâyâ, 摩耶 in Chinese) asks Ti-ts'ang to tell her what are the conditions down there in hades, for the people of Asia especially. In his answer, Ti-ts'ang gives an account of the eternal law of recompense and the horrors of the punishment in hell.

"'This is the state of affairs in southern Asia, with regard to the recompense for sin,' he says. 'There are children who are disobedient to their parents even up to the point of killing their father and mother, and who therefore must sink down into that hell where the pangs have no relief and whence through countless kalpas they can never escape.

"'There are others who pierce Buddha's messengers on the earth. Still others who speak with scorn of the three holy values, and have no reverence for the holy scriptures. All these must sink down to that hell where there is no cessation of anguish and whence through endless kalpas there is no escape. Or there may be people who devastate and destroy the holy collections of scriptures, who dishonour monks or nuns, or in the monastery buildings give themselves up to the lusts of the flesh, killing and hurting. All these must sink down into that hell where the pangs have no relief and whence, through countless kalpas, they can never escape.

"'Or there may be people who have become Buddhist monks under false pretences, for in their hearts they are not monks, and therefore misuse the monasteries,

TRUTH AND TRADITION IN BUDDHISM

harass and deceive the laity, and commit all sorts of evil. These all must sink down to that hell where there is no cessation of anguish and from which, through endless kalpas, there is no chance of escape.

"'The people who have become guilty of any of these crimes must sink down into the five different hells where pain has no cessation, and where not even for a moment is there any relief in the anguish.'

"Once more the woman Mâyâ spoke and asked Ti-ts'ang: 'Why are these places called the "endless hells"?'

"Ti-ts'ang said: 'Holy mother, with regard to the various hells, there are eighteen large hells within the "Iron-Encircled Mountain" (T'ieh-wei Shan, 鐵 圍 山). Besides these, there are five hundred smaller ones, all with different names. In addition there are one thousand more, one hundredth part of the others in size, all with different names. In the large hells, there are great cities of eighty thousand li in circumference. The cities are entirely built of iron, with an iron wall that is ten thousand li high. From this wall there blazes up a mass of fire. Everywhere flames can be seen. In the centre of this city all the divisions of hell come together, each with his own name. In the innermost circle is the "endless hell," eighteen thousand li in circumference and with a wall ten thousand li in height.[1]

"'Everything is of iron, with tongues of flame which dart up and out on all sides. There are iron snakes

[1] The picture is taken from the ancient Chinese cities, where there often was an inner city, also surrounded by a wall. One li is about one-half of a kilometre, or one-third of an English mile.

[122]

MASSES FOR THE DEAD

and iron dogs, from whose mouths dart tongues of fire. They reached out greedily after their victims and are in a ceaseless hurrying chase to east and west. In the middle of this hell is arranged an endless row of iron beds and on each bed one sees portrayed the various pains which the unhappy sinners must undergo. All see their own punishments clearly before their eyes. There are hundreds and thousands of hideous devil-hangmen with teeth as long and sharp as swords. Their eyes gleam like flashes of lightning. Their hands are changed to copper claws with which they seize their victims and hurry them off. There are other devils who carry long spears with which they bore through people, either piercing through mouth and nose, or through stomach and back, now casting them up in the air, now catching them again on the point of the lifted spear.

"'There are iron eagles, which pick out the eyes of sinners, and iron snakes which coil themselves round their necks. Every joint in the body is spiked through with iron nails. The tongue is drawn out, and the victim is pulled about by it, like a draught animal. The bowels are drawn out and hewn in pieces. Melted copper is poured down their throats, and glowing bits of iron are laid over their bodies. They die and live again in ceaseless torment, with new pains and tortures.'"

From this nerve-racking description of the punishments of hell, it is a relief to come to more quiet and peaceful matters in the second section of the book which paints the "great meeting of the saved."

TRUTH AND TRADITION IN BUDDHISM

Here it is told how Ti-ts'ang, like a true bodhisattva, has "divided his body," i. e., incarnated himself in various kinds of beings in order to save men (Chinese: fên-shên, 分身).

A translation runs as follows:

"At that time those beings who had seen saved from perdition, thanks to the compassionate heart of Tathagata (Ju-lai, 如來), met together with Ti-ts'ang in the Tao-li heaven for a great assembly. In every section there were countless millions. They all came with incense and flowers, which they offered before the face of Buddha. These multitudes who now flocked around Ti-ts'ang before the throne, never again need return to evil; for they have attained the highest and most all-embracing wisdom. These multitudes who have passed through endless kalpas of birth and death, birth and death, and have wandered through the two regions of pain, now stand in the Tao-li heaven (忉利天) with the proof of experience, for Ti-ts'ang's solemn pledges and his great all-embracing mercy have proved themselves effective. After having attained this place, their hearts are filled with the most unspeakable joy.

"Now without turning away their eyes for a moment, they look up to Ju-lai, with holy veneration. And the 'world-honoured one' [Buddha] stretches out his golden arms and blesses the various forms in which the bodhisattva Ti-ts'ang has incarnated himself through the endless kalpas. He lays his hand on their heads and says: 'As I stand in the five unclean worlds (wu-cho wu-shih, 五濁惡世) and try to instruct and influence the refractory creatures there, I find that out

MASSES FOR THE DEAD

of ten there are usually one or two who cling to evil. It is for this reason that I constantly take various forms and make use of countless different methods to save the unfortunate. I change myself into a heavenly god like Brahma, into a god of transmutations, into a king, a minister, or a relative of a minister. I manifest myself as a "pi-ch'iu" or a nun, as a man who devotes himself to Buddhism in the quiet of his own home, as a woman who gives herself to meditation in the stillness of home. I do not hold obstinately to my Buddha body.[1] I take upon myself all the above-mentioned bodily forms in order to be able to save all. You see how through these continuous kalpas I have tried, with pain and unceasing effort to save all these rebellious creatures, and bring them to obedience, so that they may give up the false, and devote themselves to the true. Nevertheless there still remain some who are under the burden of sin's retribution. If they should fall completely into the power of evil, it would be a frightful time for them.'

"'As I stand here in Tao-li heaven I call upon all, both those who now live in this world of sorrow, and those who shall live in that new world which shall issue forth at Mi-lo Fu's (Maitreya's) appearance. I desire to save all, so that they may escape from grief and want, and receive Buddha's mark on their bodies.'

"At this time all the various bodily incarnations of Ti-ts'ang were gathered together from the different worlds into one body. Tears ran from Ti-ts'ang's eyes

[1] Cf. St. Paul's word about Christ in Phil. 2:6, 7.

[125]

TRUTH AND TRADITION IN BUDDHISM

and nose, as with heart-felt longing and deep sadness he looked up to Buddha and said:

"'For endless kalpas I have been under Buddha's special guidance, so that I have received unspeakable divine strength and wisdom. This has prepared me to enter into the most varied physical forms. I have revealed myself in the most widely different worlds, in number as many as the sands of the river Ganges. In every one of these worlds I revealed myself in millions of forms. Every single incarnation has saved millions of people and led them to a reverent understanding of the three great values (Trikaya: Buddha, the doctrine, and the society) as well as to eternal redemption from birth and death, and into the state of joy of Nirvana.[1]

"'Moreover, if there should still be anything lacking in the way of good works, be it but a hair's breadth, a grain of sand, or a speck of dust, I will carry it all on to completion.

"'Therefore, thou world-honoured one, be not anxious for the generations that are to come! Be not anxious for the generations that are to come! Be not anxious for the generations that are to come!'

"Then Buddha lifted up his voice and praised Tits'ang, saying: 'Good, good—I share your joy! When you shall have fulfilled this great promise and after endless kalpas shall have finished this work of salvation, then will you truly have shown yourself to be the possessor of the tenderest heart and the highest wisdom!'"

[1] Nirvana is described here clearly as the state of joy.

CHAPTER V

THE "PURE LAND" SCHOOL (CHINGT'U, 淨土)

The great sect of "school" within the Buddhist body of China, which goes by the name of "Chingt'u," (淨土) (the "Pure Earth" or the "Pure Land"), is of very ancient date, probably the oldest of all the schools.

The principles of the school can be traced back all the way to the famous patriarchs and masters Asvaghosha (Chinese: Ma-ming, 馬鳴) and Nagarjuna (Chinese: Lung-shu, 龍樹), who were the principal leaders when Buddhism passed through its great renaissance and (as far as the northern regions were concerned) became distinguished as Mahayana.

In the famous book "The Awakening of Faith" (Chinese: "Ch'i Hsin Lun," 起信論), which is so dear to the "Pure Land" people, the following interesting passage occurs:

"First consider those who begin to study the five methods of this chapter and desire to get right faith, but are timid and weak. As they live in this world of extreme suffering, they fear they cannot approach Buddha continually and contribute personally to his service. Thus they fear they cannot attain to this perfect faith and they have a mind to renounce the search after it.

"These should know that Ju-lai (如來) (Tathagata) has most excellent means for strengthening their faith. By having the mind set only on the things of Buddha

TRUTH AND TRADITION IN BUDDHISM

and being constantly with him far from all evil, one attains this end. As the sutra says, 'If a man sets his mind to think only of Amitabha Buddha who is in the happiest realm of the West, and if his good deeds are in the right direction, and if he desires to be born in the happy paradise, he will then be born there, and as he is always in the presence of Buddha, he will never fall back!'

"If we reflect on the eternal nature of Amitabha Buddha and constantly practise this method, we shall in the end reach the place of future wisdom."[1]

Nagarjuna was a clear thinker who liked to refute the traditional, formalistic Buddhism with the most biting negative criticism. He succeeded in a really remarkable way in gathering peoples' thoughts together around loftier and more spiritual values. His philosophical treatises should be looked upon for the most part as necessary works of destruction. The ground had to be cleared for the more highly spiritual and psychological understanding of the great questions of life.

Here is a sample of his negations:

"No birth, no death,
No continued abiding, no extinction,
No unity, no multiplicity,
No future, no past."

Nagarjuna's pupil, Vasubandhu, gave a richer and deeper meaning to his master's ideas and made the figure of Amitabha a truly living one.

[1] "The Awakening of Faith," Chap. 4, translated by Dr. Timothy Richard.

ENTRANCE TO CHAN-YUN MONASTERY, LÜ SHAN, KIANGSI

THE PURE LAND SCHOOL

This tendency to get down to the root of the matter and not to be content with outward formulæ and abstractions has been characteristic of the "Pure Land" School even to the present day. On the one hand, this school has given an important place to faith and sincerity; and on the other hand, with a sharp and almost cynical sense of reality, it has probed into all the accepted dogmas and forms. It is for this reason that this school is so feared and admired; and it is for this reason, too, that it has been able to increase as no other has done in a time like ours, which requires unequivocally clear thinking, as well as a warm heart.

As was mentioned before, it was a Chinese who really established this "school," namely Hui-yüan (慧遠) (333-416), a northerner from Shansi. His original name was Chia (賈). To begin with, he was a zealous Taoist and as such went to great lengths. When, however, he had met representatives of the new religious movement which had already stirred many hearts in northern China (Buddhism), he was very quickly won over, for it seemed to lead still deeper into the tao's (the life principle's) mysterious nature. Hui-yüan seems to have been to quite an unusual degree a deeply religious personality. He consecrated himself with the greatest devotion to the cause of Mahayana Buddhism.

During a long life, first as a wandering pilgrim and later attached to the holy Lü Shan (Lü Mountains) in Kiangsi province, he came to be one of the central figures in Buddhism. Chinese Buddhists began first to find themselves in him, for through Hui-yüan the "foreign" religion received its Chinese form. His words and actions, often taken right out of the writings of the Taoist master Chuang-tse, brought many new and mystical ideas into homely relief.

It is no wonder that when he settled down pilgrims gathered about him in large crowds. He found a beautiful place for himself, first in the Tung-lin (東林) Monastery in the foothills of Lü Shan, and later in Hupeh, in the year 373, in the afterwards famous Lu-feng Monastery. Lovely ponds covered with white lotus-blossoms stretched before the temple. From this the school took its early name, as for many centuries it was called "Pai-lien Chiao" (白蓮教), the "White Lotus Religion." A secret political society, however, adopted the same name in the beginning of the fourteenth century, and the school was forced to change its name in order to avoid being drawn into the many agitations and complications of this society. They therefore took the name which is used down to the present day — the "Pure Land" School.

With Hui-yüan, China's ancient and powerful conception of the "way" or the "life principle" (tao, 道), found its way into Buddhism. We have it in such expressions as "yü-tao" (遇道), to become a monk; "tê-tao" (得道), to become a saint (arhat); and "ch'êng-tao" (成道), to be perfected, to become a buddha. The same term appears again in the name which describes the ceremony of the masses for the dead "tso-tao-ch'ang" (做道場) to perform mass so that the life principle may work on behalf of the dead. A place that is sacred to these masses, where good

[130]

THE PURE LAND SCHOOL

spiritual powers may work for the benefit of mankind, is called also "tao-ch'ang" (道場), the place of worship. In the "Pure Land" hymns and poems the wish is often expressed: "May the four corners of heaven be transformed into a 'tao-ch'ang.'"

These are only a few outward signs of Taoism's influence on Buddhism in China. The inner aspect of this influence will appear as we go further into the underlying ideas and thought connections of the "Pure Land." Here we shall merely emphasize the fact that Hui-yüan and many of the best Taoists of that period found an answer to their deepest religious longings in the central figure of the purified form of Mahayana, namely Amitabha, the All-Father of the "Pure Land" School.

The next great leader in the "Pure Land" School was the monk T'an-luan (曇鸞) who lived from 502-549. He still further elaborated the conception of Amitabha. The same was the case with Tao-ch'o (道綽), who died A.D. 646.

Beginning with the work of Shan-tao 善導 (died A.D. 681) still more positive lines of thought came into the conceptions of the "Pure Land." Through his writings and poems which are preserved to us, the thought of the eternal life, and of a vicarious saviour, were added to the conception of Amitabha. The expression "Ju-lai" (如來) became more common. It was used of Amitabha himself as well as of the two great revealers of his power and grace, Ta-shih-chih (大勢至) and Kuan-yin (觀音), respectively. The holy trinity from the West appears more distinctly. At the same time it is stated more clearly than ever before that salvation takes place through faith in the threefold "Fu" (佛).

When one recalls the fact that Shan-tao lived near the Nestorian sphere of activity and just at that time when the Nestorian Church was proclaiming its "good news" with its primitive power and strength, it is very easy to see evidence of a clear influence from the Christian mission at this point. It is also an incontestable fact that just at this period, a quiet but sure inner process began to work within Chinese Mahayana, pointing to a more monotheistic Amitabha-concept.

In Japan, which in a short time joined in the "Pure Land" movement, with its three highly esteemed and holy fathers, Gonshin (941–1017), Genku Honen (1133–1198), and Shinran (1173–1263), traces of the influence of the Christian mission can be seen very plainly, and it redounds greatly to the honour of Japanese scholars that they are coming to acknowledge it more and more openly.

Among the adherents of the Amida[1] School in Japan it is particularly Shinran's own special section, "Shin-Shu," which cultivates the "Pure Land" idea (Jodo) with the greatest zeal and vigour. There are few things in the history of oriental religions which can compare in interest with this man's life and system of thought. Born in 1173 near the capital, Kyoto, of noble family, it would have been natural for him, like

[1] Cf., on this point, H. Haas: "Amida Buddha Unsere Zuflucht," 1910. A. K. Reischauer: "Studies in Japanese Buddhism," 1918. L. Fujishima: "Le bouddhism Japonais," 1889. L. de la Vallee Poussin: "Bouddhisme, Opinions sur l'histoire de la dogmatique," 1909.

THE PURE LAND SCHOOL

the other sons of noblemen, to be sucked in by the whirlpool of court life; but deeply religious as he was, he chose the life of a monk. He went to the old master Honen, who at the age of ninety-nine had already begun to preach the power of salvation through the name of Amitabha. Shinran, however, was the first to go the whole length and declare that mankind can be born again and enter into the "Pure Land" only through faith and calling upon the name of Amitabha.

He stood forth in that time of great confusion as a reformer of the first rank, and like Luther preached his *sola fide* (by faith alone). After himself experiencing the effects of conformity to the legalism of the old system, and like the other Japanese monks of his time being stunted and crippled in the innermost longings of his soul, he found his way out through the conception of "righteousness by faith without the works of the law." With indomitable courage and joy he sang the praises of faith all the rest of his life, to the great blessing of his own and future generations. As in the case of Luther, the liberation of his human nature enabled him to take the lead in establishing a home, so also Shinran, at the age of thirty-one, married the daughter of Prince Kujo Kanezanes, and thereby established the connection between Buddhism and living humanity.

This shining example of Shinran's has been of the greatest significance, particularly in present-day Japan. The "Pure Land" School is attempting to adjust itself as a living religion, seeking to embrace

TRUTH AND TRADITION IN BUDDHISM

modern Japan and fill it with idealism and spiritual power. The first condition for this, then, is that the home shall receive its consecration from the sanctuary itself, at the hands of men who themselves live the life of the home. China has not been able to follow her former pupil in this matter, but the same forces are at work. The spiritual powers of the "Pure Land" exercise their liberating and transforming influence here also in the most varied spheres.

We shall deal with this point in a separate chapter. Meanwhile, let us quote a few specimens of literature from the "Pure Land's" rich collection of litanies and poems. We shall take the majority of these excerpts from the Chinese Buddhist society's great book of common worship ("Ch'an-mên Jih-sung," 禪門日誦) which in various editions is used in all the different schools and sects in China.

In reading through this remarkable book of chants, where lovely Chinese poems and hymns of worship alternate with gloomy incantations rendered in obscure transliterations of the Sanskrit texts, one gets a vivid impression of what enormous significance the "Pure Land" system of thought has attained. Almost everywhere the "Pure Land" ideas shine through, while the most spiritual poems, full of the deepest religious feeling, come from this same source.

Here appears quite frequently also the significant expression about Kuan-yin: Kuang-ta ling-kan Kuan-shih-yin (廣大靈感觀世音), Kuan-yin, who acts in spiritual form far and wide—all unmistakable traditions from the distant time when the Nestorian Church

[134]

AN ANCIENT, FAMOUS PICTURE OF KWAN-YIN, BLESSING HER ACOLYTE (善財童子). NOTE THE SPIRIT DESCENDING AS A WHITE DOVE WITH A ROSARY IN HIS MOUTH

THE PURE LAND SCHOOL

and the "Great Sun Religion" set their stamp on Chinese Mahayana. Kuan-yin has become the holy spirit.

The book contains, besides, important sections of the larger classic sutras, together with the necessary parts of the various masses for evening, morning, confession of sin, penance, misery, renewal, and consecration.

What particularly interests us, however, is the collection of many beautiful poems which shed light on the "Pure Land's" system of thought. These were written from the tenth century down through the sixteenth century, and thus reflect spiritual conditions through a long period of time. Many otherwise unknown authors appear here. Solitary, highly gifted monks, each in his own manner, have given a variety of expressions to the great thought of Amitabha's compassion and the glory of the "Pure Land." Each one has given voice to this deep longing to be "born into the pure land," oftentimes in the most compelling and affecting words. There is no very great advance in thought to be noted, but so much the more noticeable becomes the advance in spirituality.

In the very centralization of thought around the above-mentioned subject lies their strength. It is as if one had found a common denominator to which all lines of thought could be reduced. The form of the majority of the verses is taken from the oldest poems, written by masters like Hui-yüan. His own deathless "White Lotus Ode" found in a monastery in Chekiang, stands highest of all. We shall give a

TRUTH AND TRADITION IN BUDDHISM

free translation from this, as well as a couple of others in the following pages:

THE WHITE LOTUS ODE ON THE "PURE LAND" IN THE WEST

"What words can picture the beauty and breadth
Of that pure and glistening land?
That land where the blossoms ne'er wither from age
Where the golden gates gleam like purest water—
The land that rises in terrace on terrace
Of diamond-clad steps and shining jade—
That land where there are none but fragrant bowers,
Where the Utpala-lotus unfolds itself freely.
O hear the sweet tones from hillside and grove
The All-Father's praise from the throats of the birds!

"And the ages fly by in an endless chain,
Never broken by summer's or winter's change.
The burning sun can never more frighten.
The icy storms' power long ago is subdued.
The clouds full of light and the green mantled forests
Now cradle all things in their endless peace.
Now the soul is set free from the haunts of darkness
And rests secure in the dwelling of truth.
See, all that was dim and beclouded on earth
Here is revealed, appropriated, secured.

"There ne'er was a country so brightened with gladness
As the Land of the Pure there far off to the West.
There stands Amitabha with shining adornments,
He makes all things ready for the eternal feast.
He draws every burdened soul up from the depths
And lifts them up into his peaceful abode.
The great transformation is accomplished for the worm
Who is freed from the body's oppressive sorrows.

THE PURE LAND SCHOOL

It receives as a gift a spiritual body,
A body which shines in the sea of spirits.

"And who indeed is it with grace in his tones,
Who sends his smile out to the dwellings of the suffering,
And who indeed is it whose glance is like the sun
Who shows his compassion on life and is victor?
Yes, it is God himself, who sits on the throne
And by his law, redeems from all need.
With gold-adorned arm, with crown of bright jewels,
With power over sin, over grief, over death.
None other is like to our God in his greatness,
And none can requite his compassion's great power!"

The following little verse from "Masses for the Dead" is of special beauty. It, also, is addressed to Amitabha.

"Thou perfect master,
Who shinest upon all things and all men,
As gleaming moonlight plays upon a thousand waters at the same time!
Thy great compassion does not pass by a single creature.
Steadily and quietly sails the great ship of compassion across the sea of sorrow.
Thou art the great physician for a sick and impure world,
In pity giving the invitation to the 'Paradise of the West.'"

At the evening mass the following poem is used, which on the one hand gives expression to that deep pessimism which characterizes the Buddhist society, and on the other hand makes reference to the three eternal values which fallen humanity can hold to in the strife of life.

[137]

TRUTH AND TRADITION IN BUDDHISM

A few persons sing:
> "One more day is ended
> Of my quickly outrun span,
> Like a fish dying in waterless caves
> My day passed in joyless strife."

All join in singing:
> "Ought we not all to make haste as one
> Who has touched the glowing stone?
> Let go pleasures, comfort, rest.
> We hurry from this abode of vanity
> And assemble our spirits in the old song:
> 'I dedicate myself to thee, *Amitabha*.
> Would that all created things
> Might understand the great life principle
> And grasp the things that come from above!
>
> "'I dedicate myself to *the great life principle*.
> Would that all creation might immerse itself
> In the depths of the scriptures and attain that wisdom
> Which is vast as the sea!
>
> "'I dedicate myself to *the holy society*.
> Would that all creation might in great close ranks
> Stride forward toward the great assembling
> Of all the Saints!'"

In connection with the evening mass, the full litany of the "Pure Land" is often read. We quote the following characteristic passage, written by the monk Yün-ch'i (雲棲):

> "Thou great guiding master,
> Who dost conduct all creatures over the happy land (at thy invitation),

THE PURE LAND SCHOOL

I bow my head in assent,
And I make this solemn pledge:
I will journey toward that land
In order to be born therein.
May thy mercy and compassion help me on."

(This introductory verse is called "The Desire for the Western Paradise," Hsi-fang-chieh, 西方偈).

Then it continues with the real "Pure Land's Prayer" (Chingt'u Wên, 淨土文):

"With all my heart I dedicate myself
 To the life in the Western Paradise under thee, Amitabha.
 May thy pure light enlighten me.
 May thy merciful promises (of his forty-eight sworn pledges) protect and fortify me.

"I have attained the right understanding
 And that deep longing to be able to call upon God's name
 As it should be done,
 And I therefore pray most earnestly:
 Let me be born in the pure land.

"My prayer is in accord with the precious promises of mercy
 Which thou, Amitabha, has made:

"If there is any creature
 Who desires to be born into my kingdom,
 And who in glad assurance of faith
 Dwells upon my name in tenfold invocation,
 Not one of them
 Shall be shut out from that great experience.
 All shall attain to an understanding of my plans,
 Yes, shall attain to God (tê-ju Ju-lai, 得入如來).

"Through these precious promises, as extensive as the sea,
 All sinners may be able to gain the absolution of their sins,

[139]

TRUTH AND TRADITION IN BUDDHISM

All on account of that power
Which proceeds from God's mercy.
The good root in them will grow strong,
And when the close of life draws so near
That they themselves know it plainly,
Then without bodily pain or sickness,
Without desire in the heart,
Without a trace of vacillation,
And with the deepest assurance of soul,
They will enter into the great meeting
With God and all the saints.
See, Amitabha himself will come to meet me
With the golden seat in his hand.
In a moment shall I be lifted up upon it—
And thereby be born into paradise.

"As a flower that suddenly bursts into bloom,
So is my eye opened,
That I may see God
And understand his perfect law.

"Again in a moment,
See how my soul is filled
With perfect wisdom and an earnest desire
To have a part in the great work of salvation
For the redemption of the whole creation."

Perhaps at this point it may be well to give a sketch of the "Pure Land" doctrines and outward forms of expression, as they have developed on Chinese soil.

From the twelfth century on, the "Pure Land" doctrine began to take on special significance in the Chinese Buddhist community. Like a still, pure, bubbling spring, it gushed out over the arid desert of legalistic systems and ascetic practices which

THE TYPICAL PICTURE OF AMITABHA, USED IN THE HOMES AND IN THE TEMPLES OF THE PURE LAND DEVOTEES

THE PURE LAND SCHOOL

characterized that period. No wonder that so many of the noblest and greatest spirits in the society sought that spring.

There was ample opportunity for this, too, for traces of this remarkable school were found everywhere, in literature, in the ritual, and not least in the brotherhood (society). A great many of the itinerant brothers stayed by preference at the big monasteries and temples in Kiangsi and Chekiang provinces where the "Pure Land" doctrines were especially cultivated at that period, and later, during the quiet evening hours, these "travelling brothers" told of the tremendous religious impression they had received in these places. Thus, although there was no specially planned propaganda carried on for the "school," its ideas and thoughts were carried round to all the outposts of the Buddhist community in the various provinces. They awakened ferment, opposition, reflection, new orientation; none could entirely get away from the new ideas.

Had not Amitabha himself been solemnly designated by Gotama Buddha as the great saviour of the world in the great "Sukhavati Vyuha Ching" (Chinese: "Wu-liang-shou Ching," 無量壽經) one of the "Pure Land's" fundamental sutras?

The story of Amitabha runs as follows:

"Now there was a line of eighty-one Buddhas, beginning with Dipankara and ending with Lokesvararaga. During the period of the latter, a bhikshu, or monk by the name of Dharmakara, formed the pious intention of becoming a Buddha. He went to Lokesvararaga, chanted the usual praise of the Buddha,

[141]

TRUTH AND TRADITION IN BUDDHISM

and then proceeded to ask him to become his teacher and to describe to him what a Buddha and a Buddha country ought to be. Lokesvararaga gave the desired information, upon which Dhamakara requested that when he should attain to Buddhahood, all the qualities of the Buddha countries be concentrated in his own. He then went away, but, after a long meditation, returned with a series of forty-eight vows, whereby he would undertake to become a Buddha only on condition that he be able to save all beings and to establish a kingdom of perfect blessedness in which all living creatures might enjoy age-long happiness and wisdom.

"The eighteenth vow is the most significant: 'When I become Buddha, let all living beings of the ten regions of the universe maintain a confident and joyful faith in me; let them concentrate their longings on a rebirth in my Paradise; and let them call upon my name, though it be only ten times or less; then, provided only that they have not been guilty of the five heinous sins, and have not slandered or vilified the true religion, the desire of such beings to be born into my Paradise will surely be fulfilled. If this be not so, may I never receive the perfect enlightenment of Buddhahood.'"

The same doctrine of salvation through faith in Amitabha is contained in the other two great sutras of the "Pure Land" School, the small "Sukhavati Vyuha Sutra" (Chinese: "O-mi-t'o Ching" 阿彌陀經) and "The Amita Yurdhyana Sutra" (Chinese: "Kuan-wu-liang-shou Ching," 觀無量壽佛經).

[142]

EAST WALL, YÜIN-KANG, TATUNG, SHANSI

THE PURE LAND SCHOOL

Was not the term "Chingt'u" (the "Pure Land") introduced by Hui-yüan himself when he wanted to describe the new state of mind which a real entrance into Mahayana brought with it? Had not the word "faith" been already set up as the highest word in the ancient writing "Ch'i Hsin Lun" (起 信 論), "The Awakening of Faith"? Everywhere people were forced to admit that this way of salvation was willed and foreordained by the compassionate Buddha, who always thinks only of that great goal: the salvation of all living things.

It was not until later, therefore, that the opposition to the "Pure Land" doctrines really began to take shape. There was, however, no very great number of monasteries and temples which the "Pure Land" School could claim as belonging entirely to their branch. They did not lay special stress on propaganda. This practice has continued down to the present time. The other Buddhist schools were recognized, as all had the one Chinese Tripitaka, of which each individual school emphasized its favourite scriptures as fundamental; all held in the main to one philosophy, and acknowledged one pantheon. The inviolable teachings concerning transmigration, and its orders, were axiomatic for the adherents of the "Pure Land," and finally, everything led back to the historical Gotama Buddha, as the earthly founder and lord of the society. For this reason the school was able to carry on its fruitful work through several centuries without any break with the old order.

TRUTH AND TRADITION IN BUDDHISM

Its influence, however, was not limited to the narrower Buddhist circles. From the twelfth century on, one finds that literary production in China began to be touched by the new ideas. Thence its influence gradually spread to the field of art.

The drama has always had a strong influence on the life of the Chinese people. It has been a means of transmitting ideas to the masses, who, in a way which seems quite incomprehensible to us Westerners, can pick up songs of enormous length from these theatrical programs, and recite them by heart.

The school also worked directly on the great mass of people. Through the "Pure Land" School, that prayer began which down through the centuries has gathered the petitions of millions of people in East Asia in a common "Our Father." It is the well-known prayer "Nan-mo O-mi-t'o Fu, 南無阿彌陀佛 (Japanese; Na-mo Amida Butsu: Korean: Na-mo Amida Pul). "I turn to Amitabha, in reverence and trust." Like a great rush of water, this prayer extends from South China up to Manchuria, from Japan and Korea to the borders of Siberia. All the soul's need and longing, sighs of despair, and songs of praise and thanks are gathered up in this supplication. Buddhist monks greet one another with these words, laymen murmur them either sincerely or mechanically, both at work and at play. They appear as a refrain in the masses, they are repeated many thousand times a day during the procession round about through the corridors and halls of the temple. They are inscribed on stone tablets and engraved on

THE PURE LAND SCHOOL

trinkets. They are written and printed in papers and books.

Through the "Pure Land's" great prayer, "Nan-mo O-mi-t'o Fu," it is as if a great door were opened into the heart of the All-Father, to the "name above all names,"—that name through which hope and salvation gleam upon the human race, that name through which every individual may find himself, and finally be absorbed into "Fu" (Buddha), indeed become "Fu" himself in the land of endless bliss, the "Paradise of the West."

It is no wonder that this phrase came to be a synonym for personal honour and piety. How often in China have I heard a man who wishes to assure one that a certain person is especially pious and honest, say, "He is a regular O-mi-t'o Fu," and again comes the familiar gesture, the laying of his hand upon his heart! For everybody understands that when a man is in earnest about this prayer, it means that his conscience is in control of his life, it means that he has returned to his original nature, that he stands openly before the eye of "Heaven."

For this reason, the word "O-mi-t'o Fu" is one of the most sacred terms in the consciousness of the people of eastern Asia, it is a bright guardian angel hovering over human souls, it is the holy reflection from the secret chambers of the life of conscience. It gathers within itself both the creator and the creature in harmonious reunion. Only when one keeps this clearly before the eye can one really begin to understand a little of the secret of Mahayana's inner meaning. One begins to see how it is possible that millions of the learned and unlearned through many centuries are never tired of using this name, meditating upon it by the hour together, reciting it even many thousand times a day. It is nothing less than the ancient *unio mystica* from the mystics of the church in the Middle Ages, which appears here again on the soil of Asia—that inner contemplation and merging of the self with God, the very soul of meditation. It is "to see light in God's light." It is for this reason that there are so many verses and poems from the time of the Ming dynasty which remind one quite strikingly of the holy meditations of Thomas à Kempis.

We have already tried to point out some of the explanations of this phenomenon. In the first place, we stand here before one of the deepest well-springs of our common religious life—well-springs which are uncovered in the highest religions outside of Christianity also. (Cf. Sufism within Mohammedanism and the Bhakti movement within Hinduism, etc.) In the second place, the Nestorian Church had a chance to give Mahayana some of the golden nuggets of the Christian faith, just at the time when Mahayana was assuming its definite form in China.

Mahayana's conception of Amitabha was perhaps among those most influenced by the Christian ideas of God. This is apparent in no other school so unmistakably as in the "Pure Land" School. And this school in its turn gives the best and highest representation of Mahayana. For this reason, Mahayana's favourite picture is used so often and with so much

THE PURE LAND SCHOOL

feeling in the "Pure Land" School,—the picture of the great ship of mercy, manned by the All-Father and his two helpers, sailing over the "sea of sorrow" and rescuing all men in distress.

As we have now touched upon more of the inner side of the "Pure Land" thought system and possibilities of spiritual fruit-bearing, it may be permitted to give some account of our experience in personal association with those who stand in the closest contact with this school. We think of the many thousands of monks, nuns, and lay folk who either in the monasteries or in private homes have consecrated themselves to the special worship and special study which the "Pure Land" School requires. It is only through these living human beings that one can come to any conclusions regarding this school's ability to form character or minister spiritual strength and comfort for life's battle and death's pain. "The tree shall be known by its fruits." This universal law must also hold good here if we are to arrive at a fair judgement in regard to this school.

It is clear that a thorough and sincere investigation of these conditions will be of the greatest interest both for religio-philosophical research and for the man who from a Christian standpoint desires to gain a correct understanding of the matter.

First of all one must realize that it is impossible to give a true answer to such questions after only a short visit in a monastery or temple or from chance association with Buddhists in their homes or in the streets. This is true of the Buddhist faith as a whole, but even

TRUTH AND TRADITION IN BUDDHISM

more true of the company of monks, nuns, and laymen who especially cultivate the "Pure Land" movement. How often have we met these agitators, these cocksure free and easy judges, whom one so often hears or sees in print in connection with these matters! These expressions of opinion come usually either from godless, materialistic travellers who after a hurried stay in a place send home dashing descriptions to the papers, or from those who in their misguided zeal for Christianity outstrip one another in demolishing everything that has to do with Buddhism.

The truth of the matter is that if there is any place where one must not try to cut everything after one pattern it is just here. If one does this one commits just as great an injustice as if one should assert that all Christians are "rice Christians" because there unfortunately are some who answer to this description.

We shall in a later chapter give a more detailed account of the moral and religious life among Buddhists in general. Let us here merely point out the fact that in the large company of monks and nuns there are many bad elements, too, many unworthy members, who by their scandalous lives and their dull and mechanical religious practices, to a large degree bring the Buddhist religion into disrepute. This is true of the adherents of the "Pure Land" also. As one might expect, there are among them, no less than among other sects, light-minded individuals who, more or less consciously, "sin against grace," because they say that Amitabha in his boundless mercy will certainly know how to save them, no matter how bad

THE PURE LAND SCHOOL

their lives may be. One finds here, just as one occasionally finds in the homelands in "ultra-evangelical" circles, a curious laxity with regard to ethical demands, even while men cling to an imperfect conception of faith and grace.

It cannot be denied either that some of the "Pure Land" adherents, in their contempt for the old formalistic systems, have become "free-thinkers" to such an extent that they disregard the most elementary things in the moral order of the world. Herein lies the deepest ground for the quite strong reaction which in the last two centuries has arisen against the "Pure Land" party from the more legalistic schools. A good many of the "fathers" in the Buddhist society saw with increasing disquiet how many of the "Pure Land's" spokesmen explained away or rewrote the old objective basis. It seemed to them that nothing was certain any longer. Everything was being spiritualized. The historical Buddha became principally an enlightened man, who had only a historical interest. Indeed, Amitabha himself became often only an idea, a spiritual figure of speech who was dissolved in abstractions when one really tried to set forth his nature. The same was the case with the other Buddhas and the two assistant figures in the trinity. They became simply personifications of the various sides of the Absolute nature. The "Paradise of the West" became a spiritual condition quite as thin and negative in its conception as the ancient colourless Nirvana (Chinese: Nieh-p'an, 涅槃). All systems of salvation, all religions, became merely human attempts

TRUTH AND TRADITION IN BUDDHISM

to portray the metaphysical, all alike relative, all alike imperfect.

For these reasons the "pillars of the church" within Chinese and Japanese Buddhism felt themselves in solemn duty bound to give a warning. This movement, which threatened to undermine Buddhism from within, must be stopped.

Even greater reasons for such a reaction lay in the advancing moral deterioration which people seemed to see in connection with the "Pure Land."

The reaction came. With great vigour, the "fathers" in both China and Japan began to inveigh against the "Pure Land" School. New parties were formed to fight against it. Not faith, but works of salvation with worship according to the old instructions, meditation, and asceticism, were emphasized. And most important of all, the scriptures must be read and thoroughly studied. Only after such study and a long period of ascetic practice, could one cautiously appeal in faith to the name of Amitabha. Preferably, however, one should go to the original historical Buddha. He was the great merciful lord, but first of all, he was perfect wisdom, who by his example could draw men out of the shadowy life of illusion into the real life of unselfishness.

Unostentatiously, the whole of Buddhism was to be turned back to Hinayana's old narrow tracks. The reaction has continued right down to our own times. It has not, however, succeeded in getting back to the ancient forms. In Japan there are two schools which are entirely Hinayanistic; in China there is none which

[150]

THE PURE LAND SCHOOL

can be precisely designated by that name, but we have in the great "Lü-tsung" (律宗), the Legalistic School, and in some branches of Ch'an Tsung (禪宗), the Meditation School, a movement which very clearly tends in that direction.

In China most of the schools have come to a sort of compromise, and as is often the case in compromises, no real solution has been found, but on the contrary, the deepest confusion has been created. I can report from personal observation cases of the most bitter conflict of soul among the more idealistic and truth-seeking members of the Buddhist community. Over and over again I have met within the monastery walls, monks and lay Buddhists who in unspeakable inner conflict and grief were about to give up hope of ever reaching clearness and peace, "for the systems contradict each other and we know no way out!"

Such instances occur particularly in the large school known as the "Ch'an Tsung" (禪宗), the "Way of Meditation." This is naturally the case, for it is there that one finds the practice of assembling two or three times a day for prayer out in the main hall before the images of Amitabha, Sakyamuni Buddha, and Yao-shih Fu. By calling upon the names of the triune Buddhas and bodhisattvas, salvation may be obtained. Every mass is supposed to close with a procession round through the corridors and in between the prayer stools, in order to recite "Nan-mo O-mi-t'o Fu" five hundred or one thousand times. It is by invoking this great name in faith that final salvation will be found.

TRUTH AND TRADITION IN BUDDHISM

Shortly after this the group of monks is led into the hall of meditation (which is here called the "hall of wisdom") and there they are met by the "instructor" (wei-na, 維那), who declares that herein no prayers may be said to Buddha. His name must not be named. One must simply concentrate one's thoughts on the question, "What was my original nature?" (父母未生以前如何是我本來的面目藉此話頭可以返本還原). Some take a vow that they will not leave the hall before they have fathomed this mystery (K'ai-chio-wu, 開覺悟). This is often called "breaking through natural thought" (p'o-pên-ts'an, 破本參). The instructor paints in glowing colours the great joy which accompanies such an experience. The very aspect of such an "enlightened" person shows that he is different from others. He can associate with all, help all, bend to the lowest sinners (thieves, prostitutes, etc.) without being tempted himself. He is like the pure white fragrant lotus which shoots up from the muddy bottom through the unclean water, but is never besmirched.

Many struggle for years to have a share in this experience. They achieve the necessary outward preparation when they have learned the difficult posture of meditation; indeed they can even take pleasure in it, sitting with the hands folded together and half-closed eyes, with legs crossed under them (Chinese: Ta-tso, 打坐, or Ta-p'an-chiao, 打盤脚). Perhaps they can even arrive at the next stage: they succeed in concentrating their minds in reflection so that they can let their thoughts glide up and down

[152]

THE PURE LAND SCHOOL

on the given scale. Thus they set in order both the outward and the inward technique of Buddhist meditation. But enlightenment and peace...? The most difficult point is to determine the relation between worship of the merciful Buddha and self-sanctification through meditation. If only one dared take the lovely gospel of Amitabha's grace with him into the hall of meditation! If only one dared try the way of faith when thoughts become heavy and contradictory! But that, an honourable monk, trained in the legalistic schools, would never dare to do.

Therefore, among the truth-seeking monks within the Buddhist society of the East, one finds the same old experience, which we know so well from the accounts of the New Testament and of church history,— compare a Paul, an Augustine, a Luther,—the old experience of the fact that honest soul-searching and deep serious reflection will always work depressingly, even to despair,—an experience which has found its classic and undying description in the seventh chapter of the letter to the Romans. "When the commandment came, sin revived," when "I see another law in my members, warring against the law of my mind, and bringing me into captivity,"—so one must cry out "Wretched man that I am! Who shall deliver me from the body of this death?" It is in this fearful drama of the soul that one finds use for the gift of faith as in the eighth chapter of Romans, with its deep joy at salvation. It is for this reason that it is so difficult, even for such a deeply spiritual school as the Meditation School, to lead the many pious and serious

TRUTH AND TRADITION IN BUDDHISM

Buddhists to true enlightenment and deep peace. At the best, it produces a passive, weak, dreamy religiosity, which may perhaps have some worth and meaning for the individual, but can never put steel and will into character so that a man begins a purposeful life-work for the uplift and edification of humanity. In many cases it does not produce even this. Religion becomes purely outward, using a stereotyped jargon, which thrives quite well by the side of a low morality. Or else men attempt to restrict their religious practices to the least possible; for they have become wearied with Mahayana's many systems of salvation and cannot find their way.

Among these last are a good many with great practical ability. One observes that as a rule they are absorbed in external activities. They become the "strong men" of the society, practised in intrigue and the arts of diplomacy. They thus work their way up into the highest positions, take pains to get control of the common funds, lands, etc. They are known and feared in the courts, and both take and give bribes. The service in the larger or smaller local temples in city and town is usually in the hands of such persons and of the inferior type of monks, and such are most often met in China. The many pious and high-principled monks live withdrawn in their cells and are unknown to the world. We, however, who have had a glimpse behind the scenes, know that there are such, and that they are not inconsiderable in number. They, too, must be taken into account when the Buddhist society is judged.

[154]

GENERAL VIEW AROUND THE GREAT BUDDHA, YÜIN-KANG, TATUNG, SHANSI

THE PURE LAND SCHOOL

Against this background of religious confusion, the "Pure Land" School stands out in brilliant relief, and one can understand the reason. The "Pure Land" has one central idea, which completely governs and binds together the different lines of thought. This is not first of all a system of dogma or a long and elaborate ritual. It is a person, in whom is found glowing compassion and grace. The way to his heart is not through offerings nor through self-discipline, study, asceticism, or meditation. It is through the invocation of his name in faith. Not that study and meditation are debarred. On the contrary, the more intensely pursued the better, if only they are pursued in the right way. It must be a study of Amitabha, so that one may see how the whole of existence, oneself included, is absorbed in him. It must be meditation which has Amitabha as centre and clue. It is for this reason that the hall of meditation in the "Pure Land" monasteries is called "Nien-fu T'ang" (念佛堂), the "Hall where Fu Is Studied." It is not enough simply to name Buddha's name and worship him. One necessary condition for the attainment of enlightenment and peace is to "break through natural thought."

One can easily understand the enormous superiority of the "Pure Land" Buddhist's position. He is not troubled by uncertainty, nor by the many other angles of vision from which salvation may be seen. He sees all, must see all, from one aspect only and that is in the light of the "One, eternal in time, in light, and in mercy," Amitabha.

TRUTH AND TRADITION IN BUDDHISM

This brings with it a firm and glowing faith and a great inner joy. As has already been mentioned, there are those in the "Pure Land" party who have wholly misunderstood its philosophy, or not taken it seriously and therefore "sin against grace." Some are lost in disintegrating atheism. But there is also quite a considerable body of monks, nuns, and lay Buddhists who throughout their lives show that they are inspired with a pure and strong spiritual power so that they not only become good and pious people, but also are a help and blessing to society in general. We have met them not only in Japan, where a really admirable philanthropic work, with Sunday schools, young peoples' associations, prisons associations, orphanages, etc., is carried on by the "Pure Land" School, but in China also. The monks whose philanthropic activities have recently attracted public attention have all come from this school. Many of China's leading men of letters at the present time, men who have studied abroad and are now taking part in the social and national renaissance, have drawn their religious inspiration from the doctrines of the "Pure Land" School.

It may well be the case that some of these were awakened to a real understanding of this teaching for the first time by coming into contact with Christianity. It may be that the "Pure Land" philanthropy and stress upon genuine spirituality began to make real headway only after modern missionary work was beginning to make itself felt. The fact remains, however, that of all the Buddhist schools, the "Pure

THE PURE LAND SCHOOL

Land" alone had the spiritual qualifications needed to emulate Christianity.

In Japan it is not easy for the people to accept Christianity since national considerations are an important factor and consequently the power of judgement is perverted. The same has been the case to a considerable extent in China also. At the beginning of the modern era, the famous "Pure Land" abbot, Chu-hung (袾宏), in the Yün-ch'i Monastery (雲棲寺) near Hangchow, opposed, in several well-written letters, the well-known missionary veteran of the Roman Church, Matteo Ricci. Finding that Christianity was very much like the "Pure Land" faith, he thought it his duty to warn the people not to be deceived by this heretical and corrupt form of religion.

During the last years of the Ming dynasty the same attitude was taken by one of the famous Buddhist devotees, Hsi-ming (錫明). The Catechism of the "Pure Land" doctrine, called "Chüen Hsiu Chingt'u Ch'ieh-yao (勸修淨土切要), reprinted many times during the last four centuries, quotes Hsi-ming under the significant heading, "When worshipping Buddha beware of heresy."

The text runs as follows:

"Worshipping Buddha is the only great and right way of salvation. Although one may feel that this worship is rather easy and commonplace, still the religion here spoken of [Chingt'u] is absolutely perfect. But passing through the various steps it may be found that it is not altogether easy. It is to be feared that men and women with stupid minds having trodden the first half of the road will become lazy and finally give up in disgust, being deceived into joining the Catholic Church (T'ien-chu, 天主) or some other outside sect, having come to the conclusion that the 'Pure Land' doctrine is false. In this way they commit the great sin during life, and after death pass into hell. How deplorable! What a pity! For this reason, I respectfully exhort all who call on the name of Buddha to keep on with a sincere heart, and thus gradually attain to the point when the heart cannot be disturbed any more, when the lotus-blossom will unfold itself, and the heart see Buddha. I exhort you most urgently to break off all relations with these spirits of darkness and not to pray to these gods: then your thoughts will not be bewildered by vain aspirations, in which there is not only no gain, but great harm."

The fact that Hsi-ming felt it his duty to warn against the Christian church indicates that not a few of the "Pure Land" people at that time were not only familiar with Christian doctrine, but also somewhat attracted to it. In fact, from the time of the Nestorian Church down through the centuries of missionary activities by the Roman Catholics, we meet with Buddhists, who openly oppose Christianity and exhort the people to distinguish between the two religions.

Why should they do so if not driven by the feeling that Christian thoughts and ideas were a threatening force? That many people outside the church knew the fundamental ideas of Christianity at the time of K'ang Hsi (*ca.* A.D. 1700) is incontestable. This is

THE PURE LAND SCHOOL

shown by the discovery of the touching story of Christ and His holy Virgin Mother found in the "Shên-hsien Kang-chien."[1]

Coming back to the attitude of Buddhists towards Christianity to-day, I have often met with this same point of view among the modern adherents of the "Pure Land." It is noteworthy that among such there has been a greater willingness to admit that the strength of Christianity is to be found in the incontrovertible historicity of the main facts of the life of Christ.

The fact that Buddhists are following Christianity with growing attention is shown not least in the newer magazines which the "Pure Land" School in particular are publishing.[2]

In this connection it is interesting to recall the extensive survey of systems of salvation which was issued by the monk Chi-yüan, over three hundred years ago. The book is called "Wan-fa Kuei Hsin Lu (萬法歸心錄). "All systems unite in the religion of the heart."

We must here call attention to the fact that a great number of nuns may be counted in the "Pure Land" party. A consideration not only of the essential nature of womanhood but also of the miserable social conditions in which a great many of them live, shows how natural this is. They have a feeling that they are in especial need of mercy if they are to be saved. Few are sufficiently educated to acquire all the book learning that is necessary to enter the other schools.

[1] Cf. Chap. II.
[2] Cf. the paper, the *Eastern Buddhists*, begun in 1921, published in Kyoto, Japan.

TRUTH AND TRADITION IN BUDDHISM

For them the "Pure Land's" short-cut to salvation is more than welcome. Many devote themselves with touching earnestness to the "invocation of the name," and there is no doubt that numbers of them are saved from the deepest vice and a life of degradation, by faith in Amitabha's grace. When, however, one remembers the conditions from which most of these nuns have come, it is not to be wondered at that there are many backslidings, and that now and then black shadows are thrown on the Buddhist society as a whole and the "Pure Land" party in particular, by failures in the nuns' quarters. At the same time among the initiated it is a well-known fact that great philanthropic zeal, generous self-sacrifice, and victorious and happy deaths are often heard of in these same nunneries.

Among the ordinary people there are also large numbers of women who carry on Buddhist practices of piety with zeal in their own homes and occasionally in the convents. There is no doubt that the largest proportion of money gifts comes to the society through women. Mothers and older women, in particular, who begin to feel that deep mother-yearning and family grief which is so characteristic of the more mature women of China, take refuge in large numbers in the temples. The monks often become quite intimate with them, and from these conditions very unfortunate complications often result.

Widows bear a special burden of care for their deceased husbands or children, and, since there is no school in the Buddhist society which lays such emphasis on the masses for the dead or has such a

THE PURE LAND SCHOOL

well-developed method of salvation as the "Pure Land," it is natural that they go thither. Here every year there is a special mass of forty-nine days, plus one, for the redemption of the lost souls in hades (which, as has been described before, reveals evidence of direct copying from the Nestorian Church with its fifty days of prayer for the living and the dead). In Kiangsu and Chekiang provinces where the "Pure Land" monasteries and temples are numerically strongest, enormous numbers of women gather together every year on this occasion.

If one wishes to establish the fact that a certain monastery or temple belongs to the "Pure Land" School, it is necessary to go to the great temple hall. If one there sees the triune Buddha represented *standing*, it is certain that it is under the care of the "Pure Land" branch. The group then will consist of Amitabha in the centre, with his right hand outstretched and his left hand enclosing a lotus-blossom or a small pagoda, and Kuan-yin and Ta-shih-chih, on the left and right side, respectively. The two last resemble each other very much, each often holding a lotus in one hand while the other hand hangs loose at the side. In other cases, Kuan-yin may hold her famous jar from which she pours out her life-giving water over mankind (kan-lu shui, 甘露水), while Ta-shih-chih has a lotus leaf with a stalk in his hand.

In the famous old Ling-yin Ssŭ (靈隱寺, Monastery Under the Spirits' Shadow) near Hangchow, I found a group which forcibly attracted my attention. The monastery, with its enormous temple hall, is being

TRUTH AND TRADITION IN BUDDHISM

restored at present. Besides the ordinary twenty-four tutelary gods (devas) and the great principal buddhas, I found erected, behind the high altar, twelve great figures. I immediately suspected that there must be some old tradition to explain this extremely curious arrangement. This proved, indeed, to be true. Twelve statues were to be erected of "some disciples" who wished to serve Buddha and had so far advanced as to be "yüan chio" (緣 覺), that is, on the verge of becoming bodhisattvas. As I know that the Nestorians were powerful in Hangchow in their day, I at once connected the whole thing with the Nestorian monastery in that city, which certainly must have had statues of the twelve apostles. I imagine, therefore, that the twelve disciples from the Nestorian Church and the twelve "yüan chio" known from Buddhism's earliest history have some relation to one another.

From this survey one can form a mental picture of the "Pure Land" School, and the influence which proceeds therefrom over the life of the East. While it is true, as we have seen, that the institutions and adherents of this school may be found especially in the coast provinces of Chekiang and Kiangsu, one meets in the inland provinces as well quite a number both of "lay and learned" Buddhists who are more or less influenced by it.

We have tried to give an unbiassed account of the various spiritual and moral grounds on which these "Pure Land" worshippers stand. We have seen that

THE PURE LAND SCHOOL

many of them have manifested great religious earnestness, high character, and deep charity. Just as the "Pure Land," in a certain sense, is the noblest branch on the tree of Buddhism in China, so its best adherents form a body of "élite" among the religious classes of the East.

We have seen that some of the most precious elements of Taoism and Christianity have been woven into this religion. These elements are often rendered obscure or even unrecognizable by the dark shadows of polytheism, which have also been cast over the "Pure Land" School. But still they have been strong enough to help some few people on to light, strength, and understanding, once again witnessing to the truth of the well-known words in which St. John's Gospel speaks of the *eternal logos* as a "light shining in the darkness." That same light, which of yore led the "magi" (priests of the Zoroastrians or worshippers) on to Bethlehem, leads also serious truth-seekers in the East of to-day, on towards Him in whom "tao," the life principle, has been completely incarnated and made real, Jesus Christ. For this reason it seems clear to us that in the time of reckoning, which must inevitably take place before long in the East between Christianity and Buddhism, it will be important above all things to hold fast to the fact that there is much common ground—in spite of the many and great differences.

This common possession consists of the fundamental principles of life, as they are glimpsed more or less clearly and announced by the great prophetic figures in the highest religions, principles

[163]

which have come to us in their final consummation in a living Saviour, the Christ of Christianity. With this view as a basis, the Christian missionary will have nothing to fear in the time of reckoning. He will give the Buddhists full credit for the real values which they possess. He will not be anxious when he sees similarities, like the old Catholic missionaries, who said: "This is merely veiled deviltry!" He will rather be glad, as one who sees a new evidence of God's tremendous power through His eternal word (*logos*). He will rejoice over that eternal outpouring of light, from the everlasting sources of truth and goodness, whether he finds the light in ancient holy books or in living human personalities. In this way he will "commend himself to every man's conscience in the sight of God" and do his part in "gathering together God's scattered children" into the society of the kingdom of God, without nationality or denomination.

Especially in relation to the "Pure Land" these things are actualities, and it is our innermost conviction that only by such a positive and unprejudiced attitude as *servants of the truth*, can we succeed in averting a catastrophic conflict. If these lines of action be followed, there is good hope that Chinese Mahayana and particularly the "Pure Land" School will show itself to have been a "tutor" leading up to Christ, a kind of Old Testament for those who have not had a share in the "special revelation."

In connection with the Chingt'u catechism mentioned above, it may be of interest to give a short outline of

THE PURE LAND SCHOOL

the main thoughts of this popular book, looking into the motives of the unknown author and the other pious people who again and again have given the necessary funds for the printing of the little book, and who have written the beautiful prefaces.

We find in the prefaces and the headings of the different chapters the clearly expressed intention to popularize the Buddhist doctrine through the medium of the "Pure Land" School, in this way opening an easy road to salvation for the many people who cannot enter the monastic life.

The record of the first important parts of the book will show how natural it is that the "Pure Land" has become the favourite religion of a large number of lay devotees, and scholars (chü-shih, 居士), and also how it is that many simple-minded people join together in vegetarian associations, as "chai-kung" (齋公), or become individual vegetarians, "chai-p'o" (齋婆).

The Catechism of the "Pure Land"

After several very pretty prefaces the introduction is given as follows:

"Confucius said: 'Is there a man who on removing his home to another place forgets to take his wife along?' 'Yes,' he adds; 'in fact, there are such people, not only one, but many. Not only so, there are people who move their homes to another place and forget to take themselves along.'

When looking at people with spiritually enlightened eyes, one will find that most people forget themselves when moving around. How is that to be explained?

[165]

TRUTH AND TRADITION IN BUDDHISM

From the early morning when the eyes are opened and people rise from bed until late in the evening when retiring to bed and the eyes are closed, nothing except the toil and stress of life occupies the mind. Not a single moment is set apart for the investigation of one's own person—is that not to forget oneself when removing the home?

"In regard to men's physical needs, nothing is more necessary than the supplying of food and drink to avoid hunger and thirst, and further, in regard to the different seasons, how necessary it is to provide for the cold and the hot days! So, also, in regard to the whole course of life. Nothing is more important than to be prepared for life and for death. Should not special preparation be made for this most urgent need? Why therefore maintain this indolent attitude towards these questions? This position is truly foolish. It can only be explained by the fact that you are not aware of the *great road of salvation* opened to mankind by cultivating the '*Pure Land*' *doctrine*, through which the right preparation can be made for life as well as for death.

"For instance, if a man intend to reach a place far away, he must know something about that place beforehand. If not, how can he reach the place and transact business there? It is necessary before the evening comes to know where to rest for the night. To secure a place for rest before evening comes—this is just what it means to cultivate and worship the 'Pure Land' doctrine. Then, when darkness comes and this life is finished, a dwelling-place is secured, a new birth

THE PURE LAND SCHOOL

among the lotus-blossoms is attained, and you are saved from the misery and pain of the great perdition.

"In this way we understand the relation between the 'Pure Land' and Buddha; to worship Buddha is really to cultivate the 'Pure Land' and to be born into the new and pure life about which the scripture says: 'It is a life of boundless ages, filled with happiness and without grief.' How great a thing in this way to be prepared for the life to come!

"Nevertheless, there are many people who know something about this and still do not press on to attain it. How can that be? I understand the reason: Some will say, It is because there is no sanctuary in the home, or, the people in my home do not practise vegetarianism, or, there is too much noise! Alas, you do not know that it is just under these conditions you can worship Buddha. It does not depend upon outward position, standing, lying, sitting, nor upon the presence of noise or calm. It depends upon this one thing—that your own heart be quiet and concentrated. If you have opportunity to practise vegetarianism, of course that is very good. But usually it is only people who can leave their homes who can do that permanently. If you have *a longing in your heart* to go out from the world, that is the main thing. In all cases, exhorting people to perfect outward seclusion from the world, is certainly to make the way unnecessarily difficult for the unfortunate. If only under the different conditions of life you can concentrate your mind, then you will be sure to hear *one single voice* speaking in your heart. Then you have attained the 'Pure Land.' If you rise early in the morning and sincerely practise the morning devotion, you will be able to conquer the sins which are devastating your earthly life, and when your life is past, will ascend to the life in the 'Pure Land' above.

"As to the invocation of the name of Buddha, the more you can call on him the better. But the most important thing is that under the strain of your daily duties you can reach the higher wisdom and the compassionate state of mind. Although you are busy from morning to evening, still you may find a few moments for your spiritual life. Why not take the time used for tea-drinking for this purpose? In this way busy people, weary people, all may get some time. You have not made an effort. Why, then, say it is impossible? When your last hours come you will certainly find that this effort has not been in vain.

"We find in the scriptures ["Mi L'o Ching"] these words: 'People who steadfastly keep on with the invocation of Amitabha's name will even in this life secure ten different blessings:

"'(1) Through the day and the night you will be under the special protection of the mighty, heavenly guardians.

"'(2) The twenty-five great bodhisattvas, Kuan-yin and all the other bodhisattvas, will accompany and keep you in safety.

"'(3) The heart which by night and day dwells in Buddha will be illuminated by the splendour of Amitabha's grace and made secure and steadfast.

BUDDHA PREACHING AT LING SHAN

THE PURE LAND SCHOOL

"'(4) All the devils from the yeh-ch'a (夜叉) group (masculine), or from the lo-ch'a (羅刹) group (feminine), will not hurt you, neither will poisonous serpents nor dragons harm you.

"'(5) You will be kept from the danger of fire, water, thieves, knives and arrows, prison, chains, accidents, and untimely death.

"'(6) All your former sins will be blotted out and the creatures you may have killed will cease to insist on revenge.

"'(7) During the night you will dream good dreams and see Amitabha in all his boundless splendour. Your heart will be filled with joy and this joy will make your face shine, invigorate your physical strength and make you prosperous in all your doings.

"'(8) You will naturally treat all men honourably just as you worship Buddha with reverence and in sincerity.

"'(9) At death, all fear will disappear and you will move over, straightforward in mind and thought.

"'(10) Then you will see Amitabha and all the holy ones. He will approach you with the golden platform in his hand and bring you to the 'Pure Land' in the West. There you will enjoy unspeakable bliss and happiness through everlasting ages.'

"Just as Buddha himself urges people not to tell a lie, so be sure he himself is not lying when he gives

TRUTH AND TRADITION IN BUDDHISM

these promises. People usually do not lie to gain outward profit; they lie to avoid difficulties. Buddha needs nothing; why should he, then, ask men for something? For him birth and death are empty as air; why should he try to escape difficulties? Consequently he never depends upon lying. If you believe this to be true, it is your duty to urge people to read carefully through the doctrines given here, and to give sincere attention to the four following chapters containing the description of how to cultivate the 'Pure Land.'

"*Saved to save. This is the great thing, containing boundless merit.*

"Most urgently I implore you, do not place this book untouched on the book-shelf, and do not think these things to be unimportant. If you do that, you certainly underestimate the motives which lie behind this book. If you feel that you have no affinity to Buddha yourself, I implore you to send the book on to other people who may read it, in this way helping in the work of leading the whole creation to the higher understanding, rescuing all the world from the deep waters of perdition. This is my sincere hope."

The four chapters have the following headings: (1) "Exhortation to Worship Buddha with a Sincere Heart"; (2) "Exhortation to Worship Buddha in Spirit and in Truth"; (3) "Exhortation to Strive for the New Birth into the 'Pure Land'"; (4) "Exhortation to Cultivate the Two Aspects of the 'Pure Land' (the Direct and the Indirect Side of the 'Pure Land')." In closing the Chingt'u yüan, the confessions of sin, etc. (given earlier in this chapter), are added.

CHAPTER VI

THE BUDDHIST PANTHEON IN CHINA

We have already in the foregoing chapters mentioned a number of Buddhas and bodhisattvas, but in order to obtain a general survey, we shall now give a summary of the best-known figures that appear in the Buddhist pantheon in China.

It is only with the rise of Mahayana that there grew up the idea of representing the Buddhas in sculpture or painting, and it was also in Mahayana that the present large and motley collection of gods was developed. This characteristic has always been Mahayana's weakness, since it is polytheism which has in various ways drawn this doctrinal system, otherwise on so high a plane, into the sombre shadows of animism.

Originally only the great Buddhas were painted or modelled of wood, clay, iron, bronze, etc., and afterwards, if means allowed, overlaid with gold. The finest sculpture in the East has been developed in this group of Buddhas and bodhisattvas. This is true of Buddhism's homeland, India, as well as of China, Japan, Korea, and Tibet. Through the influence of Greco-Scythian culture, forms quite Grecian were introduced into Mahayana. Therefore, as is well known, the ordinary images of Buddha have many characteristics of the statues of Apollo, but along with these, much of Buddhism's deepest mysticism is portrayed in the figures. The attentive observer, who has studied the inner life of Buddhism, will certainly trace his way through these characteristic features to a deeper comprehension of the Buddha concept,—the face with its fine lineaments, the half-closed eyes, the firm and yet wonderfully mild lines of the mouth, all speak strongly of harmony and peace of soul, of all-ruling understanding and deep sympathy with those who suffer.

Other figures from the various orders of the cycle were added later: guardian spirits, warriors with grim faces, frightful types of the damned who were saved by Buddha's grace, creatures on whom the searing marks of sin still showed, clear and living, avenging devil-hangmen, with peculiarly diabolical faces and forms, tortured victims from the gloomy dungeons of the underworld, monsters who in form and appearance are neither animal nor human. The sinister phenomena connected with spirit-worship break crudely in upon the higher religious sensibilities.

It is for this reason that, when one wanders about in one of the larger, well-equipped temples in China, one experiences such a mixture of emotions, feelings of solemnity mingled with horror and pain. How overwhelming the religious atmosphere can be in a fine temple hall, where the trinity is represented in noble and high art, or in a hall of meditation filled with smoke of fine incense, with its symbols and altars! And at the same time how hideous and distracting, indeed repellent, it is to come out into the hell-section, where the most frightful faces grin at one from among the good and noble figures!

[172]

THE BUDDHIST PANTHEON IN CHINA

A great deal of the grotesque has been imported especially from Tibet. Abstract ideas, like swiftness and attentiveness, are represented by putting many faces, many arms, many legs, and many eyes on the Buddha statues. Indeed, the idea of reproduction is sometimes portrayed in such a way that one must hang a curtain before the image. In China proper, such statues seldom stand open to the gaze. It is different when one gets up toward Mongolia and Tibet, where Lamaism begins to have power.

Thus with Buddhism's entrance into China, began the "manufacture of gods" (tiao hsiang, 雕像) and the Chinese developed this art to an altogether extraordinary degree. The first act of consecration of an image takes place while it is being made, when the pupils of the eyes are opened. This is called "opening the light" (k'ai kuang, 開光) and is accompanied by an act of homage to the great spirit who, it is thought, will take up his abode in the statue. Occasionally it is done in a more drastic way, by putting a snake or some other reptile into the figure through an opening in the back, or by smearing the blood of a cock on the breast of the statue. This, however, takes place only in the case of the lesser local gods and the Taoist gods, who, according to the Buddhist custom, have been chosen from among the people. The great images of the Fu or p'u-sa would never be treated in this way, but a heart or a gall-bladder of silver or gold or some mixture prepared of bitter herbs may be poured into the opening.

TRUTH AND TRADITION IN BUDDHISM

One will understand from this that the Asiatics, just like occidentals, look upon the images principally as visible symbols of invisible spiritual power. On the other hand, it happens among them, as so often elsewhere in the world, that the image, little by little, becomes identified with the spiritual power in question. This transition takes place the more easily in the East, since, as has been mentioned, the spirit of the god in question is thought to have been drawn into the image by a special religious ceremony. It would, however, be a great injustice to the enlightened and spiritual Buddhists to say that they believe the image is the god. Again and again well-educated Buddhists state that the images are only thought to be a help for beginners in religion; for the advanced worshipper no image, yea, no temple, is needed, because he has the sanctury in his own heart.

After these introductory remarks, let us turn to the treatment of the various divisions into which the Buddhist pantheon falls.

Chinese Buddhists have a perfectly definite classification according to rank and kind. The *highest class* consists of the *heavenly Buddhas*.

Here the historical Gotama Buddha naturally comes first. He is most frequently called by his family name (the wise one of the Sakya family), Shih-chia-mou-ni (釋迦牟尼). Only occasionally his given name, Siddattha, appears (Chinese: Hsi-ta, 悉達). Sometimes the Tathagata title (Ju-lai, 如來) is used especially of him, but this name may also be used in the trinity group,

THE BUDDHIST PANTHEON IN CHINA

which the "Pure Land" School especially emphasizes. Therefore persons who are not specialists on the subject ought to ask expressly whether or not it is Sakyamuni Buddha who is meant by this title.

He is portrayed, as a rule, sitting in meditation. With half-closed eyes, and with legs crossed under him in such a way that his hands can rest on the upturned soles of the feet, he sits on a lotus-blossom. A characteristic feature is the large ears with their long lobes. Frequently, a jewel gleams in the forehead. Often the ancient religious symbol of the "Swastika" (Chinese "sin-in," "the heart's signet," or "wan-tzŭ," 卍 字, "the hook") is engraved on the breast. It looks, as is well known, like this: 卍. Many Buddhists explain it as the sign of "a heart come to rest." As an old common religious symbol it typifies cosmic union. Behind the Buddha's head a nimbus (Chinese yüan-kuang, 圓 光), fashioned of carved and gilded wood, is usually placed.

Standing figures of Buddha occur less frequently. In a few places, however, in northern and western China, Sakyamuni appears in an upright position, as the ascetic, with long unkempt hair and beard, and clothing in rags. Sometimes one sees Buddha's entrance into Nirvana portrayed. He lies on a big Chinese bed, with a deeply peaceful expression (wo-fu, 臥 佛). Sometimes it happens, too, that one meets Buddha in the form of a little child. This is an allusion to the legendary saying from the life of Buddha: "I am now born for the last time."

[175]

TRUTH AND TRADITION IN BUDDHISM

We shall return later to the trinity group in which Sakyamuni Buddha also figures.

As *number two* among the *heavenly Buddhas*, comes Amitabha (O-mi-t'o Fu, 阿 彌 陀 佛), of whom we have already spoken so much. He is often placed in the trinity group.

In the "Pure Land" School one also frequently sees him portrayed alone, in quite a strange fashion: the large head, with noble features, rests on a comparatively slender body. The position is upright. In one hand he bears a lotus-blossom. The other arm, which is extraordinarily long, hangs free at his side, but the hand is open as if he were about to grasp something. In this position Amitabha has the special name of "Chieh-yin Fu" (接 引 佛), i. e., "the Buddha who receives and leads" into the Western Paradise. In other words, it is the figure of the great compassionate All-Father, who is here portrayed. This explains, too, why this figure is loved and worshipped as no other is. In the Buddhist circles it corresponds to the crucifix, since people often set up such a small statue in their rooms, hang a picture of this figure over their beds, or carry it with them on a cord, or in their pockets.

The *third heavenly Buddha* is called in Chinese Yao-shih Fu (藥 師 佛) and is connected, as the name implies, especially with the idea of medicine. It has been thought that he corresponds to Bhaisa Jyaguru Vaidurya in Sanskrit, abbreviated to Bhaisajyaguru. He is a very interesting but very mysterious figure. In the special book which is dedicated to him, the "Yao-shih Ching" (藥 師 經), he is portrayed as the

THE BUDDHIST PANTHEON IN CHINA

great source of light. He lives in endless light, and will draw all creation out of illusion and the darkness of despair into light and peace.

In rendering this service he has made twelve promises, of which we give a summary:

"I come in order that all creatures who are cripples, ugly, stupid, blind, deaf and dumb, hunch-backed, leprous, insane from all kinds of suffering, may, *by hearing my name*, be healed from all their diseases."

"I come in order that the incurables, the homeless, those who have neither doctor nor medicine, the friendless and kin-less, the poor and sorrowing, may, *by hearing my name*, be freed from all their sorrows and live in peace of soul and body, so that they and their homes may thrive and attain to the highest wisdom."

"I come in order that women, who on account of all kinds of miseries are driven even to hating their own lives and wishing no longer to be women, may, *by hearing my name*, be transformed into men and attain the highest wisdom."

"I come in order that those who are in the clutches of the law, bound, beaten, and imprisoned, or who have come to the place of execution, or who suffer under endless misfortunes and bitter insults, so that sorrow sears both body and soul, may, *by hearing my name*, desire my grace and find redemption from all their sorrows."

It will be seen that there is a good deal of overlapping in the spheres of activity of (Yao-shih Fu and Amitabha). There is also much that reminds one of the

[177]

TRUTH AND TRADITION IN BUDDHISM

ancient figure of Vairocana, as he was described in the "Great Sun" School of religion. The fact is, that these *all are really one*, merely giving expression to different ideas and shades of meaning in the great harmonious whole.

We shall later see that Yao-shih Fu has a special rôle to fill in the trinity concept. As might be expected, he, together with the two great Buddhas abovementioned, is the recipient of much supplication and praise, and is much invoked in sickness and need.

The two other heavenly Buddhas, Vairocana and Loshana (Chinese: P'i-lu-chê-na, 毘盧遮那, and Lu-shê-na, 盧舍那), may be distinguished from each other by the following marks: The former has hands folded over the breast with the forefinger pointing up. The latter lets the right hand rest in his lap while the left is held up to the breast, with the tip of the thumb and middle finger touching each other.

These five heavenly Buddhas are the most common. One hears less frequently of a sixth, called Jan-têng Fu (燃燈佛) (Buddha Dipankara), whose whole body is covered with lamps which burn constantly (one hundred and eight in number). It reminds one a little of the "lighted Christmas tree" with forty-nine lamps, which is sometimes lighted in honour of Yao-shih Fu (Yao-shih Têng, 藥師燈).

One must not think, however, that one has reached the end of the list of Buddhas with these six. Indeed, there are countless hosts of them. We mention here only those which are represented in sculpture and which have special significance for worship.

THE BUDDHIST PANTHEON IN CHINA

In the ritual, after the group of well-known Buddhas and bodhisattvas has been enumerated, such expressions as the following often occur: "And to you, ye other great Buddhas and bodhisattvas from all parts of heaven, to you are prayer and praise addressed."

The same idea appears at times in the arrangement of the temples. One often sees the entire main hall filled with small gilded heads of Buddhas. Sometimes there is a special hall to represent this "Wan-fu T'ang" (萬佛堂), the hall of ten thousand Buddhas. In brief, the Buddhas are the "perfected spirits" who fill the whole universe.

The Second Class

The second great group is formed by the bodhisattvas (Chinese: p'u-ti-sa-to, 菩提薩多, or p'u-sa, 菩薩). As already mentioned, these, also, are perfected spirits. That is to say, they could, if they so desired, enter into the full dignity of Buddhahood in everlasting peace and blessedness, but they do not do so, for the time being, because as bodhisattvas they can more easily reach that part of creation still under the uncertain and painful conditions peculiar to wandering souls.

The five best-known bodhisattvas, corresponding to the five heavenly Buddhas, are as follows:

Kuan-yin (觀音) is the Indo-Tibetan Avalokitesvara, the deity who heeds the cry of misery, and bends down to the suffering. This figure, little by little, came more than the other bodhisattvas to signify *the spirit*, the merciful and good spirit who kindles the desire for

TRUTH AND TRADITION IN BUDDHISM

a renewal of heart among all creatures, and who protects them against all pain and sorrow. In early times, Kuan-yin was generally considered as masculine, and one still sees in certain monasteries in China the enormous figure with beard and virile expression, which shows Kuan-yin as a man. In this form, Kuan-yin is plainly called Amitabha's son. Little by little, feminine characteristics became more prominent. This took place as the conception of the *spirit* became dominant, and all that the Chinese can conceive of in the way of motherly tenderness and womanly grace was attributed to her. She became the compassionate Madonna of the East.

Kuan-yin, like the other bodhisattvas, has taken great vows. She will incarnate herself in the most varied forms, in order to save mankind. Therefore she lets herself be born now into this group, now into that,—among robbers, among criminals in prison, among distressed seamen and travellers. We know about thirty-two different forms, "ying" (應). Her birthday is celebrated on the nineteenth of the second month; her entering into the full wisdom is remembered on the nineteenth of the sixth month; her death, or rather entering into the Nirvana, is given as having taken place on the nineteenth of the ninth month. Among the common people these three days are often spoken of as "Kuan-yin's birthday." The confusion is easy to understand. These festivals are very lively occasions. Every one is out. The temples and towns are decorated for the festival, for Kuan-yin, the Goddess of Mercy, is exceedingly popular.

THE BUDDHIST PANTHEON IN CHINA

Many legends and stories have arisen in China regarding her origin and life, but the really classical reference to Kuan-yin is in "The Lotus Scripture" ("Fa-hua Ching," 法華經), chapter 25.

Here it says (according to Dr. Timothy Richard's translation):

> "The Incomprehensible (Holy Spirit)
> She whom no evil spirit's eyes can see—
> Much less harm—
> Baffles them all,
> Granting deliverance.
> The wondrous power of God
> Is awe-inspiring, like this:—
> Should a woman desire a son,
> And reverently worship
> Holy Kuan-yin,
> She will obtain a blessing—
> An intelligent son.
> Should she desire a daughter
> She brings forth a virtuous one,
> A beauteous daughter,
> Rooted deep in virtue,
> By all respected,
> Joy without alloy,
> Immeasurable,—infinite
> Are these blessings.
> In three and thirty forms
> Herself, she manifested,
> Vowed a great vow, deep like the sea,
> A vow of holiness. Trusting in her power
> A fiery furnace becomes a cooling lake of water,
> Waves cannot drown.
> Through her kindliness of heart
> Shivered is sword of executioner.

Accursed poisonous herbs
May life endanger, but—
Think upon the Lotus Law
And you will then be healed.
Mid thunder-clouds and lightning,
Hailstones and floods of rain,
Look up to Kuan-yin.
These all shall vanish.
Kuan-yin's wondrous knowledge
Can save a world of sorrow.
'Tis mercy upon mercy—
Purest Light!"

One of the many accounts in Chinese of Kuan-yin's origin reads as follows:

"A little while after Buddha had established monasteries for monks and nuns, a royal princess (some say from Szechwan province, others from the Southern Sea) was seized with an earnest desire to dedicate her life to the practice of asceticism. Her name was Miao-shan (妙善). Her father had two other daughters, Miao-chin (妙金) and Miao-yin (妙銀).

"According to the father's wishes, these two daughters were given in marriage, but the third, Miao-shan, could not be induced to take this step. Secretly she left her home and entered a convent, no one knew where. Burning with anger, her father sent out a band of soldiers, who during the night surrounded the largest convent in the neighbourhood, a place where five hundred lo-hans (saints) were assembled. All these were burned to death in a horrible manner. As a punishment for this, the father became blind. All kinds of cures were tried to heal him, but everything

MIAO-SHAN REFUSING TO MARRY

was in vain. Finally, it became evident that one of his nearest must tear out her eyes for him, if he was to be well. This heroic act was performed by Miao-shan, who thereafter lived the whole of her life in darkness. At her death, however, she was delivered and became a bodhisattva, and came to earth again as the merciful Kuan-yin." This story is discredited by all the scholarly educated monks.

Apparently, Kuan-yin first became known in China in the region about Hangchow. From this place there was brisk trade with Ceylon and other places, where one hears of an ancient deity named Sumana, who had his sanctuary on "Adam's Peak." The qualities which are attributed to him remind one strongly of those which characterize Kuan-yin. Ceylon occasionally, however, received visits from South Arabian seamen, Sabians. They worshipped a deity, too, who "heard the cry" and "looked down in pity upon mankind," Al-Makah. Some students of the history of religion believe that there is a connection here. Others maintain that Kuan-yin was originally an Indian deity who especially received the many offerings for smallpox cases.

In China, she is constantly mentioned in connection with the sea. "She has risen from the Southern Sea" (Nan-hai, 南海). Indeed, the place where she first revealed herself is still shown. It was on the island of P'ut'o (普陀), in the Ningpo archipelago. Consequently the island of P'ut'o became a place holy above all others.

In connection with the "Southern Sea," a special type has arisen, which even many Buddhist monks confuse with the original Kuan-yin. This is the so-called "Nan-hai chun-t'i" (南海準提), who is portrayed "with a thousand arms and a thousand eyes." This rather monstrous figure, who is supposed to represent both large-heartedness and swiftness, may be one of Kuan-yin's many incarnations, but need not necessarily be so. It may also be one of the twenty-four devas (chu-t'ien 諸天), or archangels, who, in peace and enlightenment of mind, in vigilance and helpfulness, stands foremost in the ranks. Some sinologues think that the "Nanhai chun-t'i" has some connection with the Taoist goddess "Hsi-wang-mu" (西王母), or with Buddha's mother Mo-yeh (摩耶).

Kuan-yin is also incarnated as the lauded "Virgin Who Gives Fecundity" ("Sung-tzŭ Niang-niang," 送子娘娘). As such she is enthroned, usually at the back of the high altar, surrounded by a lot of plump little figures of children. There is a special altar where light and incense burn continually. This is looked after by the many childless women who daily visit this sanctuary.

It is very probable that the all-embracing Kuan-yin has absorbed quite a number of goddesses known and dear to the Chinese from old times. At the same time, new features have in this way been added to Kuan-yin's picture. It is almost certain that the idea of the Holy Virgin, the merciful Madonna of the sixteenth and seventeenth century, has also influenced this Kuan-yin picture.[1]

[1] The wonderful story of Maria and Christ, from the "Shên-hsien Kang-chien" (神仙綱鑑) given in Chap. II.

THE BUDDHIST PANTHEON IN CHINA

Kuan-yin has appeared in thirty-two different incarnations. For that reason she can be found everywhere, even among the worst class of beings. Present-day Buddhist magazines and pamphlets lay much stress upon this and often give very realistic descriptions of her doings. This has led some Christian people to the conclusion that Kuan-yin not only mingles with sinners, but commits actual sin in order to associate with them. This conclusion is as unfair as it is superficial. From her very nature, she cannot commit sin, but because she is the good spirit she can meet the sinner at the moment of crisis or of greatest darkness. She may even speak from the mouth of the victim whom the sinner is about to dishonour, and wake up his conscience.

Since Kuan-yin, as the great revealer and mediator of the All-Father, thus cares for all the needy and suffering, it may be understood how greatly she is loved and worshipped. There is scarcely a district or village where one does not find her image and temple. In many places she has been made the "tutelary goddess." She is constantly spoken of with the beautiful attributes "Ta-tz'ŭ ta-pei" (大慈大悲), "great mercy and great sympathy."[1]

Second in the list of bodhisattvas is the figure who in the purest form of Mahayana, the "Pure Land" School, is placed beside Kuan-yin as Amitabha's second son, Ta-shih-chih (大勢至). The name in its Chinese form means "the one who, in power, has

[1] Compare the Tibetan and Mongol form of greeting: "Om Mani padme hum": "Greeting, thou jewel in the lotus!" (Kuan-yin).

[185]

TRUTH AND TRADITION IN BUDDHISM

attained the highest,"—in other words, the "Strongest One."

We have probably here the Indian Mahahasthanaparapta. There is not much said about him, but what is said is so much the more important. He has broken karma's weary circle, and in some way has once for all provided an objective atonement, which makes it impossible for mankind to break loose from the cycle of soul-wanderings. *Power* is his most important attribute, the power of love, founded upon his heart of deep compassion. The mediation of his power to the individual, however, can only be accomplished through Kuan-yin. It is she who drives the soul to holy desires for renewal and salvation, and she is the mediator of this salvation through her spirit.

It is not for nothing that Kuan-yin is represented in thousands of scrolls and paintings in China as blessing a supplicant. Fine threads go down from her hands and her halo-crowned head to the praying figure. Sometimes one sees in this connection the beautiful symbol of the Nestorians and the ancient church, the white dove (the pure spirit) which Kuan-yin sends down upon the supplicant. Moreover, the dove bears in his beak a rosary, that age-old Indian symbol of prayer's unbroken chain which binds the children of time with the world of eternity.

Third in the list of bodhisattvas comes the interesting Maitreya (Mi-lo Fu, 彌 勒 佛). In his humility and compassion, he not only denies himself the dignity of Buddhahood, but often acts as a regular tutelary god. At the very entrance to the temple one meets his great

THE BUDDHIST PANTHEON IN CHINA

plump image with the broad good-natured smile on his lips, a flower in the right hand, and with the left grasping the mouth of the sack in which the future's gifts of happiness are hidden. His cloak is thrown aside so that the enormous chest and fat stomach are exposed. His image is so strange and in one way so comic that it has found its way into the homes and shops everywhere. Even in the shops of the West one may chance to see a model in bronze or porcelain. Nevertheless, there are few people who have any idea of the fact that some of the deepest thoughts and liveliest hopes of Buddhism are bound up with this figure. Mi-lo Fu is, in fact, the man of the future. He has revealed himself before; indeed, it is even said that he once let himself be born a lo-han (arhat), and there is actually a counterpart of Mi-lo Fu in the group of the "eighteen saints." His real work, however, is to come in the future, when at Buddha's command he will descend as a Buddha from the "heaven of the blessed" and establish his great "millennial kingdom." The Chinese always speak of him as "Tang-lai Mi-lo Fu" (當來彌勒佛), the Mi-lo Fu who is to come. He is, therefore, the Messiah of Buddhism. Some people have even tried to see a connection in the name itself, but this is probably etymologically impossible.

In "Mi-lo-Hsia-shêng Ching" (彌勒下生經), the scripture describing Maitreya's descent to the world, we find how this bodhisattva is solemnly appointed by Gotama Buddha to come again as the great saviour and renewer at the time when the power of evil is at its

TRUTH AND TRADITION IN BUDDHISM

height and all living things seem to be going to ruin under sin and punishment. It is at "mo-fa" (末 法), the last hour or the "final dispensation," that this great hope which dwells so unshakably secure in the heart of every Buddhist will be realized.

The two next best-known bodhisattvas are Wên-shu (文 殊), Manjusri in Sanskrit, and P'u-hsien (普 賢), Samantabhadra, the former representing wisdom, and the latter mercy. They are distinguished from each other by the fact that the one, Wên-shu, rides on a lion, while the other, P'u-hsien, rides on an elephant. Both of them have gained native rights in China, since they are believed to have occupied two of China's holy mountains. P'u-hsien travelled up to Szechwan province and settled on the ancient picturesque O-mei Shan (峨 眉 山), while Wên-shu went to the north-east where he found for himself a holy and peaceful spot on Wu-t'ai Shan (五 台 山).

As Mi-lo Fu (彌 勒 佛) is very often counted among the "tutelary gods," Ti-ts'ang (地 藏) (the bodhisattva of the underworld) is therefore counted as the fifth in the list of bodhisattvas. As we have already, in the chapter about masses for the soul, given a sketch of him and his work of salvation in hell, it is unnecessary to say more here.

The Third Class

The third great group is that of the so-called arhats (Chinese: lo-han, 羅漢). There are any number of these in the Chinese pantheon, since most of the disciples who followed Buddha were later classed in this group.

THE BUDDHIST PANTHEON IN CHINA

First in the class come *Buddha's first ten disciples* (shih ta ti-tzŭ 十大弟子):

1. Shê-li-fu (舍利佛) (Sariputra), the disciple of wisdom.
2. Mu-chien-lien (目犍連) (Maha Maudgalyayana), the disciple with the greatest divine power.
3. Mo-ho-chia-yeh (摩訶迦葉) (Maha Kasyapa), also called Chia-shi, the disciple who became a leader among the monks.
4. O-na-lü (阿那律) (Aniruddha), the disciple with the heavenly eye.
5. Hsü-p'u-t'i (須菩提) (Subhuti), the disciple who can understand and explain the great emptiness.
6. Fu-lou-na (富樓那) (Purna), he who proclaims salvation.
7. Chia-chan-yen (迦旃延) (Kutyayawa), the great explainer.
8. Yu-p'u-li (優婆離) (Upali), the mediator of the law.
9. Lo-hou-lo (羅睺離) (Kahula), the mystic.
10. O-nan-t'o (阿難陀) (Ananda), also called O-nan (阿難), the questioner.

In connection with these ten great disciples of Buddha are named also the twelve who had not yet attained complete "enlightenment," the so-called yüan-chio (緣覺). They play a very modest rôle, and their images are seldom seen in the temples.

Ananda and Kasyapa (Chinese: O-nan and Chia-yeh) hold a special position as the two who most often stand directly before the image of Buddha. They act as heralds or spokesmen. The Chinese sometimes call Ananda by the special name he received because he was born on the day of Buddha's spiritual awakening, Ch'ing-hsi (慶喜), that is, "Congratulation." Kasyapa received the name of Yin-kuang (飲光), because of the rays of light that proceed from his body. This light is

[189]

TRUTH AND TRADITION IN BUDDHISM

connected with the full insight which he attained during the famous meeting on Ling Shan (靈 山), the mountain of spirits, where Buddha revealed his teaching.

In the course of time, however, a world of difference has arisen between the "saints" (lo-han) and those beings who are pressing on toward the condition of bodhisattvas, a difference which discloses the peculiarities of Hinayana and Mahayana. The so-called "lo-hans" became increasingly associated with Hinayana, the name coming to stand for the secure self-complacent condition into which the adherents of Hinayana entered. They themselves were redeemed and renewed; not, however, for an active life of loving and merciful service, but for a life of pleasant contentment in undisturbed rest and well-being. It has therefore become a term of reviling among China's monks to say, "He is a 'lo-han.'" It means he is a person who does not trouble himself over the needs of others.

This fine irony is seen also in the artistic representation of the best-known "lo-han" groups the so-called "shih-pa lo-han" (十 八 羅 漢)—the eighteen saints.[1] This body of choice individuals representing the most villainous robbers as well as the best men, who have been saved by the grace of Buddha, still bear for the most part the disfiguring marks of sin, and yet, over them all, spreads an expression of the greatest self-satisfaction and well-being. On old scrolls one sees them giving themselves up to taking care of their health or amusing themselves, often in the most

[1] In Japan only sixteen are counted.

[190]

THE BUDDHIST PANTHEON IN CHINA

childish manner. Besides these, however, there are drawings of groups where their dignity is more apparent.

As this lo-han group is very well known and is to be seen in all the larger temples and monasteries, we shall give the full Chinese name of each one:

1. Pin-tu-lo-pa-lo-to (賓度羅跋囉惰)
2. Chia-no-chia-fa-ts'o (迦諾迦伐蹉)
3. Chia-no-chia-po-li-to (迦諾迦跋釐惰)
4. Su-p'in-t'o (蘇頻陀)
5. No-chü-lo (諾距羅)
6. Po-t'o-lo (跋陀羅)
7. Chia-li-chia (迦理迦)
8. Fa-shê-lo-fu-to-lo (伐闍羅弗多羅)
9. Shu-po-chia (戍博迦)
10. P'an-t'o-chia (半托迦)
11. Lo-ku-lo (囉怙羅)
12. Lo-ch'ieh-hsi-na (那伽犀那)
13. Yin-chieh-t'o (因揭陀)
14. Fa-lo-p'o-ssŭ (伐羅婆斯)
15. O-shih-to (阿氏多)
16. Chu-t'u-pan-t'o-chia (注荼半托迦)
17. Ch'ing-yu (慶友)
18. Pin-t'ou-lu (賓頭盧)

In certain of the larger monasteries and temples one also finds a special long and elaborate hall for the "five hundred saints" (wu-pai lo-han, 五百羅漢). This hall is also called "lo-han t'ang" (羅漢堂), the hall of the saints, and a special advantage is given the monastery which contains this building because it becomes a sort of museum for sculpture, and through it many visitors are attracted to the monastery. Rich families often provide the means for this extensive work. The statues are frequently quite large, and when one considers the fact that often each one is overlaid with gold foil and in other ways richly

[191]

decorated, one can understand that it is a costly affair. From a religious point of view these saints play a very small part. Only on especially great occasions are any offerings made to them; as, for example, on their respective birthdays. Among the five hundred statues one finds the most varied types of physiognomy. There are some nobly formed faces, full of spiritual earnestness, but most of them are ugly to look at, some of them positively repulsive and hideous. The hall abounds with criminal types and stern men of law who bear the marks of consuming zeal. It is in this group of five hundred lohans that some believe they have discovered a statue of Marco Polo, the famous traveller who, in the thirteenth century, visited so many of China's cities. A large number of the benefactors of Buddhism, emperors, statesmen, etc., may also be found in the group.

The so-called Buddhist fathers or patriarchs are usually coupled with these figures from the third class. Of these, there are six in China, and they are all connected with the Yangtze valley. One therefore finds the majority of the temples in honour of the patriarchs (tsu-shih, 祖師) in this region.

The list opens with the Indian Bodhidarma (P'u-t'i-ta-mo, 菩提達摩) already mentioned, who came over to China in the year 520 as the twenty-eighth patriarch after Buddha, and became the first patriarch in China. He worked much in Nanking and on Lü Shan in Kiangsi, but later settled on Sung Shan in Honan province. Images and scrolls with his likeness show the un-Chinese and foreign nature of his appearance.

[192]

BUDDHIST TRINITY

THE BUDDHIST PANTHEON IN CHINA

As a matter of curiosity, it may be mentioned that there are those who have wished to identify him with the apostle Thomas, who lived his missionary life in Eastern regions! The strong Jewish characteristics have been pointed out.[1]

After Bodhidharma there followed in succession, as master and pupil, the remaining five patriarchs:

2. Shên-kuang, or Hui-k'o (神光, 慧可)
4. Tao-hsin, or Ta-i (道信, 大義)
3. Sêng-ts'an, or Chien-chih (僧璨, 鑑智)
5. Hung-jên, or Ta-man (弘忍, 大滿)
6. Hui-nêng, or Ta-chien (慧能, 大鑑)

In all great monasteries there is a special hall where homage is given these six fathers. Other Indian fathers (from among the earlier twenty-seven) also appear in the hall of the patriarchs (Tsu-shih t'ang 祖師堂). Their birthdays are celebrated with especial pomp and glory.

The Fourth Class

This group is composed of the so-called *tutelary deities* (ch'ieh-lan, 伽藍) and is quite a motley and international assemblage. One finds them all gathered in the well-known group of twenty-four devas (Chinese: chu-t'ien, 諸天) who are set up, twelve on either side of the large temple hall, but several of them also appear independently in one or other sphere of activity in the temple, and one will therefore often see duplicates. Naturally, however, when they are set up separately

[1] Doré: "Recherches sue les superstitions," Vol. VII, p. 243. Also Johnston: "Buddhist China."

TRUTH AND TRADITION IN BUDDHISM

as "heads" over one or other department, their statues are larger in dimension and much finer in appearance. This is especially the case with the leader of the twenty-four devas (Wei-t'o, 韋馱), and the four heavenly kings (ssŭ ta T'ien-wang, 四大天王). This collection of gods, angels, and archangels are named as follows:

1. Tsêng-ch'ang T'ien-wang (增長天王)
2. Yen-lo T'ien-tzŭ (閻羅天子)
3. Chien-chai T'ien-shên (監齋天神)
4. Hsing-kŭng Tsun-t'ien (星宮尊天)
5. P'u-t'i Shan-nu (菩提善女)
6. Mo-i T'ien-shên (寬盆天神)
7. Wei-t'o Tsun-shên (韋馱尊神)
8. Jih-kung T'ien-shên (日宮天神)
9. Ta-pan Ts'ai-shên (大辦才神)
10. Kung-tê Tsun-shên (功德尊神)
11. Ta-fan T'ien-shên (大梵天神)
12. Ch'ih-kuo T'ien-wang (持國天王)
13. Kuang-mu T'ien-wang (廣目天王)
14. Lung-wang Shui-shên (龍王水神)
15. Hu-chieh Lo-wang (虎伽羅王)
16. O-ni T'i-nan (阿呢啼喃)
17. Kuêi-tzu Mu-shên (鬼子母神)
18. Mo-li Wen-wang (寬唎文王)
19. Chien-lao Ti-shên (堅牢地神)
20. Yüeh-kung Tsun-t'ien (月宮尊天)
21. San-chih T'ien-shên (散脂天神)
22. Mi-chi Tsun-shên (密跡尊神)
23. Ti-shih Tsun-shên (帝釋尊神)
24. To-wên T'ien-wang (多聞天王)

As one will notice, there are here, besides the four heavenly kings (T'ien-wang, 天王), also such Indian

[194]

THE BUDDHIST PANTHEON IN CHINA

gods as Brahma (Ta-fan T'ien-shên) and Indra (Ti-shih Tsun-shên), likewise the great judge in hades (Yen-lo T'ien-tzŭ); even the "kitchen god" appears under his Buddhist title of Chien-chai T'ien-shên. All these devas have a part in the protection of the Buddhist society and its sanctuaries.

Acting with diplomacy and tolerance, the Buddhists put Confucius and the god of literature, Wên-ch'ang (文昌), into this group. They have also placed here the god of war, Kuan-shên (關神), beloved by the people.

The four heavenly kings (ssŭ ta T'ien-wang, 四大天王) grouped together, run as follows:

1. Tsêng-ch'ang T'ien-wang (增長天王)
2. Ch'ih-kuo T'ien-wang (持國天王)
3. Kuang-mu T'ien-wang (廣目天王)
4. To-wên T'ien-wang (多聞天王)

Along with them must also be mentioned the two fierce guardians, standing at the outside temple door (Hêng Ha êrh chiang, 哼哈二將).

1. Hêng (哼)
2. Ha (哈)

A subdivision of this class is the group of guardian angels, also called cherubs (Chin-kang Shên, 金剛神) known from "The Diamond Scripture" ("Chin-kang Ching," 金剛經) and other writings. Of these cherubs there are eight who, each in his own fashion, serves those who draw near to Buddha with a sincere heart. Their names are:

1. Ch'ing-ch'u-tsai (青除災)   5. Ch'ih-shêng-huo (赤聲火)
2. P'i-tu (辟毒)   6. Ting-ch'ih-tsai (定持災)
3. Huang-sui-ch'iu (黃隨求)   7. Tzŭ-hsien (紫賢)
4. Pai-ching-shui (白淨水)   8. Ta-shên (大神)

Four great "Chin-kang p'u-sa" (金剛菩薩).

1. Chüan (眷)   3. Ai (愛)
2. So (索)   4. Yü (語)

Further, it may also be mentioned that these four angels sometimes are portrayed with different expressions of countenance in order to show the four great qualities of Buddha's nature:

1. Tz'u (慈)—mercy   3. Hsi (喜)—love
2. Pei (悲)—sympathy   4. Shê (捨)—liberality

As one will notice, the quality of mercy is the one which is all-dominating in a Buddha. Quite true, he is holy, wise, thoughtful, and just, but the most important thing about him is that he is full of mercy. He is not concerned with vindicating the authority of the law, the punishment of sinners, etc. These functions are left to the great objective powers of the universe, represented by the impersonal powers working through the tao (道), logos, or quite vaguely through a heavenly god like Indra, and an archangel like Wei-to.

The laws of life work entirely impersonally. They go their way and there is no encouragement to attempt to disturb them. But it is necessary that people, on life's journey, meet the good powers as they reveal themselves in the great and merciful Buddha spirits.

[196]

THE BUDDHIST PANTHEON IN CHINA

As already mentioned, there is an endless number of named and unnamed Buddhas, bodhisattvas, and great "masters" (mo-ho-sa, 摩訶薩) who are worshipped during the long masses. The outward forms of worship, however, are determined mainly by those described above, since it is their images which are generally seen in the temples.

One formula very much used to reach the many unnamed bodhisattvas is the following:

"Nan-mo ch'ing-ching ta-hai chung p'u-sa—南無清淨大海眾菩薩
"Hail, ye pure and peaceful bodhisattvas round about in the great ocean!"

The Trinity Groups

From the very earliest times of Buddhist history, the trinity groups have been prominent. Without doubt, Hinayana itself took over this arrangement from the oldest representations of the Indian religions. Not that there were in the beginning any images which were represented as a trinity, but the ideas and thoughts about the supernatural, the divine, almost of their own accord divided themselves from the first into three.

Nothing was more natural, therefore, than that Buddhism, even during the lifetime of the historical Buddha, was considered as a synonym for the "three values" (san-pao, 三寶; Sanskrit: trikaya), Buddha, the doctrine, and the society. Ordination and the daily worship in Buddhism therefore came to be connected with the well-known triad which, in simpler or more complicated form, has been repeated again and again: "Kuei-i Fu, kuei-i fa, kuei-i sêng" (皈依佛, 皈依法, 皈依僧), "I dedicate myself to Buddha, to the doctrine, to the society."

Buddha, Sakyamuni is usually set as the representative of "Fu," but Amitabha can also take his place. The "doctrine" (fa) is represented by Vairocana (P'i-lu-chê-na, 毘盧遮那) and the "society" (sêng, 僧) by Loshana (Lu-shê-na, 盧舍那).

After Mahayana came into power and images and pictures of the gods (shên-hsiang, 神像) became the fashion, these "three values" each received a resplendent image. It is seldom that one sees these three statues together in the main hall, however. Vairocana's statue stands, as a rule, in the lecture and education hall, and Loshana is rarely to be found. The reason for this is that the "society" is supposed to be represented most logically by the group of monks who go in and out of the monastery. Sometimes, however, one finds his statue as the central figure in the main hall, as, for example, in the famous old monastery of Pao-hua Shan (寶華山) belonging to the Legalistic School in Nanking, while Kasyapa (Chinese: Chia-yeh, 迦葉) and Upali (Yu-p'u-li, 優婆離), another of Buddha's disciples, stand as the side figures. It sometimes happens, too, that Sakyamuni stands alone with his two favourite disciples, Ananda and Kasyapa, a little in front of him, like heralds. Their statues are then much smaller, so that evidently no idea of a real trinity is thought of.

In all temples of the Meditation School (Ch'an-mên, 禪門) one finds Sakyamuni Buddha as the central

THE BUDDHIST PANTHEON IN CHINA

figure, with Yao-shih Fu (藥師佛) on his right and Amitabha on his left side. It has become the fashion, probably since the appearance of Herr Hackmann's book, "Buddhism as a Religion," to deny that in this grouping the idea of the three great periods of time, past, present, and future, is involved. Even Couling's otherwise so exact "Encyclopædia Sinica" denies the correctness of this idea. Nevertheless one cannot get away from it so easily. It cannot be denied that many of the cleverest "fa-shih" (法師), interpreters of the law, within the Buddhist society, firmly maintain that in this grouping, besides other considerations, the periods of time within the world era are thought of. Yao-shih Fu, then, is looked upon as the king from the East. Indeed, I have heard him described as the king of the lost "Eastern Paradise," although this is sharply denied by others. Buddha Sakyamuni, as is so often emphasized in the scriptures, is the king or lord in this present world of sorrow (so-p'o shih-chieh, 娑婆世界), and Amitabha is the king of the "Western Paradise," the future "kingdom of god" into which he has pledged himself to draw all creatures.

In this connection, we ought to say a few words as to the resemblances between the Christian and the Buddhist ideas of the trinity. There certainly is a resemblance, but the differences are also quite apparent, as Dr. Hodous has stated in his last book on "Buddhism and Buddhists in China," 1924 (page 60): "We should note that the first person of the Buddhist trinity would correspond to God as the absolute or the impersonal background of universal Being. The

TRUTH AND TRADITION IN BUDDHISM

second corresponds to the glorified Christ and the third to the historic Jesus. There is no counterpart either to God the Father or to the Holy Spirit." The conception of the trinity which Dr. Hodous has here mentioned is derived from the well-known fact that the Mahayana Buddhists, in their thinking and scriptures, constantly return to the conception of the "essence-body" or Dharmakaya (Chinese: fa-shên, 法身), the impersonal power from whom all the different forms of living beings emanate. The second "person" is the Sambhogakaya (Chinese: pao-shên, 報身). This is the heavenly emanation, full of bliss and splendour, giving exact expression to the secret characteristics of the everlasting dharma (fa, 法). The third is the Nirmanakaya (Chinese: hua-shên, 化身), the earthly reflection of the pao-shên, taking innumerable forms according to the nature of the ever-rotating wheel of dharma, drawing all beings into the deep unity of creation. Hence comes the mystical saying, "Fa-lun miao chuan" (法輪妙轉), "the mysterious rotation of the dharma wheel."

This abstract conception of the trinity idea receives its concrete manifestation in the three well-known sentences in the daily ritual:

> Nan-mo ch'ing-ching fa-shên, P'i-lu-chê-na Fu.
> Nan-mo yüan-man, pao-shên, Lu-shê-na Fu.
> Nan-mo ch'ien-pai-i, hua-shên, Shih-chia-mou-ni Fu.
> 南無清淨法身毘盧遮那佛
> 南無圓滿報身盧舍那佛
> 南無千百億化身釋迦牟尼佛
> "I take my refuge in the lucid and pure body of the law, Vairocana.

THE BUDDHIST PANTHEON IN CHINA

I take my refuge in the perfect body of the celestial revealer, Loshana.

I take my refuge in him, who through innumerable ages appears bodily on earth, Sakyamuni."

There is in the Mahayana philosophy another expression of the trinity idea, which undoubtedly comes much nearer to the Christian conception than the trinity given above. Although it is more abstract, it nevertheless points to the great spiritual realities, commonly felt and expressed in all higher religions. This is the saying in the "Ch'i Hsin Lun" (起信論) that behind the universe which can be seen, three different manifestations of spiritual power are in action. The one is *the underlying essence*, called "t'i" (體). The second is *the image*, or hsiang (相), the different manifestations of that essence. The third is the yung (用), the essence in action, the energy working through the universe. Here is a real resemblance to the Christian idea of God the Father, the Son, and the Holy Spirit.

In the "Pure Land" School there is a classical trinity group, consisting of Amitabha in the middle, Kuan-yin on the left, and Ta-shih-chih on the right. All are represented standing.

Outside the main hall, in the "Pure Land" temples, occasionally groups may be found consisting of Mi-lo Fu, Kuan-yin, and Yao-shih Fu.

In the more legalistic schools, one often sees Buddha as the central figure and the great bodhisattvas Wên-shu and P'u-hsien, respectively, on the left and right sides. They ride on their favourite animals, the lion and the elephant. Wisdom and mercy are supposed to be represented in this combination: the heavenly Buddha looks down upon this "world of sorrow," full of wisdom and grace (Wên-shu representing wisdom, and P'u-hsien, grace).

Besides the statues above-mentioned, a great number of images may be found of local figures that have gained merit and fame for themselves in some special locality.

CHAPTER VII

BUDDHIST LITERATURE IN CHINA

Owing to the fact that Buddhism in China has taken a typical Mahayana form, our subject might be called "The Mahayana Literature of China."

We cannot, of course, attempt to give here any exhaustive description of this literature. It is far too extensive. We must limit ourselves to general summaries, for, as is commonly known, there is no religion which has a "Bible" so extensive as that of Buddhism. It may be stated on a conservative estimate that the Buddhist Tripitaka itself is seven hundred times larger than the Christian Bible. In addition to this there are the immense collections of classic commentaries and essays, only a small fraction of which have been properly examined and translated into any European language. As a large part of the Hinayana writings has also been included in the Mahayana collection, it will be seen that China, Japan, and Korea at present have the largest literary treasury in Eastern Buddhism.

Quite naturally a new section has been added to the original collection of scriptures, so that in connection with the Chinese Tripitaka (literally translated into Chinese, "San-ts'ang," 三藏, Three Baskets) there is a section which might be called the fourth basket and is termed "tsa" (雜), i. e., miscellaneous works.

The first three "baskets" (sections) are called in Chinese (1) ching (經), the scriptures; (2) lü (律), the law; and (3) lun (論), dissertations or essays; these

[203]

TRUTH AND TRADITION IN BUDDHISM

correspond to the well-known Sanskrit terms, (1) dharma, or the sutras proper; (2) Vinaya; and (3) Abhidharma.

Only a few of the scriptures of the Chinese Tripitaka have been translated from the Pali texts. The great mass came, as might be expected, from the north where Sanskrit was the undisputed religious language. Not only translations, however, are to be found in the old monastery libraries of China. Original Sanskrit texts have also been discovered. Even Chinese Turkestan has yielded valuable documents.

According to the spirit of Mahayana the most varied systems of salvation (fa-mên, 法門) are recognized. For this reason there has been no desire to change the texts, even though they pointed in an entirely different direction from Mahayana itself.[1]

In most of the monasteries of China as things have developed Hinayana has come to be described as the first order to which a man is ordained, after which he enters the higher orders. It is therefore difficult to find anything more heterogeneous or more complex than the Mahayana collection of scriptures. This is the case in the first place with regard to form, as it contains religious rules, doctrinal books and treatises, as well as commentaries, catalogue lists, and poems from earlier Chinese poets (as Han-Shan-Tse's collection of poems). It is also the case with regard to the substance, the most atheistic views being expressed side by side with pronounced theistic and polytheistic systems of thought.

[1] Cf. Chih-k'ai's original theory of harmonizing the systems.

[204]

BUDDHIST LITERATURE IN CHINA

For this reason the collection gives a complete presentation of *the ways of salvation* which are preached and practised in modern Buddhism: Bhakti (surrender in faith), Inana (knowledge), Yoga (meditation), and Karman (holiness through works). All roads are open.

It has already been mentioned that Gobharana and Matanga, the first two priests who came to China from India, began very soon after their arrival to translate the Indian sutras. The life of Gotama Buddha is probably the most important among these early translations. The book "Buddha Charita Kavya" ("Fu-pên-sing Ching," 佛本行經), which is ascribed to Asvaghosha, was translated quite early on. Another life much more extensive and also much more legendary in character, appeared in India during the first period of Mahayana and was soon brought to China. This is the well-known "Lalita Vistara." The new views of Mahayana here colour everything. Buddha, by his own power, after a long preparation of the universe for this great event, permits himself to be born. He enters his mother's womb as a white elephant, and later emerges from her side. His long life of strife and victory, goodness and purity, is described in the most sublime and dramatic style. In the modern editions which are now used in China ("Shih-chia Ju-lai ying-hua Shih-chi," 釋迦如來應化事蹟), "The History of Tataghata Sakyamuni," there are many illustrations which show the great man's "Leben und Treiben."

Another book which has been extremely important, i. e., Mahayana, "Sukhavati Vyuha Sutra" (the great and the little), was already translated into Chinese in

TRUTH AND TRADITION IN BUDDHISM

A.D. 147–148. Some scholars have thought that this translation is the work of the Parthian prince Arsaces and the Indian monk Lokaraksha. (The prince's name in Chinese is Anshikao. Anshi is the Chinese for Parthia, so this name may be a corruption of Arsaces, the founder of the dynasty of the Arsacidæ.) Unfortunately this old translation has been lost, but as the book was extremely important, it has been repeatedly retranslated, first by Samghapala and later under the famous Kumarajiva, who has enriched China with so many excellent translations. The book received through him the name "Fu-shuo O-mi-t'o Ching" (佛說阿彌陀經), "The Sayings of Buddha About Amitabha."

A well-known Chinese pilgrim, Hsüan-chuang, also made a translation directly from Sanskrit with the title: "Ch'êng-tsan Chingt'u Fu Shê-shou Ching," (稱讚淨土佛攝受經), "The Book of Praise of That Buddha in the Pure Land Who Saves and Protects."

The pilgrims already mentioned, both Indian and Chinese, expended enormous efforts both in securing the Mahayana scriptures, and transporting them long distances to China, and later in translating them there. Few can fully realize the enormous labour which has been expended on this work, both in Loyang, the old capital, and in the monasteries throughout the country. Diligent monks and highly gifted literati co-operated in the most harmonious way to make the style as clear, dignified, and noble as possible. We therefore find that from a literary standpoint most of these books hold a high place.

BUDDHIST LITERATURE IN CHINA

In order to set forth the many alien ideas and fine shades of meaning, new expressions had to be created and characters had to be used in a new and specific sense. Not only had Indian sounds to be represented in symbols, but also special modes of thought and shades of meaning had to be expressed. Therefore many of the Buddhist books are difficult reading—and the ordinary well-trained scholar will stumble after reading a few lines. It is necessary to become familiar with the special terminology of the Buddhists before one can get any real benefit from the reading of their scriptures.

It is possible to trace the history of the translations of these Sanskrit texts all the way down to the eighth or ninth century of this era, to Amogha one of the last and greatest of the translators. At this time the Mahayana Tripitaka is found to be fairly complete. Later additions come specially under section tsa (雜), miscellaneous, consisting of commentaries, dissertations, and poems. Not the least numerous are the last mentioned. Great numbers of them were produced during the Yüan and Ming dynasties. If one is to understand Buddhism during those centuries and get an impression of the influence which it exercised, these poems and ritual hymns must be given careful study.

Some of them have great beauty and breathe a deep religious feeling. But there is at the same time something extremely monotonous about them and one looks in vain for an author who draws from new wells. The poems are like the classic scriptures, and follow a

TRUTH AND TRADITION IN BUDDHISM

traditional form. The setting is a great gathering, when Buddha calls together, in a garden or on a mountain or sometimes in the centre of the thirty-three heavens (Tao-li T'ien, 忉利天), the hundred thousand myriads of the ten thousand Buddhas and bodhisattvas. These gather from the whole universe like dust motes in the atmosphere. The whole gathering is lighted by a flash from the hair between Sakyamuni's eyebrows—and unlimited brilliance and heavenly melody embrace all things.

Gods and devils, Buddhas and bodhisattvas, great masters and miserable creatures from all the hells and orders of mutation, meet and stand listening breathlessly. One of Buddha's disciples (Ananda, Hsü-p'u-t'i, Wên-shu, or P'u-hsien, or sometimes the mother of Buddha, Chinese Mo-yeh, Mâyâ) comes forward and asks a question on some abstruse subject. Then the "Enlightened One," the "World-Honoured One" (shih-tsun 世尊), gives his explanation in exalted expressions and flowery language. Often a dialogue develops. Again classical portions of the old sutras are quoted and sometimes a whole sutra is woven into the speech. This is one of the reasons why Tripitaka is so excessively voluminous.

The first act closes with a short poem which gives the essence of the instruction. These little poems have frequently wonderful beauty and depth, as, for example, the following.

After a long speech about the feeling of solidarity with all who suffer, this significant verse occurs:

Lo-han T'ang, Ling-yen Monastery, Shantung

BUDDHIST LITERATURE IN CHINA

> Listen, all ye "pi-ch'iu"[1] and go
> Out into the sorrow-filled world,
> Preach that all now can attain salvation,
> Relief, and strength on the way.
> The fire of mercy
> Lights all hearts.
> The law of salvation they must hear,
> Then the closed doors are opened.
> Glorious is the law from first to last,
> Glorious in the middle parts!
> Glorious is the wording—and sure.
> Bringing salvation and happiness.
> Therefore, ye "pi-ch'iu," tell in action and words
> How immeasurably great is the law of God.

In the next chapter the same truths are varied, new illustrations are introduced, new incarnations of the merciful bodhisattvas are described, till finally the book closes with a short hymn of praise.

Large sections are given up to the great vows and solemn oaths which the different Buddhas and bodhisattvas make concerning the salvation of the whole creation. These sections are frequently introduced with a dramatic description of the appearing of Buddha in light and glory. The sight of him makes such a strong impression on the disciples that they, too, are fired with a holy longing to attain the same profound peace and majestic calm and glory (chuang-yen, 莊嚴), the same fulness of divine power (shên-t'ung, 神通), and the same quiet, strong, and mysterious activity (wei-miao, 微妙). And the road to

---

[1] Sanskrit, bhikshu: Those who have attained to the second step of initiation.

TRUTH AND TRADITION IN BUDDHISM

this is through the sacrifice of oneself for creation. This idea of inspiration sheds light on the deeper significance of the bodhisattva, being derived from the actual sight of Buddha or bodhisattva.

"*The Basket of the Law*" (*Lu*, 律)

This work is of course still more stereotyped than the poems. Here we first have the old law of Hinayana *(pratimokshas)* with the ten cardinal commandments called the "Sha-mi Shih-chieh" (沙彌十戒) and the two hundred and fifty special ones for the "pi-ch'iu" (比丘). In connection with these there are long explanations.

"The Book of Brahma's Net" is the book of special Mahayana law ("Fan-wang Ching," 梵網經). This contains the fifty-eight commandments, ten difficult ones and forty-eight easy ones, which lead up to the highest order of ordination. It was the well-known Kumarajiva who in A.D. 406 translated this book. He himself was deeply affected by the book, for "Mahayana had given him gold. What he had formerly seen in Hinayana was only copper." The original Sanskrit text which Kumarajiva used has probably disappeared, for the book which now bears this name in the collection moves along different lines of thought.

"*The Basket of the Essays*" (*Lun*, 論)

The section ("basket") which shows the greatest variety, both as to text and ideas, is undoubtedly that of the essays. Here much of the well-known Buddhist philosophy is found, especially as it has been developed

BUDDHIST LITERATURE IN CHINA

in Mahayana, with its infinite hair-splittings. Here are found, put together, spiritual analyses of the soul, bold theoretical combinations — glimpses into the depths of spiritual life by the mind of a genius, together with absurd postulates and leaps of thoughts. The purpose is to give a foundation and a standard for genuine spiritual work like meditation, in such a way that one may be able to penetrate behind the forms and outward appearances and see "*das Ding an sich.*"

The oldest catalogue which is found in the Buddhist society in China dates from A.D. 520. In this, 2,213 works are mentioned. Of these, only 267 are extant or can be identified with writings now known. The next catalogue was prepared about A.D. 730 and is called "K'ai-yüan mu-lu" (開 元 目 錄). It is therefore only relatively correct to say that the Chinese Tripitaka was completed at such and such a time. The fact is that it was at all times kept up to date with the stage of development of any given period.

The year A.D. 972 is generally reckoned as the year in which China got her whole collection; for in that year it was printed for the first time. In the more than twelve collections, which have since been published (at first only copied by hand, but printed with wooden blocks since A.D. 972), many differences are to be found. Earlier fragments have been cut away or completed, some doubtful passages have been removed, the order has been changed so that "Sutra Pitaka" (the doctrinal writings) come first and occupy most

TRUTH AND TRADITION IN BUDDHISM

space—three quarters in fact, of the whole collection—a characteristic feature of Mahayana thinking.

The present canonical collection got its definite form under Hung Wu, the founder of the Ming dynasty, about A.D. 1375, the next edition, under Yung Lo, is only slightly different in the number of the Chinese writings, which belong to the fourth section. These important collections bear the names of "The Southern Canon" (printed in Nanking) and "The Northern Canon" (printed in Peking).

The last revision under Yung Chêng (雍正) and Ch'ien Lung (乾隆) have added fifty-four Chinese works. The total number of writings in the Chinese Canon has now been fixed at 1662.

A more modern edition was published in 1913 (the Hardoon edition). In Japan some very beautiful and handy editions have also been published. We may mention the Tokyo and Kyoto editions. Here the colossal collection of writings, printed on strong brown paper in small but clear type, has been reduced to a manageable size so that it can find a place in a private book collection.

In this connection we must mention the great service which the learned Buddhist priest, Bunyiu Nanjio, from Hongwanzi in Japan, has rendered to the world by producing, under the auspices of Oxford University, a new modern catalogue of the different sections. This has been rendered more valuable by being supplied with an index of Chinese titles by Dr. E. D. Ross. Some critical remarks have been added to the collection. Thus we read of No. 1657, a sutra

BUDDHIST LITERATURE IN CHINA

written by the empress Shan-hsiao of the Ming dynasty: "This sutra is doubtful and probably spurious." And when the expressions are too much opposed to the principles of Buddha, there is added, as for example of No. 1300: "This is not the teaching of Buddha."

The first time Tripitaka was printed in China in 972 under Tai-shü, one hundred and thirty thousand wooden blocks were used. With this in mind it is not strange that one can still find in old monasteries enormous rooms stacked with wooden blocks. These have now only a historic interest, for, as in the Hardoon edition, modern printing is now used. A Chinese physician in Shanghai, Dr. Ting Fu-pao, has in late years printed handy modern editions of some of the most important scriptures. He has also issued a quantity of Buddhist tracts.

In the monasteries, the scriptures are kept in enormous bookcases fitted with solid carved copper-studded doors. There are, as a rule, ten such cases in the library hall (Ts'ang-ching-lou, 藏經樓, or Ts'ang-shu-lou, 藏書樓). The library is usually on the second floor in order to prevent moisture and mildew from affecting the books. It is generally a very dignified room with special altars and statues usually of Vairocana, Kuan-yin, Amitabha or Sakyamuni Buddha. Solemn adorations take place there if the room is in a special degree holy. The books, carefully catalogued, lie in the cases and only the responsible functionaries may take them out. On certain days of the month, other monks and novices are allowed to "dust" and "inspect" a part of this rich literary

[213]

TRUTH AND TRADITION IN BUDDHISM

treasury (fan ching, 翻 經). This all takes place with great veneration and precision.

The monks in their own rooms also treat the scriptures with a touching veneration. They are often put away carefully wrapped in a piece of red-embroidered cloth under the image of Amitabha. This is specially the case with the scripture which is used in the daily devotional exercises. The other scriptures which happen to be in the monk's cell lie in a little bookcase.

In A.D. 544 a pious Chinese layman among the Buddhists, named Fu-hi, happened on the idea, that if one could construct a little house for the scriptures, a house which would swing round on its axis in such a way that the collection of scriptures was set in motion, it would be a meritorious act. This ought, he thought, to be equivalent to reading it all through and considerably easier. He had such a small octagonal swinging house constructed and fitted up with shelves. Its chief merit was that a single person could set it all in motion with one lever. Formerly these swinging houses were much in use in China, but now they are hardly to be seen. They are, on the other hand, extremely common in Japan.

In these days one finds such technical helps for study as **dictionaries** and encyclopædias. The recently published encyclopædia, "Fu-hsüeh Tz'u-tien" (佛 學 辭 典), ought here to be mentioned. It is quite an extensive work, and is probably based largely on the big Japanese edition. It has been published and printed by Dr. Ting in Shanghai.

[214]

BUDDHIST LITERATURE IN CHINA

Finally we shall give a little survey of the most commonly used scriptures in the Buddhist society in China at present, beginning with the large and famous "Hua-yen Ching" (華嚴經) (Sanskrit: Buddhavatamska-mahavaipuliya Sutra). This appears in eighty-one large sections and in three great divisions. It is an enormous work to read through, but is none the less interesting, for it gives in a detailed way the whole development of thought from primitive Buddhism up to the complete program of Mahayana, opening up as it were a previously closed world full of religious mysticism.[1]

In the first division (shang, 上) the development of Sakyamuni Buddha and the calling of his disciples are described. The second division (chung, 中) gives an analysis of human nature. The third (hsia, 下) points to the true road of redemption, the doctrine of Emptiness.

The importance of this book may be understood from the fact that an abbreviation of it has been made in China. This is, in a way, an "Introduction to Hua-yen Ching" or "The Theology of the Hua-yen Ching," the Chinese name being "Hua-yen Hsüan-t'an" (華嚴玄談).

Another writing which is greatly esteemed in China is the "Leng-yen Ching" (楞嚴經), the so-called "Suraangama Sutra," dealing with the great gathering on Ling Shan, the mountain of the spirits, where Ananda comes forth and asks many questions of

[1] Cf. the often-used expression "Hua-ts'ang miao-mên" (華藏妙門) "The door into the secrets of the Hua-yen Scriptures."

[215]

TRUTH AND TRADITION IN BUDDHISM

Buddha; and where the "World-Honoured One" gives many profound explanations about the different religions in the universe.

Parts of this sutra are used every day during the morning mass in the temples. Often long sections are quoted in a phonetic transcription of the Sanskrit texts. These parts are said to be of the greatest importance in order to cleanse the heart for the new day. They work almost like a magic formula. Here the Mahayana ideas are fully expressed.

Next in importance is the "Lü-tsung's Law-Book," where the commandments and rules already mentioned are to be found with explanations and summaries.

The law-book of Mahayana ("Fan-wang Ching," 梵網經), Brahma's net, and also "The Scripture of the Patriarchs," or "The Book of the Six Patriarchs" (Chinese: "Liu-tsu-t'an Ching," 六祖壇經), have been included among Mahayana's commonly used literature.

We have already dealt with the books which have the greatest importance for Mahayana in general and the "Pure Land" School in particular, namely "The Greater and the Smaller Sukhavati Vyuha" and the "Amita Yurdhyana Sutra." The Chinese name for "The Great Sukhavati Vyuha" is "Wu-liang-shou Ching" (無量壽經), "The Great Scripture of the Endless Life," and for the small "Fu-shuo O-mi-t'o Ching" (佛說阿彌佛經), "The Sayings of Buddha About Amitabha." Both are used very commonly in private worship and meditation as well as in the great masses for the dead. The latter work especially, which is really only an **extract** from the former, is used very much in the temples during the evening mass.

Here we read:

"In the great gathering in the She-wei kingdom (舍衞國) in the garden called Ch'i-shu-chi-ku-tu Yüan (祇樹給孤獨園), Buddha reveals the gospel of the saving mercy of Amitabha. Heaven and earth, hades, and all the depths resound with joy when they hear about the solemn vows, which will make it possible for the whole creation to be released from sin, sorrow, punishment, and suffering, and to be born into the "Western Paradise," Sukhavati (Chinese: Hsi-fang Chi-lo Shih Chieh, 西方極樂世界)."

In very flowery language the "Western Paradise" is described with imagery which strongly reminds one of the Apocalypse, chapters twenty-one and twenty-two. It is, of course, an Oriental heaven filled with shining jewels and treasures, dotted with beautiful groves, and fragrant trees where the birds sing their songs. Every place is adorned with lotus flowers. All sin, strife, and pain have disappeared and while the most wonderful music fills the ears, one can rest in peace in the shadow of the trees by the quietly flowing rivers. In this book we also get the common explanation of Amitabha's origin: before becoming a Buddha he was a bodhisattva named "Dharmakara." Through his vow to save all living creatures he gained so much merit that he became the "Buddha of unlimited life and light." It is as such that he continues his great work of salvation by drawing the whole creation to himself in the "Western Paradise," where he now lives and reigns.

TRUTH AND TRADITION IN BUDDHISM

The next important scripture on which the "Pure Land" School bases its doctrine is the famous "Amita Yurdhyana Sutra," which in Chinese has the name of "Kuan-wu-liang-shou Ching" (觀無量壽佛經): "Reflections on the Boundless (Eternal) Life." This is, in general, much like the two former books, except that the references to the bodhisattvas, especially Kuan-yin and Ta-shih-chih are a more prominent feature.

All these writings can now be had in English in "The Sacred Books of the East" series, Volume XLIX. We must add about the last-named "Kuan-wu-liang-shou Ching," that it gives one a unique opportunity penetrating into the fundamental mysticism of the "Pure Land" School; but trained minds and appreciative hearts are needed in order fully to grasp the fine things in it. Time and again one has met in the monasteries religiously minded Confucianists who were absorbed in this scripture and who have spoken about it with much enthusiasm.

The other great work, "Fa-hua Ching" (法華經), or "Miao-fa Lien-hua Ching" (妙法蓮華經): "The Lotus Scripture of the Mysterious Law" (Sanskrit: Saddharma Pundarika Sutra"), has been spoken of before. A number of Mahayana sects regard it as the most important scripture and is in many respects unique. No other Buddhist writing contains so many great thoughts, and it is therefore quite natural that it has moved and still moves countless hearts in the East to a holy affection. It was translated by Dharmaraksha into Chinese for the first time about A.D. 310.

BUDDHIST LITERATURE IN CHINA

Later it was translated by Kumarajiva and still later, in A.D. 610, by other "fathers." It is now to be had bound as a book in foreign style and is used as a pocket Bible by great numbers of people. It is about as big as the four Gospels and the Acts, and contains twenty-eight chapters.

It should be noted that some of the translations now to be found in Japan, Korea, and China, differ very much from the Sanskrit form, translated into English by Kern. A thorough investigation, conducted along historical lines, would very probably throw some light upon the vexed question of the origin of the spiritualization of the original text.

The sixteenth chapter concerning Ju-lai's nature and work is one of special beauty and depth:

> I am a secret,
> I possess miraculous power,
> As I was truly born of God,
> Like him my age is infinite —
> Millions upon millions of years.
> Even in ordinary affairs
> I do the Incomprehensible,
> According to necessity
> In all places, saying,
> My name is various,
> My age is various.
> Rejoicing in the elements of Faith,
> Where good deeds are but few
> And misdeeds many—
> Whether speaking of Myself
> Or of others,
> Whether directing Myself

TRUTH AND TRADITION IN BUDDHISM

Or others,
Whether My own affairs
Or those of others—
Whate'er I say
Is true.
Wherefore?
Because I truly see
The spiritual forms of the three Realms.
Without birth or death,
Whether retiring or coming forth,
I am not of these worlds.
And as to My death and translation,
'Tis neither real nor unreal,
Not like, yet not diverse,
Unlike the three Realms
But visible in all three Realms.
With these signs
You see clearly who I am,
Without mistake!
The Divine works I do
Are not passing illusions.
I am the Truth,
Who am the Same,
Yesterday, To-day—For ever
Without birth, or death.
The Illumined appear on the earth
But are not quickly recognized.
Since the Beginning when I dwelt with God,
Long ages past,
My life unmeasured is—
Through all Kalpas of Time.
I never perish,
The Way of Saints I follow,
Which Life secures for evermore.
My life is not ended
But multiplied.

ATTENDANT BODHISATTVA

BUDDHIST LITERATURE IN CHINA

I have Medicine
To cure all sicknesses
As God, dwelling upon earth."[1]

In truth a wonderful parallel to the eternal Logos, "Logos spermaticos," described by many names, Life, Light, Truth, Way, in our glorious Gospel of St. John! It may easily be understood why some scholars have tried to find a connection between this and the spiritual life and environment where the Gospel of St. John originated. These attempts have not so far been successful, but the parallel stands there in its bright beauty, showing that God in truth has not left the people of the Orient without witnesses, but in a wonderful manner has prepared the way for the kingdom of His Son.

We may further call attention to Chapter XI describing "The Places Where God Dwells," the various kinds of "ferry-boats" in which he takes all living beings across to the happy land, and the hymn of praise ("Holy, holy, holy") which sounds forth from these places. Here Sakyamuni Buddha is represented as the one who "opens the seven seals," whereupon an enormous chorus of voices is heard. (See note.)

The "Yao-shih Ching" (藥師經), "The Scripture of the Great Physician" (Yao-shih Fu; Japanese: Ja-ku-shi) has been mentioned before. It is quite short and is largely composed of the twelve well-known promises of salvation and redemption for all these who

---

[1] Quoted from Dr. Timothy Richard: "The New Testament of Higher Buddhism," T. and T. Clark, 1910, Edinburgh, p. 207 pass. "The Lotus Scripture" has been translated into French by Burnout and into English by Kern and Dr. Richard.

[221]

sigh in the pains of purgatory and carry the heavy cross of life. It is significant that one daily hears this refrain in the temples: "Nan-mo hsiao-tsai, yen shou, Yao-shih Fu" (藥師佛): "Hail to the great Buddha-physician, who annihilates calamities and lengthens life."

Another sutra which is extremely popular and widely used in eastern Asia is "The Diamond Scripture" ("Chin-kang Ching" (金剛經) (Sanskrit: Vagrakkhedika Pragnaparamita). We here meet Sakyamuni Buddha giving instruction while the disciple Sulehuti asks questions and propounds problems to the master. Many of the profoundest thoughts of original Buddhism have found their way into this book. It is here one finds the famous sentence: "Wu wo-hsiang, wu jên-hsiang, wu chung-shêng-hsiang, wu shou-chê-hsiang" (無我相無人相無衆生相無壽者相), "No more I-image, no more man-image, no more race-image, no more unlimited life-image."

On the basis of such profound expressions as these it is quite natural that Sulehuti voices to the master the fear that men in future ages may not be able to understand these high things. To this Buddha, according to the Chinese text, answers that this will not be the case: "For five hundred years after my death there will appear one who will fulfil all right-eousness, one who has not only the good root in him of one, two, three, five, ten, or a thousand Buddhas, but who has that of ten thousand [that means in Chinese: has all perfect goodness in himself]. Therefore when he comes, hear him!"

BUDDHIST LITERATURE IN CHINA

According to the statements of the well-known Sanskrit scholar, Professor Steen Konow, of Norway, there is here a divergence from the Sanskrit text, as the latter refers not to one but to many, who after five hundred years will arise and *completely understand* and practice Buddha's directions for salvation.

This book is much used in the masses, and by pious lay devotees, for the dead. This is very remarkable because this Hinayana-coloured writing, which is of fairly recent date, contains no mention at all of Amitabha. Some have thought that its popularity is due to the obscure prophecy quoted above concerning the new era which would be inaugurated five hundred years after the death of Buddha, the great era of the rise of Mahayana when the "King of the Western Paradise," Amitabha, the "King from the West," should open the way for all who were oppressed. The additional scriptures which are connected with the masses for the dead, "Yü-lan-p'ên Ching" (盂蘭盆經), the "Ullambana Sutra," the book of Ti-ts'ang: "Ti-ts'ang Pên-yüan Ching" (地藏本願經) and "The Book About the Feeding of Hungry Spirits": "Yü-chia yen-k'ou" (瑜伽餒口) have been previously treated.

A special group of Buddhist literature is formed by the books of penitence, "Ch'an-hui-wên" (懺悔文 Sanskrit: "Upavasatha"). The most popular is the so-called: "Ta-pei-ch'an" (大悲懺), "The Penitential Mass of the Great Compassion." Here Kuan-yin plays the main part as mediator of Amitabha's mercy. In the masses for the dead which are subscribed for in the temples, this book is much used. For instance, in the great Liu-yün Monastery (留雲寺) in Shanghai several bands of monks are incessantly occupied in reading this penitential hymn to the pilgrims who gather there in great multitudes.

From the books of penitence we quote the following extracts:

"I am without any glory, I am miserable and have nothing in the world whereby I can fully express my desire for adoration. I have wicked cravings and evil plans, and harbour vain thoughts. May my protectors think of me [. . . here comes the name] in mercy. I surrender myself to you, my conquerors; as a son, I adore you; make me your slave."

Or:

"All the evil I have committed in the past time, all the endless sin of wicked desires (t'an, 貪), evil plans (ch'ên 瞋), and vain thoughts (ch'ih, 癡)—all that I have *done, spoken,* or *thought* wrongly I will to-day abstain from.

"All the sin which has arisen in my heart is now mourned by the same heart. When the heart mourns the sin, it is thereby exterminated. The sin being exterminated, is forgotten and the whole has become nothing.

"Behold this is truly repentance and conversion."

Among the more cultured and educated Buddhists the "Wisdom" books play a great part. Here the famous "Ta-pan-jo Ching" (大般若經), "Mahapragnaparamita Sutra," where the highest wisdom (pan-jo, prajna) is sung and described, comes in the front rank. It is called a "roaring lion" (cf. Wên-shu who always

[224]

rides a lion) and this wisdom is gained by quiet, reverent meditation (san mei, 三昧).

A more abridged form of this wisdom teaching is to be had in the well-known book "Hsüan Fu P'u" (選佛譜), "The Guide to Buddhahood," translated by Dr. Timothy Richard. Here the stages and gradations of thought are clearly set forth,—the ten worlds (shih-ti, 十地) through which a bodhisattva has to pass before he attains perfection.

Compare here the four sworn pledges of the Mahayana novices:

"I swear to lead all beings without exception onward to salvation."
"I swear to end all pain and all suffering."
"I swear that I will study the countless teachers."
"I swear that I will perfect myself till I reach the highest glory of the Buddha."

Another wisdom book is the so-called "Nirvana Scripture" ("Nieh-p'an Ching," 涅槃經), which expounds mystically the conditions in Nirvana and the road by which it is attained.

Finally we may mention "Wei-mo Ching" (維摩經), which gives the spiritual reflections of a pious monk on the deep teachings of Buddha.

If one desires to see something of the sublime philosophy which during the seventh and eighth centuries was introduced into China, one ought to read "Wei-shih Lun" (唯識論), "Vidyama-trasiddhi." Here the deepest philosophy and the most phantastic magic formulæ (tantras) have been closely interwoven.

TRUTH AND TRADITION IN BUDDHISM

There has in recent years been established a special "school" among the scholars in China, for the cultivation of this branch of Buddhist philosophy. The leader is the famous Ou-yang Ching-wu (歐陽竟無), of Nanking. This last work brings us to the category of the dissertations. Most important of these for Mahayana is the famous "Ch'i Hsin Lun" (起信論), translated into English by Dr. Richard with the title "The Awakening of Faith." As has already been mentioned, Asvaghosha has long been supposed to be the author of this remarkable book. There are some, however, who believe it was written by one of his disciples. Liang Chi-chao thinks it is a genuine Chinese work. Dr. Beal calls the book a "pseudo-Christian work." This opinion is difficult to establish, even though a great many details seem to indicate Christian influence. The book is not large, about the size of the Gospel of Mark, and it is full of fine and exalted thoughts. The first part is strongly philosophic, the latter part concentrates on that which is the essence of all deep religious life, the wonderful faculty of faith. It is like a hymn of praise to faith and the inner life. Not in an external intellectual way comes the great transition which leads up to a higher kind of life, but through the surrender of the heart in faith.

It is no wonder that this book has been a source of the greatest blessing to many of the best educated people in the East. For the growth of Mahayana the book was epoch-making. As far as we can tell it was translated by Paramartha about A.D. 540.

BUDDHIST LITERATURE IN CHINA

As an example of various writings collected in one volume, let us refer the reader to the Buddhist books of ritual which are used in the monasteries. Especially inclusive and characteristic is the "Ch'an-mên Jih-sung" (禪門日誦), "The Daily Mass Ritual of the Meditation School."

We have here mentioned only the most important works. There is besides an enormous mass of dissertations, histories of local monasteries, and hymns of adoration which we cannot here even enumerate. What we have seen, however, may give us an impression of the enormous literary treasure with which Buddhism in the Far East is endowed.

CHAPTER VIII

MONASTIC LIFE

We shall in this chapter try to draw a picture of the throbbing life of the Buddhist society in China, as it is lived both inside the temple walls, and also outside them, in the lay circles that definitely gather round this religion.

It is in a peculiar sense the monks and nuns who form the basis of the society. These constitute a brotherhood, as in the case of the religious orders in mediæval Europe which, like our monks and nuns of mediæval times, is isolated from the rest of the people. Their celibacy, their completely vegetarian diet, the dress of the monks, and their residence, the monastery, all serve to make the distinction clear and strong. It is therefore significant that the technical term for becoming a monk or a nun in China is "ch'u-chia" (出家), i. e., to leave the home; and the popular term for such people is "ch'u-chia-jên" (出家人), i. e., people who have left the home, in contrast to the ordinary members of the secular society, who are called "tsai-chia-jên" (在家人), i. e., those who live at home.

On the calling cards of the monks there is no family name given, only a literary name, "ming tzŭ" (名字), chosen from the Buddhist world of ideas, and in addition a name for daily use (hao, 號), derived in the same way. Sometimes they place instead of the family name the character "sêng" (僧), corresponding

MONASTIC LIFE

to the Sanskrit word "Sangha," which means the "Society." Or they take the first character of the name for the historic Buddha, calling themselves "shih" (釋) after Shih-chia-mou-ni (釋迦牟尼), Sakyamuni. Theoretically and formally the break is complete, and many times actually so, especially if the monk enters the monastery when he is quite young. Then he does not know his family name. But for those who have entered in later years and who desire to maintain a certain connection with their homes (su-chia, 俗家) there is, as a rule, some opportunity to do so.

It is these monks who, down through the ages, have maintained the Buddhist society and, by means of scriptures, temples, and monasteries, have been the mediators of that strong, spiritual influence, which has flowed from Buddhism into Chinese society.

Where have these monks and nuns come from? What has driven them to enter the Buddhist society?

To these questions different answers must be given. It is, in the first place, a well-known fact that some parents who are in straitened circumstances and who think that they can do without a child, give little boys as early as possible to the monasteries. Or perhaps the parents die and the relatives give the boy to a Buddhist monk who wishes to adopt a novice. For it is frequently the case that the older monks take novices who become like sons to them. The suppressed, but none the less deep, yearning for home and affection, and for some person who will cherish one's memory, and offer incense and prayers at one's urn, makes it a common practice to secure at least one novice for one's self.

Often a very affectionate relationship is established between master and novice (shih-fu, 師傅, and t'u-ti, 徒弟). The monk looks after the education of the youth. If he is a good and enlightened monk he sees that the pupil is given good schooling, preliminary to the special instruction which leads on to ordination. In return, the young novice will constantly try to take care of and protect the master, when old age and sickness come. I have known cases where the novice was for years tied to the bedside of the sick master till the latter died, and during this time nursed him faithfully and patiently. When the novice grows older he follows in the footsteps of the master. He gets a novice for himself and the "family" continues in that way. When this is the case, there naturally follows the keeping of family registers and working out tables of the "fathers." This is done to a considerable extent in Chinese monasteries. This is the case not only in China, however, but also in Korea and Japan. Even to-day one may see the different "chia" (家), families, that have been formed in this way, after certain periods of time sending their representatives far away to do reverence to old deceased masters. Thus representatives from "monk families" in Japan are often sent to China to worship at the place where the old head of that family lived.

Besides this first line (adoption) there are two other lines which are of considerable importance in the structure of the Buddhist society. *These are the line of ordination* and *the line of succession to the office of abbot.*

Even those who enter the Buddhist society at a mature age must have a master, who in some respects becomes their adopted father, for it is required that there shall always be one monk to stand sponsor for each individual who enters the society. He both introduces and guides the newcomer. On the other hand, it is self-evident that the more independent, cultured, and mature the novice is, the more the relationship to a master becomes a matter of form.

One finds the most widely different motives leading young men to enter the Buddhist brotherhood. A great many have had their first hard fight in life's battle, and sorrow and disappointment have entered so deeply into the young hearts, that life in the monastery with its calm, deep peace, away from the hard, cruel world, seems the only salvation. In periods of war and famine, and in troublous times, therefore, the influx is always the greatest. This has been especially true in recent years. Some have become sick of life on account of the bloodshed they have seen. Perhaps they themselves have taken part in the most awful orgies of war. Then disgust with themselves and weariness of life arise, and drive them into the great calm of the monastic life. A not inconsiderable percentage of military men, both officers and privates, end their lives in monasteries.

Many come from very doubtful motives. Not seldom criminals and others, who have made themselves impossible in society, come to the monasteries to hide, and, by one ruse or another, worm their way in. Of course, many of these remain doubtful characters who often earn for the monasteries a bad reputation and involve them in all sorts of complications. At times, such temples and monasteries as prove to be out and out robbers' dens are closed by the authorities. But we must also, in truth, say that some of these bad characters are in an amazing way changed by the monastic life. They repent and become new men, who with intense fervour concentrate on meditation and worship. I have several times had a chance to verify this.

There come to the monasteries, also, others with a genuine desire to find religious light, comfort, and peace. If they enter one of the well-disciplined brotherhoods and the sincerely religious circles, such find a place for themselves and also get some help. Very often, however, they are disappointed, for they do not need to live inside the walls very long before they find that here, too, the mercenary spirit is powerful, that intrigues thrive, and that dissension very often appears within the most holy groups. Therefore not a few leave the monasteries and return home bitter and disappointed.

Quite a number of men enter the monasteries on account of sickness, and certainly in many, many cases they are healed, the effect on the soul influencing the body for good.

Finally, there are some old and lonely men and women who enter mainly in order to find a home where they can spend their declining years in peace.

MONASTIC LIFE

and quiet, while at the same time making preparations for the life which awaits them beyond the grave.

It will be evident that the great mass of the monks come from the common people. If they have energy, desire for study, and religious zeal they can rise high both in personal piety, culture, and education. This comes not so much through compulsory instruction, for this is rather meagre, but rather through private study. The libraries are at their disposal and they have plenty of time if they will only use it. Many, however, do not avail themselves of time or opportunity and remain almost illiterate. A great many prefer to take part in the bands hired to perform masses and thereby make some money. Many others desert the monasteries, where they find the discipline too severe, preferring to rove around in their monks' habits at places where the pilgrims gather, and where, by begging, magic, and deceitful practices, they can levy a toll from the credulous multitude.

These bad elements, who are met with to a large extent at the great places of pilgrimage and outside the large monasteries, are the dregs of the Buddhist society, being equally despised by the honest monk and the ordinary Chinese citizen. They have organized themselves into secret societies and bring endless disgrace on the Buddhist society. They are known as "Yeh-ho-shang" (野和尙), or "wild monks," or even by worse names.

There remains in connection with the monasteries, however, a considerable body of the élite, refined and learned monks, who have been recruited from the

TRUTH AND TRADITION IN BUDDHISM

decent and upper classes of society. Many of the leaders and famous law-scholars (Fa-shih, 法師) come from these circles. They in turn attract highly educated lay Buddhists who at intervals come to live in the temples to study the holy scriptures and meditate on the deeper meaning of life.

The nuns are often recruited from poor and broken-up homes, or may have run away from brothels and the nunneries become asylums for them. Now and then one has met nuns from nice homes, women who rank high both in a moral and a religious sense.

It may be well to describe in some detail the course of *instruction* leading to *ordination*.

The novices often get their first instruction from their adopted masters in one of the temples or smaller monasteries. They become familiar with the routine of daily worship and assist the master. In the village temples and country places around, the young men may continue for years in this way before any proper instruction and preparation are given. Indeed, it sometimes happens that the novice continues wearing his monk's habits till he is an old man, without ever having been ordained. This is specially the case in northern China, where the Buddhist society is in a rather disorganized condition.

Where there is order and discipline, some one sees to it that the young novices are sent to a larger monastery with the right of ordination, and the older and more famous the monastery is, the more honour is it to be ordained there. Not only the fame of the

GENERAL VIEW OF YUN-YEN MONASTERY, SOOCHOW, KIANGSU

MONASTIC LIFE

monastery, is important. It must also have an abbot who is distinguished by piety, learning, and influence. From ancient times there have been such famous places, some even having a tradition that points back to the introduction of Buddhism in China, which brings a corresponding glory. The abbot who ordains becomes with his immediate predecessor (master No. 2 in the line of ordination) a "Father in God."

The ordination platform (chieh-t'ai, 戒台) plays a great part. It is of great importance to the master who sends his novice away for ordination to find a good "platform of ordination." Some hold that the most famous "platforms" in China are those connected with the old "Ku-lin" (古林) and "Pao-hua Shan" (寶華山) monasteries in Nanking. The legend says that from this place the "twelve disciples" went out. Some went northward and established in the neighbourhood of Peking the "Ordination Temple of the Western Hills" ("Hsi Shan Chieh-t'ai Ssŭ," 西山戒台寺). Others went south and established a similar platform in Hangchow. This latter is to be found in the "Chao-ch'ing Monastery" (昭慶寺). A third group went to the famous mountain "Pao-hua Shan" (the "Precious Flower Mountain") and gave half a platform to this place. This "half platform" must be particularly precious, for it is here that most monks from central China are actually ordained. Here, where the severest instruction and discipline rule, where the blows fall hard and often on the shoulders and closely shaven heads of the novices, enormous crowds gather for ordination, not only once a year, but throughout spring and autumn. Even the old "Ku-lin" in Nanking, which has been called "Tsu-t'ing Chieh T'ai" (祖庭戒台) (the "Platform of the Patriarch's Hill"), cannot compare with the "Precious Flower Mountain" in popularity. The ambitious old monk now in charge in the Nanking monastery is enlarging the accommodation there enormously, and it seems as if he were trying to outdistance the mountain with its "platform."

If the monastery which ordains is rich, i. e., owns much land, it is easy to provide for the expenses of ordination. But often the masters who send novices away for ordination have to spend a considerable sum of money. It is never so large, however, as to cover the expenses for board and the necessary ordination equipment of the candidates. Much has to be supplied from the funds of the monastery.

As we have previously seen, the supposition is that the young get their first training in small temples and monasteries—the nuns in small colonies of women, known by the name "ni-ku miao" (nunneries). Others, who happen to have a master connected in some capacity with a big monastery, attend the regular monastic schools. In this way, most novices have had a certain amount of training and teaching before they come to the place of ordination. But it happens at times that people come directly from the "life of the world" to a course of instruction before ordination. When one realizes that this, as a rule, does not last more than sixty to ninety days, sometimes even less, it is not strange that one meets many ignorant monks in China.

MONASTIC LIFE

The main part of the course is the training in the "Law." First of all the ten plus two hundred and fifty commandments of Hinayana are studied. After these the novices are introduced to the "Net of Brahma" ("Fan-wang Ching," 梵網經), the fifty-eight commandments, and get their first practice in those parts of the ritual which are used in the daily mass. A syllabus of it is given in the "Ch'an-mên Jih-sung" (禪門日誦), or the "Lü-mên Ch'ih-sung" (律門持誦), the mass books of the Meditation School and the Legalistic School, respectively. At this stage there is little question as to which "school" one wants to join. It is, practically speaking, these two schools or sects that conduct ordinations.

The course itself is severe, so severe that many cannot endure it and run away. Everything goes like clock-work. The novices get up in the morning between three and four o'clock for the first worship. At this time the instructor (Wei-na, 維那), who is always a very severe man, is often heard going from bed to bed and striking the sleepers. They partially rouse themselves and pull the quilt over their faces in order not to be hit. After worship, the morning toilet is made, and then the novices gather again in the large dark dormitories to wait for breakfast. Then the well-known sound of the beating of the wooden block announces the time for eating. The novices assemble in long rows and, chanting softly with the hands folded, they walk sedately down toward the refectory, where they sit down in silence by the long tables.

TRUTH AND TRADITION IN BUDDHISM

At a given sign they sing the "table song," a beautiful hymn, wherein the merciful Buddhas are praised and asked to satisfy all the hungry ones in the world. The abbot then comes in and takes his seat on a raised platform, where his food is served. First comes a chant, during which one of the youngest present, with the chopsticks laid together, carries some rice grains out into the open court. These are placed on a stone pillar in honour and praise of "Heaven" (T'ien, 天) that feeds and nourishes all. Here evidently an old Chinese rite has been embodied in the Buddhist ritual, for it has been deeply burned into the heart of every Chinese that it is "Heaven" that grants us food (k'ao-t'ien ch'ih-fan, 靠天吃飯). When the young novice has returned, the meal is begun. Deep silence prevails. Only the attending brothers walk round with big vessels filled with rice and vegetables fried in vegetable oil. At times bean-cakes (soya-beans) are added.

The novices leave the table in a procession, again singing, and return to the dormitories. Here and in the adjoining rooms the instruction is begun. Sentence after sentence is explained and taught, at some times to groups, at others to the whole body. There is much scolding and beating. The bright ones have an easy time, but the dull are miserable. It is a definite rule, however, at some places (for instance, at the famous "Precious Flower Mountain," Pao-hua Shan) that everybody has to be disciplined, for only in this way is it possible to attain to that calm of heart, discipline, and submission which are so important for Buddhist monks.

MONASTIC LIFE

I have often seen the blows fall like a shower on diligent and good novices, but they stood immovable, for they knew that this was a part of the course, and they said, as generations before them have said: "He who strikes me loves me."

At times, the abbot comes down to examine. He also may be severe, but I have never seen an abbot so unreasonably severe as many of the young and indifferent, or over-zealous instructors. At intervals the abbot says some words of encouragement or of sweet exhortation. I have heard them speak with real enthusiasm of the rest and peace of spirit, the inner enlightenment and joy, to which the novices will attain, if they will now in earnestness and sincerity take to heart the instruction they are getting. I have heard them say as the last word before the much-longed-for rest of the evening: "Now go to bed nicely and keep Buddha in your heart, so that you will not be disturbed by evil dreams and vain thoughts."

In this way, the time of instruction passes, broken only by examinations and ordination rehearsals. The novices march up to the sanctuary, each one is assigned a definite place; everything is practised minutely, so that everything may run smoothly and without a hitch on the great days of ordination which are in store. The two ablest ones are chosen to lead the procession. They are called "sha-mi-t'ou" (沙彌頭), and it is a great honour to be one of these.

The ordination itself lasts for two or three weeks. It is widely announced by posters that such and such a monastery has "chieh-ch'i" (戒期), a time of ordination, at a certain date. It is the occasion of much bustle and many preparations. Sometimes monks from other monasteries have been present all the time as assistants and instructors, but for the ordination itself two of the most venerable "elders" among the neighbouring monks are invited to assist, one as a confessor (ch'ieh-mo, 羯 麼), and one as an examiner (chiao-shou, 教 授); and, in addition, seven others act as witnesses (tsun-chêng, 尊 證). The confessor is, as a rule, an old and venerable man.

In former days, the rule that the novices must be twenty years old before they could be ordained was strictly adhered to. Now boys of fifteen, sixteen, or seventeen are frequently ordained. In the same way, the rule that a considerable time should pass between the three degrees of ordination has been set aside. This is done for practical reasons, as the long and inconvenient journeys would otherwise make things too difficult.

The first act makes the young man a novice in the true sense of the word. The two "sha-mi-t'ou" open the ceremonies by going up to the abbot and asking permission to take the vows and be ordained (ch'iu-chieh, 求 戒). This takes place in the reception room of the abbot, where temporary seats have been arranged for him (in the middle) and the two assisting elders, the confessor, and the examiner on each side. At a table sit the seven witnesses.

The novices promise to keep the five great commandments:

MONASTIC LIFE

1. Not to kill any living being.
2. Not to steal.
3. Not to commit adultery.
4. Not to lie.
5. Not to take intoxicating liquors.

One often sees laymen and laywomen take part in the first act and be consecrated. These are they who, though not wishing to be monks or nuns, yet desire to consecrate their lives once and for all to Buddhist practices and studies. They receive a hood and a certain kind of coat which they later wear on solemn occasions. They are called "shou-wu-chieh-ti" (受五戒的), i. e., such as keep the five commandments. They form vegetarian groups and are found to a considerable extent throughout China. They are in many cases looked up to and act as "assistant priests" among the people in general. Some of them are very pious. Others use their "consecration" as a means to make money and gain influence.

This act is followed by the first real step in the ordination (or consecration), the one that takes the novice into the first degree of holiness, that of sha-mi (沙彌), or sha-mên (沙門) (Sanskrit: Sramanera). The laity step aside, and the novices, nuns, and monks, are conducted by their several elder "sisters" or "brothers" into the big open temple court in the front of the main temple in order to "shou sha-mi-chieh" (受沙彌戒) (become a deva, a holy one of the lowest degree). The abbot, with the two elders and the witnesses, sits at the entrance of the temple hall. It is an extremely lengthy performance. First comes an enormously long mass-litany. Thereafter follow the different questions and the great vows.

These latter begin with the remaining five of the decalogue of Buddhism, viz.:

    6. Abstinence from perfumes and flowers.
    7. Abstinence from song and dancing.
    8. Abstinence from the use of big (comfortable) beds.
    9. Abstinence from taking meals at regular intervals.
    10. Abstinence from acquiring or possessing valuable things.

The abbot puts the questions to the whole body collectively, and the answer is given in ringing unison from the twenty, forty, one hundred, two hundred, or one thousand novices who are kneeling on the cold stone pavement under the open sky. I have seen them kneel like this for hours in mid-winter, for the whole *pratimoksha*, the two hundred and fifty monastic rules of the Hinayana, must be read and assented to.

After this follows the much-longed-for ceremony: the last little tuft of hair which is left on the otherwise clean-shaven head is shaved off by the assistants who walk around with knives performing this operation. Later, bundles with the outfit for each individual are carried in: the begging coat (chia-sha, 袈裟), which gives the right to perform altar service, the kneeling rug (chü, 具), which is to be used on solemn occasions, and the begging bowl (po, 鉢), which symbolizes the complete break with the world. Everything is touched by the abbot and his assistants and a benediction is chanted. One of the assistants then goes round the circle of those kneeling, lightly touching the new begging gown, the long folded rug, and the little brown bowl of each one, and pronounces the last blessing over them. Again a mass is said, and the great sha-mi act is finished. The whole closes with a feast.

Six to ten days later comes the second great act, the "shou pi-ch'iu-chieh (受比丘戒). This is the entrance into the first degree of Mahayana as a bhikshu, which means one who is completely holy, an arhat (lo-han, 羅漢). It can be gathered from the preparations required that this is a bigger affair than the first. Clothes have to be changed from top to toe and all must bathe. Furthermore, all must go to confession (ch'an-hui, 懺悔) and be absolved. In a quiet, secluded room a high platform is erected. The three and a half famous places of ordination have imposing granite platforms of enormous size and with fine decorations. Even in the common monasteries, care is taken to give solemnity and dignity to the act and to all arrangements which are connected with these platforms. One feels that here one is standing at the entrance to the real sanctuary of Buddhism. While crowds and spectators are allowed to witness the first act, only the three elders with the seven witnesses are present on this occasion. A quiet solemnity, which has no parallel in the usual Buddhist worship, rules. As a special privilege, I was allowed to stand in a corner for a few moments and see and hear what took place during this part of the ordination. The platform was covered with the finest carpets and beautiful draperies hung round it. The three elders, dressed in their best garments, sat like living Buddhas, with their feet drawn up under them, on cushions right in front of the entrance. Along the sides the seven witnesses sat in the same manner. The oldest legitimate head of the monastery (lao-ho-shang, 老和尚) sat with the elders in the seat of the abbot. The abbot himself was meanwhile conducting in the novices, three at a time, for the solemn ordination. While the novices knelt, the vows, according to the "Net of Brahma," were read and assented to with a loud "Yes." The blessing was given in a low impressive voice.

I have talked with several monks who have said: "That was the greatest moment of my life. I experienced something indescribable."

This act is also closed with a feast. Some days elapse before the third rite begins. During this time a less important but interesting ceremony takes place: the two sha-mi-t'ou kneel at a table covered with dishes and chopsticks and, on behalf of the whole group of ordained novices, invite the three elders and the others to a feast of gratitude. This is provided by all the novices.

Then comes the third and closing act, the great consecration to bodhisattva (p'u-sa, 菩薩). It is called "shou p'u-sa-chieh" (受菩薩戒). This takes place in the temple hall itself where the leading actors sit as previously described (the witnesses round a table, and the three elders on raised seats). The act begins at noon with a very long mass. Previously there has been a special ceremony of confession with absolution, a bath, and a change of clothing. With great solemnity the candidates for ordination pledge

MONASTIC LIFE

themselves to live and work as bodhisattvas, i. e., not as Hinayanists, not in the intermediate stage as holy ones (lo-hans), *but as those who have entered the higher Buddhism with sympathy and love for all living things.* They pledge themselves to look down upon all other stages to which previously they have been ordained as of less value, and solemnly pronounce the following bodhisattva vows:

1. To lead all beings without exception to salvation.
2. To make an end to all pain and suffering.
3. To study the works of the countless teachers.
4. To perfect themselves in such a way that they can attain the highest glory of the Buddhas.

The early part of the day is an easy time for the candidates. It is not until evening that their ordeal begins when they give proof that they are willing "to suffer" for the sake of others. They then receive "Buddha's marks on their foreheads by branding" (shao chieh-pa, 燒戒疤). There are indications that this practice of branding was known to a certain extent in India in the second century. In China, it seems that the custom first came into vogue in the eighth century (by the work of Amogha).

As it gets dark the candidates gather in small groups round the older monks, who are ready with ink and hollow reeds. A reed is dipped into the ink and put on the shaven heads of the kneeling candidates. In this way small rings are marked. An attempt is made to distribute these as evenly as possible, three in a row, across the head from forehead to crown. Three are enough, but most candidates take nine, others twelve or even up to eighteen.

When the litany is finished, long tables are set up on which lie small disks of turnip and other articles. Besides these, there are small saucers with wax and some strange red parcels. These contain small cone-like pieces of charcoal covered with combustible plant pollen. The candidates kneel down on praying rugs before the tables, with their arms on the tables and the hands clasped together. Monks stand behind them holding their heads with a firm grasp and pressing their thumbs against the temples. On the other side of the table stand older monks with lighted incense sticks. The mass begins again, while everybody sings "Na-mo pên-shih Shih-chia-mou-ni Fu (南無本師釋迦牟尼佛), "I take my refuge in thee, thou original master Sakyamuni Buddha." At the same time the cone-shaped pieces of charcoal are firmly fixed with plant-wax on the heads of the candidates just where the ink rings have been marked. While the candidates and the other monks sing a mass, the charcoal burns down into the wax and deep into the scalp. The men are marked for life. On some faces convulsions of pain may be seen; others show nothing, but often the singing reveals what is felt, being changed to a cry of pain to the "original master." To assuage the pain the pieces of turnip above mentioned are placed on the burns. When everything has burned down, one of the monks brushes the ashes off the wounds and orders the candidates to go with lifted heads into the cool walks outside. At the door stand monks with

MONASTIC LIFE

baskets of oranges, of which every one gets a share, "for oranges cool."

Thus the candidate is finally ordained, so that the next day he can come up and worship in his own right before the face of Buddha. After a final mass the great gathering scatters. Only the staff of the monastery remains, with perhaps a few newly ordained men who happen to be engaged for service there. Now they wear for the first time the big gown, outside the regular monks' dress (ta-i, 大衣).

Happy and free, with his big, beautifully decorated certificate of ordination and with the equally beautiful book of recollections from the mother monastery, containing names of the great new master, the abbot and his nearest predecessors as well as those of the confessor, examiner, witnesses, and all the "schoolmates," the newly ordained monk can now begin his career. He can either go "home" to his first master or launch out on a pilgrimage, or go to the great common home, assured of being well received wherever he comes. With his begging gown and kneeling rug carefully folded up, and with the begging bowl and the certificate of ordination in good order, he will be able to go through the whole of China, and even visit some of the neighbouring countries where Buddhism prevails. Such a wandering monk can put up for at least three days at a time in the different temples and monasteries that he comes across. This is called "kua-tan" (掛單), "to be registered," and is practised to a large extent in China.

TRUTH AND TRADITION IN BUDDHISM

During his pilgrimage he may be engaged for shorter or longer periods in different positions in the monasteries, beginning with the lower occupations, and then rising in the ranks. If he has a good education and is a good pious monk, he can be sure of getting a good position. If he is poorly educated he must be satisfied with the "rougher" work. Honesty and piety will, however, bring him at last to a good place. But if he does wrong he will soon deteriorate and sink to the lowest level.

It is considered the best sign when a newly ordained monk goes as soon as possible to one of the bigger monasteries to "chu ch'an-t'ang" (住禪堂): enter the hall of meditation, for a half year or more. Before ordination, there is no chance to begin this sacred exercise, which the Buddhists regard so highly. We shall, in another connection, treat what, in Buddhist phraseology, is called "yung-kung" (用功), "doing the real work" or meditation. Here we shall only mention the fact that few temples and monasteries will never consider engaging a young monk for the more important activities, unless he has already spent at least six months in the hall of meditation. It is taken for granted that the monks who only stop in passing take part in the daily masses.

The department for guests ("kua-tan-yüan," 掛單院, or "yün-shui-t'ang," 雲水堂) and pilgrims is located in such a way that they can keep much to themselves. In this department, where old friends meet and new acquaintances are constantly made, all news is passed on and questions of common interest

CHAI-T'AI MONASTERY, WESTERN HILLS, PEIPING

MONASTIC LIFE

reported and discussed. It is a combination of meditation hall, reception room, and common sleeping-room. Very appropriate, therefore, is the name "yün-shui-t'ang," the "hall of the clouds and the water" (which always are in motion).

In order to get a clearer idea of life in a Buddhist monastery in China we shall here give a description of the plan and arrangement of the monastery compound. It is evident that it must be difficult to generalize in this case, as in others; for the monasteries vary by reason of their site, size, equipment, etc. But everywhere some common points are found, and these will appear distinctly if we describe a common, medium-sized monastery in central China.

As a common trait, we may mention the fact that the Buddhists have a predilection for the most naturally beautiful places as sites for their temples and monasteries. We are not here thinking of the ordinary municipal temples, which in enormous numbers are scattered over the countryside and in the villages of China; these have often been squeezed in among the houses, or at best have been built on some small open space in the neighbourhood of the town. We are thinking of the places which the Buddhists themselves have chosen. They have occupied the most picturesque mountain-sides, the most attractive hill-slopes where bamboos or other trees grow thickest, the most beautiful islands in the big rivers, or the most smiling river-banks. The tendency is always to get away from the tumult and traffic into the calm and beauty of nature, so that the mind is attuned to reverence and

[249]

TRUTH AND TRADITION IN BUDDHISM

worship. With a fine understanding of these things, the old masters have chosen the sites and let the architectural features which are most typical of Buddhism blend with the landscape in such a way that it forms a panorama of incomparable beauty.

In many instances, Buddhism has, through its strong ritualistic system and its great spiritual power, taken possession of the Old Holy Mountains of China. This is the case with Nan-yü Shan (南嶽山) in Hunan and to some extent with T'ai Shan (泰山), two of the oldest places of worship in China, not to mention their own holy mountains: The P'ut'o (普陀), Chiu-hua (九華), Wu-t'ai (五台), and O-mei (峨嵋) mountains, and the many other less well-known places. If one wants to see Buddhism at its best one must go to such places. But, as we shall see, these same places are for this very reason exposed to the danger of becoming secularized and commercialized.

The first thing that strikes one, when one sees the monastery from a distance, is the beauty of the whole scene, including the monastery itself and its environment. I have often seen monks, who have struggled up the steep hill-sides or the endless stone steps, at the sight of the distant monastery, put their hands together and whisper in ecstacy: "Nan-mo O-mi-t'o Fu."

As we get nearer, the details become clearer: the strong wall, which surrounds the compound, the beautiful lines of the roofs, the arrangement of the buildings in terraces up the slightly sloping ground, etc.

We come to the main gate, above which is written in large characters the name of the monastery and the

MONASTIC LIFE

special school to which it belongs. A couple of old monks welcome us with folded hands; they bow and say: "Nan-mo O-mi-t'o Fu." We enter the first gate and come to an open court, either completely paved or with a paved walk across it to the monastery proper. On both sides of the walk we may see ponds, one filled with lotus the other with quantities of fish. The lotus is the holy symbolic flower of Buddhism. In the same way that this beautiful flower grows up from the mud and floats with its big leaves on the dirty water, pure, beautiful, and fragrant, so shall the life of men be in an evil and impure world. It shall unfold itself in beauty and purity. The fish in the other pond swim actively about. They also have their significance. They have been carried here, it may be from a great distance, by pious pilgrims who would like to take part in the work of salvation on this earth. Such a fish may well be a human soul in transmigration. To bring it up here means that it not only is saved from being eaten, but also that it is taken to a holy place, where the daily masses and meditation will make it possible for it to attain release. Pigs, goats, and other animals are often given to the monasteries for the same reason.

At the inner gate the two fierce-looking guardians, "Hêng Ha êrh chiang (哼哈二將), one on each side, keep watch. After having passed through that inner gate we come to the first little sanctuary. Here we are met by the smiling and thriving figure of Mi-lo Fu (彌勒佛). This is meant to express the beautiful thought: Every one who comes here shall know that there is hope for him. Mi-lo Fu will finally come with his regenerating power and in his endless mercy he looks on the whole creation with hope. Here the monks and the pilgrims make their first obeisance.

We are to be reminded not of mercy only as we enter. The severe guardians of the law also are here in the first little chapel. These are the four heavenly kings, ssŭ-ta T'ien wang (四大天王), two on each side, who in different armour and with severe, grim faces look down on the visitors. There we see the "Guardian of the East," Ch'ih-kuo (持國), with his black face and long black beard, with the sword in the right hand and the golden ring in the left. The next is the "Guardian of the South," Tsêng-ch'ang (增長), with white face and short beard, holding the "balloon guitar" in his hands. The "Guardian of the West" is Kuang-mu (廣目), with beardless red face, holding a snake or a dragon in the right hand and with the left raised up in the air holding a jewel. Lastly, we have the "Guardian of the North," To-wên (多聞), with a pink face without beard, holding an umbrella in his right hand and a rat in his left.

After crossing a little open court we come to that part of the temple where the patron god proper has his place. This may of course be one of several (Wên-shu, P'u-hsien, Ti-ts'ang, etc.), according to the Buddha or bodhisattva who has established himself here. With his back to the patron god, but separated by a board wall, stands another image, often in shining golden armour. This is the "archangel," the head of the heavenly guard, "Wei-t'o T'ien-tzŭ" (韋馱天子). We later see his image again among the twenty-four chu-t'ien (二十四諸天) devas, but there as a rule on a smaller scale. He and his altar face the inner temple hall. This is for a special reason. "As a guardian of the sanctuary and the upholder of the law he is always tempted to blaze up in righteous anger, and consequently might easily consume the many sinners that enter by the main gate." For this reason it has been decreed that Wei-t'o shall always stand in such a way that he sees the face of Buddha, from which grace and goodness shine.

The court which divides Wei-t'o Tien (韋馱殿), the temple of Wei-t'o, from the main temple is pretty and is paved with stone slabs. Often a couple of very small fish ponds are to be seen on either side of the wide stone walk that leads to the temple hall. This, as a rule, is a little higher, and broad stone steps lead up to the sanctuary. We stand here facing the well-known holy "triratna," the hall devoted to the "three values" or "jewels" (san-pao, 三寶): Buddha, the doctrine, and the society. Buddhists in China as a rule use the designation "ta-tien" (大殿), the "great temple," for this hall. Or it is given special names, as, for instance, the "Precious Hall of the Great Hero" (Ta-hsiung Pao-tien, 大雄寶殿). It is a large building, the pillars are immensely thick, and enormous amounts of money and work have been expended on the carved rafters and the massive beams. When new temple halls are now built, it proves difficult to get large enough timber in China. It is therefore usually ordered from the United States (Oregon). This was the case during the

[253]

TRUTH AND TRADITION IN BUDDHISM

recent restoration of the "Foremost Temple" (Ch'ien Ssŭ, 前 寺) at P'ut'o and the "Temple Concealed by the Spirits" (Ling-yin Ssŭ, 靈 隱 寺) at Hangchow.

The three great Buddha figures have been placed each on his own platform. They form one or other of the trinity groups, differing according to the different schools that control the temples. The most common are Amitabha, Buddha, and Yao-shih Fu. In some newer temples only one mighty Buddha, Sakyamuni, is to be seen, with the two disciples, Ananda and Kasyapa, in positions of service before him, and in much smaller dimensions. In front of the group is a large altar, adorned with big candlesticks, incense urns, and the different holy articles typical of Buddhism. Often fine silk draperies hang from the ceiling, and the whole place has a festive character. This is particularly the case at ordinations and similar solemn occasions. Praying mats and instruments used during the worship lie on the altar or have been placed on separate stands.

On both the long sides of the hall, twenty-four other images, twelve on each side, have been placed. This is the holy collection of gods, angels, kings, and judges that have been united in the well-known deva group (Chinese: Chu-t'ien, 諸 天). Here the four heavenly kings reappear with Wei-t'o, Brahma, Indra, Yama, (Yen-lo), etc. The list has been given in the chapter on "The Buddhist Pantheon in China." Some have a mild and noble appearance. Others are hard and austere. Each is connected with some particular

[254]

object, or has a special position of the hand, which makes it possible to distinguish him.

Behind the main altar, but with the back to the trinity group, there often stands a separate image of Kuan-yin. She is surrounded by a host of little children and constantly receives the adoration of pious wives and mothers. Or another trinity group more influenced by the "Pure Land" tendencies may stand here. In the corners behind the main altar there is often to be seen an image of Ti-ts'ang or some other tutelary god such as Kuan-yü (關羽), etc.

In central China Kuan-yin receives her special worship in a separate hall just behind the main temple hall. She is represented in virginal beauty and grace like a madonna, either standing alone or as a central figure in a trinity group. At the sides repose the eighteen lo-hans (十八羅漢) (arhats), in their self-satisfied and indolent calm.

As mentioned above, large temples often have side halls for the five hundred lo-hans, but as this demands much space and is an expensive arrangement, most monasteries must do without a "lo-han-t'ang" (羅漢堂). Often there are other fine temple halls, however. Thus at times there is to be seen a separate lecture hall with a pulpit, tables, and benches and with P'i-lu Fu (毘盧佛) (Vairocana) as a protecting Buddha over it all. Sometimes his place is taken by Mi-lo Fu.

In the temples of the Legalistic School the "Buddhist society" (sêng, 僧) may be seen represented by Lu-shê-na (盧舍那) (Lochana). He sometimes

TRUTH AND TRADITION IN BUDDHISM

appears as a central figure between the two great disciples of Buddha: Yu-p'u-li (優婆離) (Upali) and Chia-yeh (迦葉) (Moha Kasyapa). Others of the ten great disciples of Buddha may be met with in the temples, for example, Shê-li-fu (舍利佛) (Sariputra), but in general they are not so prominent as one might think.

A very important chapel is the so-called Tsu-t'ang (祖堂) (the hall of the patriarchs). Here one usually sees beautiful scrolls depicting the famous Bodhidharma (P'u-t'i-ta-mo, 菩提達摩) as the central figure. In the same or an adjoining hall are placed the images of those who have in a special way earned the gratitude of the monks as a whole (chia, 家) or of that particular monastery.

The buildings have lofts, as a rule. These rooms, besides being used as dormitories and store-rooms, are generally used in the masses for the dead. Sometimes a single room may be changed into a temple hall; such as a "Wan-fu tien" (萬佛殿), that is, a hall for the ten thousand Buddhas. Walls and ceiling are then seen studded with Buddha heads. Above an altar hangs a big picture of Kuan-yin. This signifies the fact that she must mediate the prayers which are to reach the myriads of unknown Buddhas.

The hall on the second floor, which interests us most, however, is the library hall (Ts'ang-ching-lou, 藏經樓). Here are the ten big cases where Tripitaka, carefully catalogued, has been placed. Incense burns incessantly on the larger and smaller altars. Some books, carefully wrapped, lie on the tables. The

MONASTIC LIFE

statues of the holy Buddhas here are not large, but have a pleasing and attractive appearance. This room has a distinguished look and there is a purer atmosphere about everything. There is no loud talking. Everything is done with great reverence. In side rooms in some of the old monasteries rest the enormous stores of carved blocks with which the oldest editions of the Tripitaka were printed. Old manuscripts and modern tracts and essays are also placed here.

The next section of the compound is the so-called "Fa-t'ang" (the law hall), where the abbot and the different ex-abbots reside. The latter have still the decisive influence in important questions. Here are one or more reception rooms and, besides these, are the private rooms of the leaders. The rooms are clean and well ordered. This is also to a certain extent true of the other buildings in the compound. The Buddhists attach considerable importance to outward order and cleanliness, and it is regarded as praiseworthy to be neat about one's own person as far as ablution, bathing, and clean clothes are concerned. As a sign of the authority of the abbot the "fragrant boards" (hsiang-pan, 香板), nicely carved, are placed at the main seat in the reception room. These are instruments of punishment and point to the fact that corporal punishment is practised to a considerable extent in the monasteries.

The room that is in one way the most inspiring is the "hall of meditation" (ch'an-t'ang, 禪堂), also called the "hall of wisdom" (pan-jo-t'ang, 般若堂), because it is here that one attains the deeper understanding of the fundamental essence and meaning of life. It is significant that in the Legalistic School this hall is called "pan-t'ang" (板堂) (the "hall where one receives punishment"). It is a big hall with an altar and a Buddha figure in the middle. In the cement floor certain lines and marks have been made, in order to show where to go during the running and quick marching which always precedes every long period of meditation. Along all the walls there are wide couches on which cushions are placed. Here the meditating monks are to sit. Behind the couches a platform is built around the room. This has been arranged in such a way that the meditating monks can put their bedclothes and other articles in toward the wall and at night spread their bedclothes and sleep there. A slip of red paper above the platform states the name of the meditating monk.

In the big monasteries there is, beyond this hall, or beside it, a separate room for old monks, a place that they can use for a living room and a meditation hall. In some cases, each one has something that looks like a cage in which to sleep and meditate. In other places, there is only an open hall. On the back side of their little kitchen and garden, and farther up the hills, stand the solemn chapel with a little pagoda where the many urns containing the ashes of the cremated bodies are put. It is only a few steps up here from the "home of the aged" (yang-lao-yüan, 養老院). An atmosphere of preparation and expectation pervades the place. If one wants to see systematic preparation for death one

MONASTIC LIFE

ought to go to this hall. It is as if every step reminded one of the controlling motto *momento mori*.

The crematorium itself is a small stone house, a covered chimney with a couple of big earthenware pots. The small urns with the ashes are catalogued and put on shelves and in niches in the place of rest.

Often there is a big pagoda at the back of the monastery (Chinese: pao-tʻa, 寶塔, the precious tower; Sanskrit: stupa). The original idea of the pagoda was to commemorate one of the great Buddhas. Often a relic was buried underneath it. Later it became more of a place of worship, and many beautiful thoughts gathered round this fine edifice. The pagoda became the visible symbol of the human soul in its longing and reaching out after full understanding and peace, its development toward Buddhahood. As the pagodas rise into the air in rounded storeys which diminish as they ascend, so the development of the holy ones shall reach up towards Nirvana. The Chinese name of the pagoda also denotes a deep meaning. It is composed of the two characters "earth" and "answer" (from 土 and 答): the earthbound soul shall get, through meditation, an answer to the deepest questions of life. Another symbolic idea is this: the square foundation on which the pagoda rests represents earth, the round storeys the air, and the top storey, with the four openings, represents heaven and the four heavenly guardians. The ball at the top is perfection, becoming one with Buddha. The fortunate numbers in China are always uneven, therefore the pagoda has from

[259]

TRUTH AND TRADITION IN BUDDHISM

three to thirteen storeys. The most usual numbers are seven and nine.

Very significant, also, are the small copper plates and bells which have been hung along the sides and which are moved by the wind. In this way, a "music of the spheres," which is known in the symbolic language of the Buddhists, is produced. As was to be expected, a special significance was accorded to these strange structures by the geomancers. Gradually it was assumed that the pagodas exercised an influence on the weather and the prosperity of the different places. They controlled the laws of "wind and water" (fêng-shui, 風水) in a beneficial way. The result was that all places of importance, all centres of administration, built their big pagodas, and the small places followed the lead. Indeed, the enthusiasm for pagodas became so great that individual families in the country districts built smaller ones for their own private benefit. A pagoda is often to be seen, even at the centre of the state religion, the residence of the official, or "yamen," and a Chinese landscape can hardly be imagined without one of these typical buildings. Lately, the enthusiasm for pagodas has, however, cooled to a certain extent. This is shown by in the fact that most pagodas are very poorly kept up.

In dealing with the buildings and equipment of the monastery, mention must be made of the cells which have been fitted out for the monks who "pi-kuan" (閉關); i. e., allow themselves to be locked up in order to be able to give themselves completely to meditation. There are still quite a good many who do this. The

PAGODA, SUNG-YU MONASTERY, HONAN

MONASTIC LIFE

door is walled up and sealed. Their food is put in through a small opening. Outside there is occasionally a small court like a garden, but often nothing but the cell. Generally the monk makes a vow to meditate in solitude for one to three years. Very long periods are rarer and solitude for life still more so. One or more scriptures are taken with the monk, these form the basis for the daily prayer services, but the greatest weight is laid on meditation. At times, a monk cuts himself off from association with his environment by merely locking his door. He does not receive any calls, nor do any business, but at certain times he meets the nearest brethren of the monastery.

The ordinary rooms (cells) of the monks are very plain. It is only the monks permanently connected with the monastery and visitors of superior social position who get such "one-family houses." The majority have to live in the hall of meditation or the large common rooms. A monk's cell may be both attractive and clean. The prohibition of comfortable beds, flowers, etc., has been entirely ignored. These belong to the poor "child's learning" of Hinayana. A table, a bookcase, a little private altar, a favourite sutra wrapped in a piece of beautiful embroidered cloth, some pictures on the walls, or, in recent times, photographs, a letter holder and writing outfit, and a few chairs for himself and visitors, these he has. The old deserving monks and ex-abbots often have rooms that are particularly beautifully situated.

The outer rooms, kitchen, store-room, wood-shed, etc., as a rule lie at the side of the main buildings with courts of different sizes. The kitchen, which is in charge of a respected monk, has an interest all its own. Huge pots and frying pans are ready for use. In many places, there is also quite an ingenious water system, which carries the water either through bamboo tubes or through open water troughs to the kitchen, washing room, and bathroom. The whole of this important department is under the big "business department" (k'u-fang, 庫房) which plays such an important part in the monasteries.

The picture we here have drawn is that of the more ordinary monasteries which have a working staff of thirty to fifty monks. During times of ordination and special festive occasions there may, of course, be many more, even up to three or four hundred. Beside these ordinary monasteries, there are some still larger ones, as, for instance, T'ien-ning Ssŭ (天寧寺) at Changchow. At ordination times, there are often as many as two thousand monks there, in truth a "shih-fang ts'ung-lin" (十方叢林) (a monastery for all the world). In these great monasteries one may find special activities such as homes for the blind and the sick. The rise and phenomenal growth of the T'ien-ning Ssŭ under the long administration of the pious Chih-k'ai (治開) is an illustration of the old truth that men are always drawn to those who, by self-sacrificing love, give a living testimony to the power of religion and sincerity. It shows that in Buddhism, also, it is the persons that make the institutions. For this reason many finely equipped monasteries are comparatively

MONASTIC LIFE

empty, while smaller places with poorer equipment draw the masses.

Beside the "shih-fang ts'ung-lin" (十方叢林) (the big monasteries which in the stricter sense of the word are the common property of the whole Buddhist brotherhood, and as such stand open to every honourable monk), there are also many of more or less private monasteries, called " tzŭ-sun ts'ung-lin" (子孫叢林), i. e., monasteries which have been taken possession of by a special clan (chia, 家) among the Buddhists. The monks in these monasteries are often very exclusive and do not care for the opening of a "hall of hospitality" (kua-tan yüan, 掛單院), where the travelling monks can put up. They do not "k'ai tan-k'ou" (開單口) (open up resting places), as it is called in Buddhist language.

In some of the monasteries there are places for binding and storing the scriptures. The printing is done in the larger private printing offices. The T'ien-ning Monastery has distinguished itself in this respect, as have also some of the monasteries in Yangchow, Hangchow, and Ningpo. We have previously mentioned the more modern printing press and bookshop under the auspices of Dr. Ting in Shanghai. It looks, however, as if the centre might soon be changed to Yangchow, where large buildings for the literary activities of the society are being erected. In Ningpo, a Buddhist magazine has been published. Similar efforts have been made in other places, but without a very long lease of life. One which still appears regularly is the well-known *Hai Ch'ao Yin* (海潮音): the

TRUTH AND TRADITION IN BUDDHISM

Sound of the Tide-Wave. The lay devotees have also their own paper.

The difference between a monastery (ts'ung-lin, 叢林) and a common temple (ssŭ, miao, an, 寺, 廟, 庵) is that the monasteries not only are homes of monks, but also to a large extent attend to the "propagation" (the ordination). Therefore, as a rule, the best men, men with a feeling of responsibility and a social spirit, are found in the monasteries, while the more indifferent and worldly, the "traders," are in the majority in the temples. This is, of course, a mere generalization. Many exceptions are to be found.

Although the temple buildings are very different in size, there are, as a rule, not more monks connected with them than are strictly necessary to carry on the "daily business" of service and masses for the dead. In addition, some monks who are on pilgrimage may come, but as a rule they only stay for a few days.

The temples which belong to the Buddhist society (ssŭ, miao, 寺, 廟) rank highest. Much more mixed and degraded are the municipal temples (kung-miao, 公廟), which abound in city and country. The dominating power in the latter is the "temple association," a very heterogeneous, and at times very irreligious, group of people. In addition, all who live in the district, even the lowest of the people, think they have a right to the place. The result is that the poor monk who has to attend to the religious side of the business is looked upon as a hired servant. The atmosphere is wholly created by the people of the locality. Therefore these temples may be used for the

MONASTIC LIFE

most unbelievable purposes, ranging from a common municipal hall of deliberation, to a school, a temporary storehouse for goods, especially coffins, and at night a gambling den. A good self-respecting monk will never accept an engagement in such a place.

The nunneries are small. They are often situated near a big monastery, which, through its trusted men, has the administrative authority over it. The nuns are ordained in the monasteries. Their small sisterhoods are governed by an old and experienced prioress; she in turn appoints the different nuns to manage the different services in the same way as is done in the the monasteries, only on a smaller scale. They have their little temple hall, etc., where they perform their services and meditations often with great piety. They often go out to the homes of the many lay Buddhists among the women and do a great work both from a religious and a financial point of view. Nobody collects so much money or pulls so many invisible strings as do the nuns. There is thus a good reason why the nunneries accompany the monasteries as the moon accompanies the earth!

Let us now look a little more closely at the services that are performed in a monastery and the life that goes on inside the high walls.

It is the duty of the abbot to engage suitable monks to fill the various positions. His success as an abbot depends largely on the fitness of his choices. The appointments are usually made about New Year and midsummer, and run for six months. Capable monks

TRUTH AND TRADITION IN BUDDHISM

may, however, be engaged for the monastery in the course of the year, as vacancies occur.

As well as the abbot (fang-chang, 方丈), who nominally is the head, there are the "fathers" (i. e., retired abbots, t'ui-chu ho-shang, 退居和尚), who still wish to remain in the monastery. Often they retire to a small temple, over which they have acquired the right of disposal. If they remain in the monastery they become "lao-ho-shang" (老和尚), or "t'ai-lao ho-shang" (太老和尚): "old monks," or "very old monks," and, as such, retain the decisive vote in all important cases. At the same time, they are so independent that they can travel where they please, or withdraw for rest and meditation when they wish.

From among the older and more reliable monks who have been connected with the monastery for a long time, some are chosen to be members of the main administration, "chien-yüan" (監院). The first of these is called "tu-chien" (都監), the others "chih-shih" (知事) or more inclusively "fu-ssŭ" (副寺), assistant managers. The number varies with the size of the monastery. These monks hold the most important and coveted positions forming the "k'u-fang" (庫房), or business department. They manage the funds and make all purchases. They have their own rooms with offices, and often their own guest room, where they receive the many monks and laymen who come to confer with them. Often they have to travel round the district to collect the land rent from those who farm the fields belonging to the monastery. Many of the monasteries have big estates which form their economic mainstay,

[266]

MONASTIC LIFE

but often these are insufficient, and the monks have to depend upon the benevolent gifts of the pilgrims and payments for masses for the dead, which, from a moral standpoint, form a rather questionable source of income.

Besides the main work of administration there is a second big department, the "k'o-t'ang" (客堂), or guest department. As the name indicates, it has to do with the reception of guests and is conducted by a very influential monk who is called "chih-k'o" (知客), main host. To assist him there is the "sêng-chih" (僧值), a term which is best rendered, perhaps, by the word "inspector." He goes round with the host and sees that everything is in proper order. Their rooms are also provided with the symbolic "beating boards." The monks have to apply to them for permission to go out. The inspector may even censure the abbot if he does not do his duty. Thus the organization of the brotherhood is both autocratic and democratic. In the guest department monks may be appointed particularly as reporters and clerks. In some big monasteries, besides a host, there is also a vice-host and quite a number of assistant hosts.

Finally, we have the department of instruction and worship, which comes under the "ch'an-t'ang" (禪堂) (the hall of meditation). Here the instructor (Wei-na, 維那) is the head. He is assisted by an older monk, who is called "t'ang-chu" (堂主) (the master of the hall). He has, besides this, a staff of helpers who are partly permanent, partly temporary (yüeh-chung, 悅眾, and shih-chê, 侍者). In consultation with the

TRUTH AND TRADITION IN BUDDHISM

abbot he arranges everything which has to do with worship and the hours of meditation, and appoints serving monks to act as "hsiang-têng" (香燈) (waiters) in the temple halls. The "sêng-chih" (inspector) and the "huei-lo" (instructor) are the most feared men, and often in their public capacities have to act very severely. The abbot has a number of young assistants who serve him; namely, a body-servant, (tʻang-yao, 湯藥), two helpers (shih-chê, 侍者), a keeper of the wardrobe and all the abbot's personal belongings (i-po, 衣鉢), and a shao-hsiang (燒香) who regulates the incense. A couple of these, carrying his insignia, precede him at the daily masses. They correspond in a way to the acolytes used in some of the Christian churches.

In the dining-room, or refectory, there are two waiters, who are called "hsing-tʻang" (行堂). They are assisted by a number of serving lay brethren (tao-jên, 道人). Laymen are often employed in the lower, serving positions, as in the kitchen (ta-liao, 大寮), but two or three monks are there, too, engaged in the cooking and serving. A number of monks also serve as attendants in the main temple, as well as in the smaller chapels and halls. They see that the incense does not burn out, that the place is cleaned and swept, and in addition receive the visiting pilgrims who come to perform their worship at the different altars. In this way they now and then get tips. They are called "hsiang-têng" (香燈). Finally monks also act as gate-keepers. At times, one sees experienced monks taking care of the landed property or occupied in other practical affairs. Monks also carry all the water and the large amount of food-stuffs needed.

In describing these things, we must also mention the distinction made in the monasteries between the "tung-tan" (東單) and the "hsi-tan" (西單): the East party and the West party. Some have understood this distinction to mean that the former attended only to the worship and the latter to the practical activities. This is not quite correct. The fact is that it is practically only in the arrangement in the temple hall and during the meals that a distinction is made between an East party and a West party. On these occasions, those who belong to the general administration and the guest department stand on the West side (the side of honour) and those of the meditation section on the East. According to the rules, the abbot in the morning stands on the East side and in the evening on the West, but this is not always adhered to. He does not come in till all have found their places. The inspector stands in the place of the abbot till he comes. After that the inspector moves round, going wherever he finds anything to correct. The West party is headed by one who is called "shou-tso" (首座), a title which he has only as long as the service lasts. All important guests of the monks stand on the right side. If a law scholar (fa-shih, 法師) happens to be present he is, as a rule, made "shou-tso," the leader of the West party, for the duration of the worship. These law scholars are, in general, entirely relieved of all practical occupations. They live in a fine room and can devote themselves to their great and proper work, that of preparing the daily expositions.

In connection with the ranks already mentioned there is also another division, which ought to be mentioned briefly. That is the superior group, from which all the higher positions are supposed to be filled. This superior group consists of the six following divisions, which have nothing to do with the actual duties: (1) tso-yüan (座元); (2) shou-tso, (首座) the "highest seat"; (3) hsi-t'ang (西堂), the "West hall commander"; (4) hou-t'ang (後堂), the "back hall commander"; (5) t'ang-chu (堂主), the "commander of the hall"; and (6) shu-chi (書記), secretaries. This grouping conforms to the old rule in China that all officials are supposed to come from the literati with degrees.

As a rule, the abbot is chosen for three years. He may, if he so wishes, retire before this term is expired, but as this is not often done it is not considered a good sign either for himself, or for the monastery. There are, on the other hand, some monasteries that prolong the term for a popular abbot, but the rule is only very reluctantly broken. Where the elders in a place are very strong and the monasteries are completely subject to the decisions made in the council of the elders, the election of an abbot must take place openly. The elders agree to nominate suitable candidates, and during a special service of prayer which at times takes the form of drawing of lots, the election is decided through the "special intervention of Buddha." In many monasteries the practice has now arisen of having the abbot with the various ex-abbots in reality decide it all beforehand. It even happens that three younger men who are considered suited to be abbots are chosen at the same time to fill the position after three, six, and nine years. By a special ordination service these men are appointed beforehand and thus a "home" (chia, 家), or "family line," is formed. These men call each other brother, and by reason of their anticipated ordination they are appointed members of the "k'u-fang" (general administration). As they belong to it in a special way, they are called "tang-chia-shih-fu" (當家師傅) (masters who have the right to decide). This ordination, with something approaching to a right of inheritance, and a legitimate right to decide about the monastery and landed property, with responsibility towards the whole society, is what is meant by the expression "chêng-fa yen-ts'ang" (正法眼藏), which perhaps may best be rendered by "legal succession." The monks concerned often wear very high caps while doing their work in the monastery. This is a sign that they, in company with the abbot (the father) and the older generations in the inner apartments (the grandfathers), are the proper stewards of the big home of the brotherhood in that place. This right they retain, even when they go to other monasteries for a longer period of time, to assist in some service. At times they come home, and in due time they succeed to the dignity of abbot. Much more could be written about the intrigues, the agitation, and the deliberations preceding these elections.

TRUTH AND TRADITION IN BUDDHISM

The religious activity in the monastery now claims our attention again. The external forms are many, and they are the product of long evolution. What does it all lead to?

Let us first consider the daily worship. It is taken for granted that as many as possible of the various functionaries take part in it, those from the East party as well as from the West party. If there are absences, the inspector will seek them out and the abbot will reprimand them publicly while he "k'u-fang" (庫房), i. e., inspects the monks at the morning or evening meal.

The fixed daily services begin very early in the morning, especially in the summer. Even in the winter one can hear the first signal for the morning mass at three o'clock in the morning. The monks then get out of bed and gather, quiet and solemn, in the big temple hall. Each knows his place, either in the East party or the West party. The instructor stands by the altar on the right side. He plays one of the instruments, and leads the chanting in a full, clear voice. A good voice and musical ear are essential for being "wei-na" (維那). Farther to the right stands the drummer and the man who beats the well-known hollow "wooden fish" (mu-yü, 木槵). Farther out in the congregation stands the one of the East party who beats the time by striking a little bell (ch'ing-tzŭ, 磬子). In some places, cymbals and other kinds of strange instruments are in use, for the "time" is very difficult. It is remarkable to hear what they can achieve with these instruments in the chants, which may last for

FA YÜ TEMPLE, P'UT'O

MONASTIC LIFE

hours. The well-known daily masses are sung without any book of ritual, but during the long extra masses the inspector and the main leaders have the books in front of them. By points and cross-lines and partly also by pictures of the instruments and other symbols, the order and time of the chant are indicated.

The service begins with a "prelude," the time being given by striking the different instruments. A signal is then given on the bell, and the whole congregation bows in silence on the praying stools or praying mats, not merely on their knees, but all the way down, so that the forehead lightly touches the floor. This is done in unison, and when several hundred monks in the same dress are seen doing this the effect is quite striking. They get up and then bend again, nine times in all. This is the holy greeting, three repeated three times (3 × 3). When bowing, they must remember to let the right knee touch the floor first, for the right side is the clean one, while the left is unclean. Therefore the cloak, which is the garment used during the mass, is only worn on the left shoulder. The kneeling rug is spread out neatly during the first prostration.

Meanwhile, the abbot, accompanied by his acolytes, has come in. He also begins with the nine-fold prostration. He may be recognized by a red patch on his gown. As soon as he has finished his silent prayer, a signal is given on the bell and the instructor introduces the mass by singing, in very low chanting tones, the first words of the sutra used. As a rule, it is the formula of greeting "Nan-mo," then comes the name of the Buddha or bodhisattva concerned, and finally "fu, p'u-sa." After "Nan-mo," all join in, supported by the beating on the instruments, and a rushing volume of chanting rises to the high temple ceilings. The first sections of praise and the holy vows which are daily renewed offer the greatest variety. Here the alternating instruments and song are most effective. Besides facing the altar, the worshippers turn several times to one side so that the parties of the West and East face each other.

Special parts of the mass are sung by the abbot. He genuflects and bends in a rather interesting way. It is when one comes to the sutra itself that the greatest demands are made upon the monks who take part. In order to get through it all within reasonable time the speed has to be increased enormously. The chant rushes along breathlessly so that everybody feels great relief when the last section is reached, where they can rest in the long tones of praise. This last part of the mass, chanted in kneeling position, is the most touching.

The chanting tones have a pronouncedly mournful character. The music and the tunes of Buddhism are known as "pei-t'iao" (悲調, tunes of woe). And yet, at times, during the great festivals, a cheerful hymn of praise may arise. To those who hear such masses for the first time the effect may be strange and eerie. But one need not have been present many times at mass in one of the larger monasteries or heard a well-drilled monk choir, before one is struck by the devotion and religious intensity of the singing. This is doubtless true of the most serious and devout of the monks,

MONASTIC LIFE

while on the other hand many only take part in a mechanical way. More than once I have spoken with monks who have talked with enthusiasm of their longing to get to certain monasteries where the singing is specially cultivated, as for instance, to Chiao Shan (焦 山), the remarkable little island in the lower part of the Yangtze, where some of the best singers of Buddhism gather. I have been present with them at several of their masses and I shall never forget the impression of noble singing and religious devotion which I there received. For here are tunes with which the Chinese feel at home, tunes which are the spontaneous product of the genius of the Chinese race, developed and refined during many centuries through the cultivation of Buddhism. Is there not a lesson just here for the Christian church in China? If Christianity is to be "sung into the soul" of China, we must also have hymns and chants composed on the lines of these Buddhist masses, and not confine ourselves to imported German chorals and light Anglo-Saxon melodies.

If it be asked: "Why do we not see larger ethical results from all this religious emotion?" I will answer with my hand on my heart: "The Chinese have the same difficulty in exchanging religious rapture and emotion for a well-directed holy life as we Westerners have. But that these masses are often ethically helpful I am quite convinced." Several Buddhists have told me: "It was not till I took part in these solemn masses that I understood what Buddhism was. I felt regenerated."

TRUTH AND TRADITION IN BUDDHISM

The mass often closes with a quiet procession round the great temple hall. The participants walk in long rows between the stools or out into the corridors, with hands folded (ho-chang, 合掌) and eyes half-closed, pronouncing a greeting to the different Buddhas and bodhisattvas by prefixing every name with the well-known "Nan-mo." Or all may be united in a five-hundred- or one-thousand-fold greeting to Amitabha. The final act takes place before the high altar, the abbot after the nine prostrations returning to his apartment followed by the acolytes, and the instructor singing the last hymns and making the last genuflections, after which everybody retires.

In some monasteries there are as many as three such services every day, but two are the usual rule, for there are many other things to be attended to, and such a service may last one or two hours.

After morning mass there is a chance to complete one's toilet, after which comes breakfast. This is often followed by the ordered masses for the dead, when a band of monks must serve again in the temple hall. Then guests come who have to be entertained, the daily business must be attended to, etc. In some places, there are special schools for the young monks and novices. All too soon it is eleven o'clock and the dinner bell calls the monks to the refectory. In the afternoon there is, as a rule, less to do, so it is easy then to get a talk with the monks. The evening mass is about five o'clock and is quite impressive. It differs from the morning mass only in including, as a rule, a part of the confession litany. The beautiful

[276]

prayer of the "Pure Land," which we have heard before, is also chanted. The sutra used is often the little Amitabha scripture (the "O-mi-tʻo Ching").

When there are no novices being educated in the monastery and all is quiet, it is considered a meritorious undertaking to have a law scholar (Fa-shih, 法師) connected with the monastery giving regular lectures or expositions of different classic writings. If the abbot himself is a law scholar he may do it, but as a rule some famous expositor from another place is engaged. This serves to bring fame to the monastery. It is announced a long time ahead, by big posters, that such and such a master is going to give lectures on some of the scriptures. "All who are devoted to Buddhism are welcomed." The master is received and treated with veneration, but not nearly so much so in China as in Korea. The lecture usually takes place in the afternoon. It has fallen to my lot to be present on many such occasions.

The master comes in, accompanied by the abbot, and takes his seat on a stage beside the image of Vairocana or Maitreya. When he enters, everybody stands up. A short mass is read as an introduction to the lecture. The master sits with his feet crossed under him like a living Buddha, and the choir boys arrange the folds of his gown neatly around him. In addition to the monks there gradually assemble a group of interested laymen, old pensioned officials, scholars, or even a group of venerable matrons. The young monks distribute copies of the scripture that is to be read, to every one present. First the master reads a passage. Then he begins to explain sentence by sentence, while he gives a general survey later. He sometimes launches out into the deep so that it is difficult for the "unlearned" to follow him, but often he gives out real pearls. His theme carries him away, one feels his deep emotion, but he controls himself and forces himself back to the usual academic style.

Without doubt these lectures do much good, especially among the monks who are led deeper into the great religious thoughts. They act as an antidote to the mechanical routine which constantly tends to blunt the mind. Some masters keep question boxes where both monks and laymen may put questions about religion. These are explained either before or after the exposition of the scripture. These masters, however, do not exercise any large influence among the common people. The whole is too academic to allow of this. Latterly, there have been some attempts to have more popular lectures given, particularly by young reforming monks. The development of this movement in Japan is far ahead of anything in China.

It remains now to say something further about meditation. This can be done either privately in the different cells or unitedly in the meditation hall. At the latter place, regular courses in meditation are given under the leadership of the "wei-lo" or the "t'ang-chu." These are meant to assist the newly ordained monks to become familiar with this holy art, but one often sees older monks also, both from among the casual visitors and those who have definite occupations in the monastery, joining in voluntarily. These older

MONASTIC LIFE

monks have their seats on the left side as one enters. Here, also, the "lord of the hall" (t'ang-chu) sits. The instructor sits on the right side near the group of young monks. He has the "fragrant beating boards" (hsiang-pan, 香板) on his side, and is placed on a separate raised seat. He keeps a close watch on all, and if irregularities occur, he gives his reprimand when the period is over, at which time the "fragrant boards" may be used. By his side he has two young assistants, who help in his work. Special beating of the big drum calls the monks together for meditation. In order to benefit fully from the holy exercise it is the rule first to take two or three quick marches to get the blood moving. The whole group makes a round of the corridors and then re-enter and take their places. At a given signal everybody gets up again, and the quick march is resumed, this time round the hall, going a certain number of times round in circles, the leader at the side of the group with a long bamboo pole in his hand. "Right about face" is ordered by a heavy stroke of the bamboo pole on the floor, after which the quick step goes in the opposite direction. This is done as many as three times. Then the big drum is again sounded, the door is shut, the participants resume their seats, and the meditation proper commences. Meanwhile, a long incense stick has been lighted in one of the outer halls. This is looked after by an attendant (hsiang-têng). Three quarters of an hour may elapse before it has burned down. When it does, the fact is announced by renewed drum beating. A new stick is then lighted, burns out, and another three quarters of an hour has passed. If the meditation is to take "three incense sticks," still another is lighted, and in this way they mark altogether two and a quarter hours. The periods in the meditation are thus divided according to the burning down of the incense sticks. This, too, expresses the thought that meditation should assist a person to concentrate his mind so that it ascends in a fine, straight line, as one sees the incense smoke rise from a stick in a closed room.

It is of first importance in meditation to get the correct posture. Without this, it is difficult to attain to the right condition of mind. The posture is the same as that of the historic Buddha when he sat under the Bodhi-tree and had his great inner experience: the legs crossed under him, the eyes half shut, the hands loosely crossed in front. If one sits quietly and immovably like this, and breathes deeply and regularly, one will have bound or chained that part of the body which mostly hinders man in the free expansion of the mind. But more is required, for though it is difficult to get accustomed to the rather uncomfortable position, this is gradually learned, particularly if one begins in youth. A thousand times more difficult is the next step: to become calm and acquire concentration. To help toward this the instructor repeatedly enjoins: "Away with all unnecessary and vain thoughts," "the heart must get to rest" (hsin kuei-i, 心皈一). Here it is that many fight a desperate inner battle, and worst of all, one is not allowed to ask Buddha for help. No, here in the meditation hall, Buddha must in no form be invoked

MONASTIC LIFE

for mercy. Here one must "yung kung" (用功) oneself, labour on to the goal. Many have given up the effort at this, the second step, and allowed it to become a merely mechanical performance.

Where, then, shall those who would attain to this calm of mind begin? The answer is: You must begin with yourself. Think of where you have come from; what you were before you were born into the world as a man. Think until you see your original face (pen-lai-ti mien-mu, 本來的面目). Then think of what you may attain to if all the illusions of the world, all the worldly and carnal desires, are annihilated. (Here drastic directions are given of how to see through the emptiness and ugliness of everything connected with the body and the senses.) Think of being delivered from all this! Think what it means to get behind all feelings of pleasure and displeasure, to be raised above the vicissitudes of life, to see clearly, to see "emptily," and face the future as one who has already conquered it. At this stage one may begin thinking of Buddha, not the historical Buddha, but the Buddha idea. And from this elevation he is seen in a new light: Buddha is not a distant personality, he is myself in my final redemption, which I now perceive from the midst of the white mist in which I am sitting. The few elect who attain to this feel as if their seats have been changed into a flowery bed of the most brilliant and fragrant lotus. Personally, I have met such persons. They long for the hour of meditation, and even continue their meditation in their own chambers until late at night.

[281]

TRUTH AND TRADITION IN BUDDHISM

From this it will be understood why the Buddhists call meditating "tso kung-fu" (做工夫), or "yung-kung" (用功); namely, work. They often measure the spiritual worth and character of a monk by the extent to which he finds his enjoyment in meditation. We have said before that there are many of the T'ien-t'ai School who are not very enthusiastic over this intense meditation. This attitude is shared, to a large extent, by Buddhists of the "Pure Land." They say this kind of meditation forces the whole question of salvation back to the Hinayana stage, and only a small minority attain their goal, while the rest become machines—or lunatics.[1] It is much better, they say, to read the great inspiring scriptures (T'ien-t'ai), or surrender oneself in prayer and faith to the great father's name, Amitabha (the "Pure Land"). The latter is the road open to all, learned and unlearned—and to the majority it is the only road. Many of the leading men of the "Pure Land" say: "We men are so permeated by sin, and our reason is so obscured, that it is impossible for us to attain salvation either by reading or meditation. There is only one universal road left, that of faith and surrender."

Just because there are these many ways of salvation (fa-mên, 法門), an acute and wide-spread tension is felt among the Buddhists of the East. During recent years particularly it is said: "All these roads are

[1] From this one can understand why the relationship between the Legalistic School (Lü-tsung, 律宗) and the Meditation School (Ch'an Tsung, 禪宗) is so good. They both rely to some extent on what is the original idea in Buddhism — Sakyamuni's way of salvation.

MONASTIC LIFE

probably necessary, because we human beings are so different and by the special grace of Amitabha they have been united in one great religion: Mahayana, the ship of salvation for all living beings."

CHAPTER IX

PILGRIMAGES

Pilgrimages play an important part in oriental Buddhism, not least in China. Indeed, it can be said that this practice first reached to the heights which it now has attained, through the influence of Buddhism. .

Certain mountains in China were, indeed, looked upon as especially holy, even in the most ancient times. Notable amongst these are the five famous old sacred places (wu-yü, 五嶽): (1) T'ai Shan (泰山), in Shantung province; (2) Hua Shan (華山), in Shensi; (3) Hêng Shan (恆山), in Shansi; (4) Nan-yü Shan (南嶽山), or Hêng Shan (衡山), in Hunan; and (5) Sung Shan (嵩山), in Honan.

The Buddhist monks were fortunate enough to secure a foothold in several of these places, and although they were not the sole proprietors everywhere, but had to share with the Taoist priests, it was they who drew up the rules for worship and gave the framework for those special festivals which later have worked so like a charm upon the religious masses of the East. The Taoists felt that if they were going to hold on to any part of the field, they must to some extent pattern their arrangements after those the Buddhists had adopted.

Besides the above-named mountains, the Buddhists very soon succeeded in creating certain great new centres for pilgrimages. Wonderful legends of great Buddhas and bodhisattvas began to circulate. It was told that this one had settled down here, that one there. Powerful rays of light had manifested themselves, great miracles had taken place on this or that mountain. The religious spirit was greatly stirred and thousands determined to have a part in building monasteries and temples in honour of these Buddhas. There is scarcely a monastery that has not some such miraculous account to point back to. The number grew with the centuries, and larger and larger became the guest halls where pilgrims could be received. Certain mountain ranges were, so to speak, overcrowded with temples and monasteries, as, for example, Lü Shan (廬山) in Kiangsi and T'ien-t'ai Shan (天台山) in Chekiang. The Taiping rebellion laid waste a great many of these, but even now the many heaps of ruins witness to this golden age of Buddhism.

There were, in particular, four mountains which, in a special sense, became sacred places of Buddhism, for on these mountains the greatest bodhisattvas had revealed themselves. Volumes might be written about each of these places. We must here confine ourselves to giving a very brief description of each.

The names of these mountains, as has already been mentioned, are: (1) P'ut'o Shan (普陀山), an island on the coast near Ningpo (Chou-shan, 舟山) archipelago; (2) Chiu-hua Shan (九華山), in Anhwei province; (3) Wu-t'ai Shan (五台山) in Shansi province, and (4) O-mei Shan (峨嵋山), in Szechwan province.

As might be expected, one will see in these places some of Buddhism's most impressive manifestations, so far as material structure is concerned. There are

[285]

TRUTH AND TRADITION IN BUDDHISM

colossal temple halls, provided with a magnificent equipment for worship to attract the pilgrims. There are whole towns which have sprung up round the sanctuary, and are entirely supported by the sale of objects needed in the worship. There are inns and guest halls, restaurants and fine hotels, all overcrowded during the pilgrim season. There are art treasures and historic documents of great worth, about which special books have been written by Chinese and Japanese, as well as by Western writers.

There are deeply affecting instances of the highest religious ecstasy, of penitence and longing for renewal to be seen in these places. But there are quite as often very offensive scenes where the grossest bartering of "gods" for the attainment of riches and material gain is carried on quite openly.

Here one finds a choice band of serious and religious monks, and also an unpleasantly large group of profit seekers, while out along the roads, and outside the large temples, is a horde of "wild monks," sinister creatures who use the worst methods for getting hold of the valuable possessions of the pilgrims.

Round about in caves and holes in the ground sit hermits who, in fanatical ecstasy, spend most of their days in reciting the holy writings. One can also find pious and learned monks living their quiet, retired lives in some solitary temple, situated on the holy site. Only one who is well acquainted with the conditions will be able to find his way to these "still ones in the land," in the midst of the great whirlpool, where

觀自在菩薩

KUNA-YIN

Painted by Wu Tao-tzu

PILGRIMAGES

everything seems to be poisoned by the cold deadly breath of commercialism.

The most beautiful and splendid sanctuary is certainly P'ut'o Shan. Access to it is comparatively easy, as there is always steamship connection with Ningpo. In the summer, extra lines with tourist boats run from Shanghai; and besides these, pilgrims come in great numbers in large and small boats from the whole coast.

The fishing population, especially from the coasts of Fukien and Kwangtung, are tireless in coming with their thank-offerings to the merciful Kuan-yin, who "blesses their trade and protects them in storm and danger on the deep waters."

The island is sacred to Kuan-yin, for which reason her statue, in enormous dimensions, is enthroned in the most beautiful way in the temples, nearly a hundred in all, with which the island is strewn.

The legend relates how she revealed herself for the first time in a cave which the waves have worn in the side of the island near the sea. This was the cave, afterwards so famous, called "Ch'ao-yin Tung" (潮音洞), the "Cave of the Roar of Billows." This event happened in the year 847 A.D., while an Indian monk was carrying on his worship in the cave. Immense crowds have stood and looked down into the cave of the billows from that day on. Many have stood there from ebb-tide, when the cave lay dry, until the waves came rushing in, filling the air with their deep powerful roar, and flooding the cave again in their engulfing waters. Sometimes an impelling force has seized them

TRUTH AND TRADITION IN BUDDHISM

so that they have cast themselves into the deep, and have either been killed on the stone bottom or have at once "been borne in upon Kuan-yin's billows to the 'Western Paradise.'" Others, feeling an irresistible longing to give some outward sign of their inward consecration, have cut off an ear or a finger and cast it into the sea.

The day the writer stood by the cave, the bottom was stained red with blood, in spite of the fact that the authorities have made proclamations strictly prohibiting visitors from "taking their lives or cutting off any of their members at the spot"! For greater security, a railing has now been set up round the whole cave.

The island, which has been in the possession of the Buddhists through all these centuries, has often been visited by both native and foreign pirates, who time after time have destroyed the sanctuary and driven the monks away to the mainland of China. None of the buildings which one sees there now dates from before the fourteenth century.

In 1572, a monk was sent down there from Wu-t'ai Shan, to restore the ruined buildings at the expense of the emperor. The island was originally under the authority of the legalistic party (Lü-tsung), but in the seventeenth century the Meditation School (Ch'an Tsung) secured the ascendancy.

At the landing-place there is a regular little town given up to the sale of requisites for temple worship, and a long row of vegetarian restaurants. The first temple enclosure, which is, in reality, a monastery

PILGRIMAGES

enclosure also, forms the famous "Temple of Universal Mercy" (P'u-chi Ssǔ) (普濟寺). It is also popularly called "Ch'ien Ssǔ" 前寺 (the First, or Foremost Temple) in contrast to the other great enclosure which lies farther inland, on the slope below the real mountain. This latter is called "Fa-yu Ssǔ" (法雨寺) (the Temple of the Doctrine which Rains Down), or "Hou Ssǔ" (後寺) (the Back Temple). One ought to go into these temples, if one wants to see impressive masses held for great crowds of pilgrims who lie prostrated in long rows. Here, also, one finds the very finest of Buddhist art. One meets something similar, though on a smaller scale, if one goes over the lower slope, up the many stone steps to the temple "Fu-ting Shan" (佛頂山), "Buddha's Peak," from which there is an enchanting view out over the ocean.

Among other remarkable places, in addition to the "Cave of the Roar of Billows," is the famous "Fan-yin Tung" (梵音洞), where a relic of the historic Buddha is said to be.

The full name of the island, "P'ut'o-lo-ch'ieh (普陀落伽), is an allusion to Kuan-yin's original mountain, the Indian Potaloka. A good many monks have settled down as hermits here or on the surrounding islets, in order to "lay up merit" for themselves during shorter or longer periods.

Buddhism's next greatest sanctuary is Chiu-hua Shan (九華山), in Anhwei, situated in one of the most naturally beautiful parts of the Yangtze valley. Further details are given in the chapter on "Masses for the Dead" and Ti-t'sang. We learn that the first hermit

[289]

settled there as early as the year 401. This was an Indian whose Chinese name was Pei-t'u (悲陀).

The original name of the place was "Chiu-tzŭ Shan" (九子山), but after the great Chinese poet Li-t'ai-pai (李太白) had been there he rechristened it "Chiu-hua Shan" for "there were not merely nine ordinary mountain peaks, but nine flowering mountain peaks."

It was, however, only after the coming of Chin Ch'iao-chio (金喬覺) in A.D. 754 that the mountain acquired its great reputation for holiness, when it became known that the great and merciful bodhisattva Ti-ts'ang was re-incarnated in him.

The Taipings destroyed a number of the old buildings, but much is still standing, among other things the great monastery of "Hua-ch'eng Ssŭ" (化城寺), dating from the eighth century. Behind this stands a pavilion which contains the Chinese Tripitaka, presented to the monastery by the emperor Wan Li of the Ming dynasty.

Besides these, the best-known feature is the great pagoda, about which the pilgrim bands march with slow reverend gait. On the open space in front of the pagoda is a big iron jar. The legend is that devout pilgrims, after two days of fasting, and clad in green, will, by standing in a certain position and gazing down into the depths of the jar, be able to catch a glimpse of the lost souls in hades and the "merciful Ti-ts'ang."

Among other objects worth seeing on Chiu-hua Shan are the old temples built on the rocks, "Tung-yai Ssŭ" (東崖寺) and "Pai-sui Kung" (百歲宮). In the latter place the skeleton of an old and holy abbot

PILGRIMAGES

overlaid with gold-foil is found. Crossing a deep valley one climbs the T'ien-t'ai Mountain (天台山), where some picturesque temples are also to be found.

The third sanctuary is Wu-t'ai Shan (五台山), situated in the northeast part of Shansi province. This rises in five terraces to a height of three thousand six hundred feet, which has given it the name "Wu-t'ai," the "Five Platforms." The tutelary god here, as has already been mentioned, is Wên-hsu (文殊), the bodhisattva of wisdom, who in ancient times manifested himself in the form of an old, white-haired man. One of his "silver hairs" still lies under the great white pagoda which adorns the spot. This is a meeting-place for the lamas from Mongolia and Tibet, and the Chinese Buddhist monks, so one sees the prayer wheels beginning to revolve here.

Of the one hundred and fifty monasteries and temples, twenty-four are occupied by the lamas. The chief director belongs to the Lama society and is called "Chang-chia Fu" (張家佛) (the "Buddha Who Is Always Renewed"). He is a very autocratic and aristocratic gentleman. As one might expect, the monastery's rites and the whole of the inner life of the place is strongly characterized by syncretism, as the two great streams of Buddhism meet. The rather difficult access to the place is accountable for the fact that there are fewer pilgrims here than is the case at P'ut'o and Chiu-hua.

The fourth great sanctuary is O-mei Shan (峨嵋山), far inland in Szechwan province. The mountain rises up like a huge cone from the plain, and with its picturesque slopes and remarkable mountain steps and buildings it is certainly without parallel in the whole world. From the six-thousand-foot crest one has the most marvellous view, not only of the fruitful plains of Szechwan, but also over the mountain wilderness toward Tibet. The mountain peak rises out of a plateau and reaches a height of eleven thousand feet above the sea.

That which has contributed not a little towards surrounding O-mei Shan with romance, is the fine mist which often lies over it, like a collar around the mountain top. When the sun breaks through, one sees the colours of the rainbow in its bursting brilliance, producing light effects of surpassing beauty.

It now passes for a true tradition that the great bodhisattva of mercy, P'u-hsien (普賢), has from ages past manifested himself on this mountain, riding on his white elephant. The emotional pilgrim who sees these light effects, naturally connects them with P'u-hsien, and believing that a vision has been granted to him is seized with rapture. Some have cast themselves in ecstasy from the outmost crest into the misty space and have disappeared in the depths. Whitened bones below tell the story of their last swift journey.

An enormous bronze figure of P'u-hsien on the elephant is erected in one of the largest temples. There are, in all, seventy temples and monasteries with fully two thousand monks. One of the most famous sights is the ruins of the bronze temple built by the

PILGRIMAGES

emperor Wan Li about the year 1600, afterwards destroyed by lightning. Of the fifty-six pagodas, there are two made of bronze, dating from the time of the Ming dynasty.

The place, a day's journey west of Kiating, is the great meeting-place for Tibetan lamas, Buddhists from Nepal, and monks from the various provinces of China.

Besides these great pilgrim centres, there is an enormous number of holy places and famous monasteries throughout China which attract pilgrims by the thousand; for example, Wei Shan in Hunan, now destroyed; Ku Shan (孤 山) in Fukien; and above all, the many beautiful monasteries and temples round Hsi Hu (西 湖, West Lake), at Hangchow. We cannot describe them all, for it would require an extra volume, but we shall give a general description of the pilgrim processions such as are found throughout the whole land.

There are, as a rule, special circumstances that send men on pilgrimages. Often it is sickness, often unfortunate business conditions or poor harvests, or such like, which lie behind these undertakings. Particular sins, and the calamities consequent upon them, are often to be expiated by such a pilgrimage. Occasionally, it is real religious need, the need of deeper spiritual experience and religious certainty, which drives them forth. The person concerned, who may be the son of the house, the father, or the brother (in many cases also a mother, a daughter, a widow, or a cast-off wife), goes first to the nearest temple

TRUTH AND TRADITION IN BUDDHISM

(preferably one dedicated to a certain Buddha or bodhisattva). There a vow is taken (fa-yüan, hsü-yüan, 發願, 許願) that the person concerned will go to a holy place, if help can be received. If help comes quickly, the pilgrimage is then an act of thanksgiving, and the promise is redeemed (huan-yüan, 還願). Often, however, it is a journey to seek help (ch'iu-ên, 求恩). Often the vow is a pledge of annual pilgrimages for so many years.

There are a great many points to be observed about the journey itself. The day of departure (usually in early summer or in the autumn) is decided, after consultation with a soothsayer (a chooser of days). A special costume is prepared, usually a yellow or a red waistcoat, upon which is sewn the Chinese character for the particular "mountain god." The red costume is generally worn by those who are going to expiate some especially grievous sins. These carry with them also a bowl in which stand sticks of incense, which must never die out. At every third step, these pilgrims cast themselves down on the ground and repeat their prayer for mercy.

When a band of pilgrims sets out, there is no demonstration; they depart in silence. There is no talking, and the eyes are not turned to left or right, as in groups of from ten to fifty they pace forward. The mind must not be distracted, neither must they let themselves be tempted to any sin, for then everything is in vain. The silence is broken only when the leader in high falsetto tones calls out a prayer formula. The rest join in on the second line.

PILGRIMAGES

The pilgrims eat only vegetarian food. Some take only a little rice porridge and water. After a few days' time, therefore, many of them present a very worn appearance. Mile after mile, day after day, the procession goes on in this manner. Often their feet become swollen, while exhaustion and sickness urge them to stop. But this is a bad sign, for it shows that their thoughts have not been held in check!

The inns along the way, during the pilgrim season, make special preparations for getting good patronage. Ornamental paper lanterns with grandiloquent inscriptions are hung out. An altar is made ready and prayer mats are laid out, for after the evening meal the pilgrims must conduct their worship. The pilgrims who travel by boat naturally carry their altar with them. A special mark on the sail, or a special pennant, signifies the fact that there are pilgrims, "hsiang-k'o" (香客), on board.

When they have arrived at their destination, they first go into an inn and wash, or preferably bathe themselves, and rinse their mouths. After that they proceed to the main temple and conduct their worship in a solemn manner. The large choir of Buddhist priests help the individuals with this. The great evening masses, in particular, with their large number of burning candles and extravagant amount of incense, have quite an overwhelming effect.

The pilgrims, by the hundred, lie upon the stone pavement in prayer while the priests stand before the altar and chant. Occasionally the pilgrims also break in with their verses of prayer.

[295]

TRUTH AND TRADITION IN BUDDHISM

The opportunity is taken at this time to enquire about the future. Dice are cast (ta kua, 打掛), lots are drawn (ch'iu-ch'ien, 求籤), slips of paper telling fortunes, are issued at a long table. In brief, the whole oracle machinery is set going, and money flows into the treasury of the monasteries and temples.

A heterogeneous mass of deities connected with the darkest animism come in for their share of worship. Social gods, and gods from other religions have their altars set up near the sanctuary of Buddhism, and they all receive homage also.

Then the pilgrims betake themselves home again and the same asceticism, the same worship, the same rules, are observed until they stand in their own door-yards once more. Death may have reaped his harvest there at home; perhaps the threads of misfortune have drawn themselves even tighter. Or it may be there is improvement to be seen. Expectation has stimulated the sick ones — and an answer to prayer is recorded. In such a case it is common to have, written or printed, slips of paper expressing gratitude, which are pasted up on walls and trees, expressions of thanks and homage to the mighty spirit, the gracious bodhisattva, who has so evidently answered prayer. Such news spreads and the "god's" fame is sung far and wide.

Perhaps this act is done in a still more solemn manner. The words of gratitude may be engraved upon beautifully painted and carved tablets of wood, and these "pien" (扁) are hung up in the temple concerned. Some temples are full to overflowing with such trophies!

[296]

PILGRIMAGES

As we have seen before, the monks themselves often go on long pilgrimages. A special book, a travellers' guide, has been prepared for them. The name of the book is "Chao Ssǔ Ta Ming-shan Lu-yin" (朝四大名山路引), "Guide for Travellers to the Four Famous Mountains."

CHAPTER X

PRESENT-DAY BUDDHISM IN CHINA

A few remarks about the special characteristics of modern Chinese Buddhism may not be amiss in conclusion.

According to recent investigations undertaken two years ago by Professor Hodous and the author, there are now approximately a million monks and nuns in China. The nuns are greatly in the minority, scarcely more than one-tenth of the entire number. An absolutely exact count is naturally difficult to make, as so many of the monks are wandering.

The greatest number are to be found in the coast provinces of Kwangtung, Fukien, Chekiang, and Kiangsu, together with Anhwei and Kiangsi. The number of monks is especially large in Chekiang and Kiangsu.

In inland provinces, like Hupeh and Hunan, however, and particularly Szechwan, there are quite a number and there are, of course, some to be found in all provinces. One also meets a good many in and around Peking, but except for the capital, there are comparatively few in northern China, and the discipline is much more lax. For example, it is quite common to find monasteries in the north in which they eat meat quite openly. The excuse is that they do not kill it themselves! Most of the temples in the north are in a very dilapidated condition.

Within the last ten years there have been enormous accessions of monks to the monasteries. This is

LOCHANA

PRESENT-DAY BUDDHISM IN CHINA

connected with the establishment of the Republic and the greater freedom which has thereby come, and also with the misfortunes of civil war and famine. It seemed at first as if the Revolution were going to inflict absolutely mortal wounds on the Buddhist society, but that was only at the beginning. Since then, the principle of religious freedom, as has already been mentioned, has won its way, and brighter times have come for the Buddhists.

Thus there is no longer so much talk of inspection by the state, and restrictions regarding the right of ordination have practically disappeared. The only thing that is stressed now is that the work shall be kept up, for if any buildings stand empty, or activities slacken, both buildings and worldly possessions are very quickly confiscated for public purposes.

The great accession of men during the last few years is probably also connected with the remarkable renaissance which in recent times has made a beginning within the Buddhist society. With no little understanding of the needs of the times, many of the best Buddhists have taken up for serious consideration the question of how the new era may best be brought in.

When Professor Hodous and the author undertook not long since a rather extensive tour of a number of the leading monasteries, they found everywhere a feverish activity in restoring temple halls and enlarging guest-rooms. This was partly due to the steadily increasing number of visits from bands of pilgrims, and the growing habit of many educated and seriously minded Confucian scholars and teachers of

TRUTH AND TRADITION IN BUDDHISM

withdrawing for shorter or longer periods of quiet contemplation and meditation in the monasteries. Special rooms are built for them. These people, who ordinarily are spoken of under the general term "chü-shih" (居士) (Buddhist devotees, "home Buddhists"), are very highly regarded. And with good reason, for one finds among them real intellectual culture combined with religious earnestness. A great deal of what often disfigures Buddhism, in the way of coarse, animistic superstition, is in a wonderful way discarded by these people, and they concentrate upon the deeper mystical and spiritual ideas in Mahayana. The better elements among the monks, especially the "Fa-shih" (法師) (explainers of the law) already mentioned, join themselves to this group of "home Buddhists," and this may lead to a greater revival still arising from among just this group.

A bridge might thus be built across that gulf which has from earlier days separated Buddhism in China from the sound, practical instinct of the people. This gulf is due to the unnatural demand for celibacy, and the consequent threat to home life. Could it be bridged, Buddhism would be bound more closely to the common life, even though it should continue to hold that some are called to the celibate life of the monk as a service to human society.

It is interesting to notice the theoretical grounds for, and the defence of, the meditation of the monks in the monasteries. When one asks the "home Buddhists" and monks, who carry on in common their holy contemplation and meditation, how they defend this

PRESENT-DAY BUDDHISM IN CHINA

quietist occupation, they will often give the answer: "This spiritual activity is in truth of the greatest importance for the race, for by it is laid up a fund of spiritual strength which is of benefit to all!" According to this idea, the monasteries should be centres of spiritual power for mankind. Thus spiritual energy, is, so to speak, generated and is available for the many who spend their lives in various kinds of work out in the difficult world.

A "chü-shih" of our time will go even further, however. He will say that periodical stays in a monastery, in the quiet practice of piety, will make him fitted for a better life-work. He has, in other, words, laid hold of the right principle. If only it could be carried out in life! As has been mentioned, one finds the majority of these "home Buddhists" in connection with the "Pure Land" School. For this reason the "Pure Land" is the most powerful school in modern Buddhism, both in China and Japan.

The leading monk in the new Buddhist movement is the famous T'ai-hsü (太虛). Besides him may be mentioned Yüan-yin (圓音). T'ai-hsü has joined forces with some deeply religious and energetic lay devotees from Chekiang, Kiangsu, and Hupeh provinces. The movement is especially strong in the Wu-han centre. There the Chü-shih have provided T'ai-hsü with the funds necessary for opening a Buddhist academy. This is situated in Wuchang and is styled "Fu-hsüeh-yüan" (佛學院). The author has had opportunity to see the place and attend some of the lectures. A group of about sixty students, mostly young monks of good education, listen daily to the eloquent and stirring lectures given by T'ai-hsü and the other "Fa-shih." The curriculum is practical and includes the study of some of the most urgent secular questions of to-day.

The chief point, however, is that the students are inspired to revive Buddhism and preach the "law of salvation" in such a way that they can meet the need of the new China. Allusion to the methods used in the Christian missions is often made and the students are exhorted to use similar methods. More than that, they are urged to study Christianity, which is thought to have some very good and helpful ideas, especially in regard to true compassion and self-denial. On the other hand, it is always pointed out that, in regard to the solution of the great metaphysical questions, Christianity is very much inferior to Buddhism. A number of handy text-books dealing with the history, doctrine, philosophy, and ethics of Buddhism have already been prepared. The lectures are afterwards printed and appear in the Buddhist magazine mentioned before (*Hai Ch'ao Yin*, 海潮音), or are published as tracts or books.

Inspired by the fervour of the young preaching bands from the academy in Wuchang, preaching halls have been opened in several streets of the Wu-han centre. In one of these halls the author recently found an immense image of Amitabha as "Chieh-yin Fu" (接引佛) (the "Buddha Who Receives and Leads On") placed in a conspicuous place facing the entrance and surrounded by a mighty number of electric bulbs. When the doors are opened for evening meeting the electric light is turned on, and the gold-covered and beautiful image beams with splendour. The impression on the hearts of the many people, who from childhood have heard about the "great compassionate Amitabha" is naturally very great.

The same Buddhists, headed by T'ai-hsü and some of the most energetic graduates from the academy, have also inaugurated a yearly "world conference for Buddhism" on Kuling, the great summer resort in the Yangtze valley. During the last conference representatives from the different Buddhist schools in Japan were present. Here on the ruins of the old "Ta-lin Ssŭ" (大林寺), where now a modern lecture hall in foreign style is built, some very stirring and interesting lectures have been given. A spirit of tolerance prevails, and the leaders very often invite broad-minded and sympathetic Christians to lecture on the Christian doctrine or any other religious topic. Similar preaching has gone on in several of the monasteries in Peking. There a special preaching work among the prisoners has also been started. A Young Men's Buddhist Association has also been formed. There is, however, a great lack of able leadership just in those circles, and the gift of endurance and steadfastness is manifestly lacking. Of a quite different character is the aristocratic Buddhist Academy conducted by the old Confucian scholar Ou-yang Ching-wu (歐陽竟無) in Nanking. He is a disciple of the famous Mr. Yang, who cultivated the

TRUTH AND TRADITION IN BUDDHISM

"Pure Land" doctrine at the time when many years ago Dr. Richard made special studies of Buddhism in the Nanking area.

During the fight for religious freedom which was waged especially in the first years of the Republic, a "fu-chiao hui" (佛教會), a Buddhist association, which was to look after the interests of the society in a more effectual manner, was formed among the Buddhists. This unification was necessary because the Buddhist society, while organically united as a single body, had never had any adequate organ for the expression of its unity. It lacked deputies elected for the purpose, who could speak on behalf of the whole society. The associations had managed with "elders" (ch'ang-lao, 長老) in each district,—a rather free and haphazard gathering of the most influential abbots and leaders. These again elected one or two to deal with the authorities in each district. The weakness of this arrangement was felt particularly when the Republic, with its well-known demagogues in power, began to put the screw upon the monasteries which had much of worldly possessions.

These difficult times have, however, given the Buddhist monks of larger vision and sympathy. They, supported by several prominent "chü-shih," succeeded very soon in forming a great Buddhist association ("fu-chiao hui") after the pattern of the Christians and the Confucians. Its establishment was perhaps not accomplished in the most democratic manner, nor was the election of officers any more so, but the main

PRESENT-DAY BUDDHISM IN CHINA

object was attained: a number of courageous and well-equipped representatives were sent to Peking, where, side by side with the Christian, Mohammedan, and Taoist representatives, they maintained the undying struggle for religious liberty.

It soon appeared that the president of the Republic, Yüan Shih-kai, as well as many of the delegates to the National Assembly, were in favour of making Confucianism the state religion, and laying heavy restrictions on all other religions. That they did not succeed in carrying this through, is owing largely to the energetic protests and agitation of the Christians and the Buddhists.

The Buddhists opened a special preaching-hall quite near the meeting-place of the National Assembly, where many of their best men were constantly and zealously working to influence the populace and the delegates. At the same time, local Buddhist associations were formed, with a central organization in the various provincial capitals. The sale of books was often connected with these. It was also at that time that the publication of Buddhist magazines, tracts, and pamphlets received an impetus.

For a while it looked as if this movement would lead to a real spiritual revival within the society, but it soon became evident that this was not being achieved. Indeed, now that more peaceful times have come, even the Buddhist association itself has collapsed to such an extent that it really has no more than a nominal existence, but should difficult times return, it would no doubt be revived and again play its part. No, revival must come from deeper sources, and there is really only one force that seems capable of achieving this end, namely the group of religious élite within the brotherhood of monks, working in connection with the best of the "home Buddhists" (chü-shih), men who have some of the power and glow of vital faith, such as we find in the "Pure Land" School.

We have quite frequently, in the earlier chapters, touched upon the various "schools" or "parties" (tsung, 宗) within Chinese Buddhism. We shall finally try to give a more condensed survey of these schools, and at the same time indicate which of the schools play any part worth mentioning in modern Buddhism.

The classification which the famous Chih-k'ai gave is largely of theoretical interest. He divides the Buddhist society into four principal divisions:

1. Shan-chiao (闡教), or the Hinayana School.
2. T'ung-chiao (通教), or the Translation School.
3. Pieh-chiao (別教), or the Mahayana School.
4. Yüan-chiao (圓教), or the Perfected School.

The following ten schools have been of practical importance:

1. The T'ien-t'ai School (天台宗), founded by Chih-i (智顗), with "The Lotus Scripture" as its principal sutra (described more fully in Chapter II).

2. The Hsien-shou School (賢首宗), founded by the monk Hsien-shou (賢首), also called Fa-ts'ang (法藏). He is said to have been the third patriarch after

PRESENT-DAY BUDDHISM IN CHINA

Manjusri's incarnation on Wu-t'ai Shan in Shansi. The school plays a minor part in northern China, but has altogether died out in the South. Its principal scripture was the "Hua-yen Ching" (華嚴經).

3. Lü-tsung (律宗), the great Legalistic School, with its principal stronghold on the famous "Precious Flower Mountain" (Pao-hua Shan, 寶華山) near Nanking. Here we have Buddhism in its most severe and ascetic aspect. Only two meals a day are eaten and nothing but tea is drunk. The monks are usually clothed in a dark gown. The school is quite prominent in the coast provinces.

4. Tz'ŭ-ên Tsung (慈恩宗), which, according to its name, emphasizes kindness and mercy, was founded by the monk Chieh-hsien (戒賢). He used the philosophical sutra "Wei-shih Lun" (唯識論) as his basis. A special form for meditation was used. It does not at present play an important part.

5. Chingt'u Tsung (淨土宗), the "Pure Land" School, described in detail in Chapter V, represents at present the most sincere and reforming spiritual power, in Japan as well as in China.

These five "tsung" (branches) are often called "chiao-mên" (教門), religious schools, in contrast to the Meditation School with its many "tsung-mên" (宗門), sub-divisions.

    6. Chü-shê Tsung (俱舍宗).
    7. Ch'êng-shih Tsung (成實宗).
    8. San-lun Tsung (三輪宗).
    9. Mi-tsung (密宗), or Chên-yen Tsung (眞言宗).

TRUTH AND TRADITION IN BUDDHISM

These four schools are now entirely merged in Bodhidharma's great and famous Meditation School:

10. Ch'an Tsung (禪宗). Of this we have already heard a good deal. The school divided out imperceptibly into a northern and a southern branch. The southern branch was the greater and produced a number of smaller divisions. These are also sometimes called "tsung," and confusion is thereby created. The right name for them, however, is chia (家), home, or family. Their names are:

    a. Wei-yang (潙仰).
    b. Lin-chi (臨濟).
    c. Ts'ao-tung (曹洞).
    d. Yün-mên (雲門).
    e. Fa-yen (法眼).

Of these, the Lin-chi family and the Ts'ao-tung family are the best known. The former is especially famous. It emerged in Shantung in the ninth century and had a great deal of influence among the educated classes. The reason for this was that the leaders of the school have constantly maintained that man in himself has the powers which are needed to attain sanctification, and can himself create his own happiness and overcome his difficulties, if only he has the right view of the true character of his human nature. This doctrine comes very close to the views of Confucius and a Confucian could therefore agree to meditation on this basis. A great many of China's monasteries and monks in our day are therefore anxious to maintain that their "home" is connected with the Lin-chi

BODHIDHARMA

PRESENT-DAY BUDDHISM IN CHINA

School. Indeed, even the officials (mandarins) of the old school adopted the rosary as a part of their official costume, to show that they were connected with this quite "Confucian meditation."

We shall mention only one of the schools that has died out or has been absorbed, the Mi-tsung or Chên-yen Tsung. As the name indicates, this was founded for the study of the mysterious. It therefore came to take up the remarkable Vairocana doctrine, which in the seventh and eighth centuries after Christ played such an important rôle in northern China. In Chapter II we have already spoken in detail of this doctrine, at that time known by the significant name of the "Great Sun Religion" (Ta-jih-chiao 大日教). Its apparent connection with the Nestorian Church (the Shining Religion) makes this school of more than ordinary interest.

It is worth while mentioning that during these last few years some of the most enterprising and religious monks in China have been very eager to revive the Mi-tsung (the school of mystery). T'ai-hsü has sent one of his ablest disciples to Japan to study this school, which in Japan's religious thinking still plays a great rôle. The monk has been sent to Japan not so much to bring back scriptures belonging to this special school (although many such scriptures still exist), but rather *to get into personal contact with the masters who have received the traditional sayings, rules, and mysteries from the old masters.* It is always stated that the real meaning of Mi-tsung can never be apprehended through a study alone, but personal contact with the masters is the main thing. These masters will be able to teach the three important things: *how to sit, how to use your mouth (in prayer and invocation), and how to think* (身口意漢相應). But the real spiritual experience will be a permanent secret between yourself and Buddha.

In Mi-tsung, all things and all conceptions can be thought of as animated by the great source of life, God, and the system may, to this extent, be called pantheistic. But all the emanations will finally return to the one centre, the heart, where the cosmic unity is revealed.

This school was early transplanted to Japanese soil, but since then the development in Japan has taken a somewhat different course. One finds there two additional schools, which really are purely Hinayana in character.

A religious awakening is to be felt in many parts of China, and the new religious life is manifesting itself in new forms, but behind them all Buddhism is to be traced. We shall only mention the fact that the greatest number of the many syncretistic religious associations, now springing up all over China, have received most of their ideas, as well as their form, from Buddhism. This is true of the "Tsai-li-mên" (在理門), which really is a special Kuan-yin cult, with the "T'ung-shan Shê" (同善社), "Wu-shan Shê" (悟善社), and "Tao-yüan" (道院).

In northern China, in the neighbourhood of China's ancient capital, Loyang, a row of colossal figures of Buddha are carved out of the solid rock. The place is called Lung-mên (龍門), and together with its counterpart in central China, Ch'i-hsia Shan (棲霞山), near Nanking, forms a regular eldorado for all students of oriental sculpture, so far as solid granite statues are concerned.

For those who study the religious history of the East with spiritual insight these figures of Buddha, hewn out of the rock, speak a language of their own. In them we see a symbol of the profound impression made by Buddhism upon the soul of the Chinese people. Deep, deep have the lines been chiselled—in thought, in viewpoint, in hope for the future, in resignation, in unutterable pain and grief, in deep longing after enlightenment and peace, in inexpressible sympathy with all that lives, and in a quiet and strong hope for the "salvation of all living."

If one wishes to understand China, one must see it in the light of Buddhism.

INDEX

Abbots (Fang Chang), 23, 157, 231, 235, 238, 239, 240, 244, 247, 257, 265, 266, 267, 268, 269, 272, 273, 274, 276, 277, 290, 304.
  Election of, 270 *ff*.
Abhidharma, 48, 204.
Absolution, 244.
Absorption into the absolute, 13.
Acolytes, 268, 273, 276.
Acts, of the Apostles, 219.
Adam, 89.
Adam's Peak, 183.
Adoption, 229–231.
Afghanistan, 30.
All-Embracing Master, The, 120.
All-Father, The Great, 112, 131, 145, 147, 176, 185.
Al-Makah, 183.
Amida Buddha Unsere Zuflucht, 132.
Amida Butsu, 144.
Amida Pul, 144.
Amitabha, 31, 33, 38, 39, 40, 41, 53, 74, 107, 112, 128, 131, 132, 133, 137, 141, 142, 144, 148, 149, 150, 151, 153, 155, 161, 168, 169, 176, 177, 180, 185, 198, 199, 201, 213, 214, 216, 217, 223, 254, 276, 282, 283, 302, 303.
Amitabha Sutra—"The Book of the Eternal in Time," 33, 53, 277.
Amita Yurdhyana Sutra. *See* Kuan-wu-liang-shou Ching.
Amogha, 89, 90, 93, 101, 107, 207, 245.
Ananda, 74, 87, 189, 198, 208, 215, 254.
Ancestors, Prayer for, 115.
Ancestors, Meditation for, 116.
Ancestors, Reverence for, 88, 229, 230.
Angels (Heavenly Spirits), 57, 59, 61, 145, 184, 194, 195, 196, 252, 254.
"Angel of the Golden Altar," The, 76.
Anhwei, 48, 114, 285, 289, 298.
Animism, 4, 105, 171, 296, 300.
Aniruddha. *See* O-na-lü.

Anshikao. *See* Arsaces.
Apes, 64 *ff*.
Apocalypse, 217.
Apollo, 171.
Apostles, The twelve, 162.
Arabian Seamen, 183.
Archangels. *See* Angels.
Archdeacon, 108.
Arhat, 51, 80, 81, 130, 187, 188, 243, 255.
Arsaces, 33, 42, 206.
Art treasures, 286, 289.
Aryans, 13.
Asceticism, 23, 150, 155, 182, 296.
Asoka, 16, 26, 27.
Associations:
  Young Peoples, 156.
  Prison, 156.
  Young Men's Buddhist, 303.
  Buddhist, 304, 305.
Asuras, 81.
Asvaghosha, 12, 29, 31, 127, 205, 226.
Atheism, 156, 204.
Atonement, 79, 113, 186.
Augustine, St., 153.
Avalokitesvara, 31, 39, 179.
Awakening of Faith, "Ch'i Hsin Lun," 30, 31, 127, 128, 143, 201, 226.

Bairath Stone, The, 27.
Bajagriha, 27.
Baptism, 58.
Baptismal Hymn, 90.
"Baskets," The Three, 203 *f*., 210.
Beal, Dr., 226.
Bells, 100, 104, 114, 260, 272, 273.
Benedict, Pope, 22.
Bethlehem, 163.
Bhaisajyaguru, 176.
Bhakti, 205.
Bhakti Movement, The, 30, 146.
Bhikshu, 141, 209, 243.
Bible, The, 35, 203.
"Bible," Buddhist, 203.
Bible references, 6, 7, 8, 80, 107, 113,

[313]

INDEX

114, 120, 125, 146, 147, 148, 153, 163, 164, 217, 221.
Blessings promised, 168.
Bodhi-tree, 280.
Bodhidharma, 16, 45, 46, 47, 49, 192, 193, 256, 308.
Bodhisattva:
  Of Mercy, 292.
  Of Wisdom, 291.
Bodhisattvas, 34, 40, 50, 51, 79, 80, 81, 94, 98, 100, 105, 109, 112, 113, 116, 118, 119, 124, 151, 162, 168, 171, 179, 180, 183, 185, 186, 188, 190, 192, 201, 208, 209, 210, 217, 218, 225, 244, 245, 252, 273, 276, 284, 285, 290, 291, 292, 294, 296.
Book of the Eternal in Time, The, 33, 53.
Book of the Six Patriarchs, The, 216.
Bouddhisme, Opinions sur l'histoire de la dogmatique, 132.
Brahmin, 29.
Brahma, 46, 125, 195, 254.
Brahma's Net. See "Fan-wang Ching."
Branding, 245 *ff*.
Bribes, 154.
Bridge of Death, 96.
Bronze Temple, 292.
Buddha, 10, 11, 12, 15, 16, 27, 29, 31, 34, 35, 36, 38, 39, 40, 44, 46, 50, 51, 52, 55, 67, 74, 86, 89, 92, 102, 103, 106, 114, 115, 116, 117, 118, 120, 124, 126, 127, 128, 141, 143, 145, 149, 150, 151, 152, 153, 155, 157, 158, 161, 162, 167, 168, 169, 170, 172, 174, 175, 176, 187, 190, 192, 195, 196, 197, 198, 199, 201, 202, 205, 208, 209, 210, 213, 215, 216, 217, 221, 222, 223, 225, 229, 239, 247, 252, 253, 254, 256, 259, 270, 273, 280, 281, 289, 310, 311.
Buddha, The Conquering, 76.
Buddha, The living, 103, 104, 105, 243, 277.
Buddha of boundless age and light, 40.
Buddha of Sweet Incense, The, 76.
Buddha of Wisdom (Father of Buddha), 39.
Buddha who is always renewed, The, 291.
Buddha who receives and leads on, 176, 302.

Buddha of unlimited life and light, 217.
Buddhas, The Compassionate or Merciful, 103, 112, 162, 238.
Buddhas, The great, 259, 284, 285, 294.
Buddhas, The Heavenly, 174, 176, 197, 276.
Buddha Candidates, 78, 79.
Buddha Charita Kavya, 12, 29, 205.
Buddha country, 142.
Buddha's disciples, 198, 256.
Buddhahood, 78, 79, 113, 120, 142, 179, 186, 225, 259.
Buddha Idea, The, 281.
Buddha Images, 15, 37, 54, 88, 102, 117, 118, 119, Chapter VI *passim*, 254, 256, 257, 258.
Buddha Incarnation, 105, 125, 130, 141.
Buddha's Mark, 125, 245.
Buddha's Peak, 289.
Buddha posture, 280.
Buddhism and Buddhists in China, 199.
Buddhism as a Religion, 199.
Buddhism, Higher, 4, 5.
Buddhism, Modern, Chapter X *passim*.
Buddhist Academy, 301, 302, 303.
Buddhist Associations, 303, 304, 305.
Buddhist brotherhood, 231, 232, 263.
Buddhist China, 110, 193.
Buddhist Councils, The Three Great, 27.
Buddhist decalogue, 240-242.
Buddhist gods, 59, 64, 66, 162, Chapter VI *passim*.
Buddhist hell, 81, 82, 85, 94, 172, 208.
Buddhist Language, 263.
Buddhist Library, 3, 213 *f*., 256.
Buddhist Literature, 2, 10, 11, 12, 13, 15, 16, 27, 28, 42, 43, 50, 51, 54, 59, 64, 72, 74, 89, 134, 141, 144, Chapter VII *passim*, 257, 263.
Buddhist magazines, pamphlets, and tracts, 185, 213, 263, 302, 305.
Buddhist missionaries, 12, 24, 32.
Buddhist Monastery:
  Plan and arrangement, site, etc., 249 *ff*.
  Rites and inner life, 291.

[314]

INDEX

Buddhist music, 274.
Buddhist Pantheon, Chapter VI *passim*.
Buddhist philosophy, 226.
Buddhist poetry and poems, 101, 134, 135, 146, 204, 207, 208.
"Table Song," 238.
Buddhist priesthood, 84.
Buddhist Relics, 11, 12, 16, 18, 42, 44, 259, 289, 291.
Buddhist Renaissance, 23, 24, 299, 301.
Buddhist Ritual, 238.
Buddhists, 7, 13, 14, 18, 24, 26, 27, 44, 46, 48, 49, 51, 59, 147, 151, 154, 156, 159, 164, 175, 188, 195, 200, 214, 248, 249, 253, 257, 260, 263, 275, 282, 284, 287, 293, 299, 303, 304, 305.
Buddhists, Home, 300, 301, 306.
Buddhist Scholars, 11, 12, 49, 212, 226.
Buddhist Schools, 303.
Buddhist Society, The, 111, 115, 149, 154, 160, 199, 211, 215, 228, 229, 231, 233, 255, 264, 299, 304, 305, 306.
Buddhist Text-books, 302.
Buddhist Trinity, 2, 102, 105, 106, 131, 149, 151, 161, 172, 174, 176, 197 *ff.*, 254, 255.
Buddhist Worship, 243.
Bunyiu Nanjio, 212.
Burma, 28, 42.
Burnout, 221.

Caiaphas, 58.
Candle Boats, 97.
Canon:
  The Northern, 212.
  The Southern, 212.
Catalogues, 204, 211, 212.
Catechism, 157, 164 *ff.*
Catholicos, 108.
Cave of the roar of billows, The, 287, 288, 289.
Celibacy, 17, 228, 300.
Ceylon, 28, 42, 183.
Chai-kung, 165.
Chai-p'o, 165.
Chang-chia Fu, 291.
Chang Chien, 10.
Chang Chi-tsung, 60.
Chang-chow, 262.

Ch'ang-lao, 304.
Ch'an-mên Jih-sung, 134, 227.
Ch'an-t'ang. *See* Hall of Meditation.
Chanting, 272 *ff.*
Ch'an-ting, or Nieh-p'an, 78.
Ch'an Tsung (Meditation School, The), 46, 47, 48, 53, 55, 151, 198, 227, 288, 308 *ff.*
Chao Ssŭ Ta Ming-shan Lu-yin, 297.
Ch'ao-yin Tung, 287.
Ch'a-ti-li, 44.
Chekiang, 48, 135, 141, 161, 162, 285, 298, 301.
Ch'en Dynasty, 16.
Chêng-fa, 87.
Cheng-fa-yen ts'ang, 271.
Ch'êng-fu, 35, 78.
Ch'êng-huang (city gods), 84.
Ch'êng-huang miao, 84.
Ch'eng-shih Tsung, 307.
Ch'êng-tsan Chingt'u Fu Shê-shou Ching, 206.
Chên-ju, 36, 37.
Cherubs, 195.
Chia (family), 230, 256, 263, 271, 308.
Chia. *See* Hui-yüan.
Chia-chan-yen, 189.
Chia-li-chia, 191.
Chia-no-chia-fa-ts'o, 191.
Chia-no-chia-po-li-to, 191.
Chiao-mên, 307.
Chiao-shou (examiner), 240.
Chia-pei-o-êrh, 56.
Chia-sha (begging coat), 242, 243, 247.
Chia Yeh. *See* Kasyapa.
Chieh (sphere), 80.
Chieh-ch'i, 239.
Chieh-hsien, 307.
Ch'ieh Lan, 193.
Ch'ieh-mo (confessor), 240.
Chieh-t'ai, 235.
Chieh-yin Fu, 176, 302.
Chien-chai T'ien-shên, 194, 195.
Chien-chih. *See* Sêng-ts'an.
Chien-lao Ti-shên, 194.
Ch'ien Lung, 212.
Chien Yüan (administration), 266.
Chih-k'ai or Chih-i, 48, 49, 50, 53, 55, 106, 204, 262, 306.
Chih-k'o (Host), 267.
Chihli, 14.
Chih-shih (assistant manager), 266.
Ch'i-hsia Shan, 311.

[315]

INDEX

Ch'i Hsin Lun, 31, 127, 143, 201, 226.
Ch'ih-kuo T'ien-wang, 194, 195, 252.
Ch'ih-shêng-huo, 196.
Chin Ch'iao-chio, 109 *ff.*, 290.
Chin Dynasty, 10.
    Eastern Chin, 14.
    Later Chin, 14.
Ching (The Scriptures), 203.
Ch'ing-chên, 60.
Ching Chiao, 107.
Ch'ing-ch'u-tsai, 196.
Ching-fêng-shan, 56.
Ch'ing-hsi, 189.
Chingt'u (*See* Pure Land School), 6, 21, 31, 32, 40, 41, 53, 55, 62, 99, Chapter V *passim*, 175, 307.
Chingt'u Wên, 139 *f.*
Chingt'u yüan, 170.
Ch'ing-yu, 191.
Chin-kang Ching, 195, 222.
Chin-kang shên (Cherubs), 195.
Chinkiang, 23.
Ch'in-kuang, 83.
Ch'i-shu-chi-ku-tu Yüan, 114, 217.
Ch'iu-chieh, 240.
Ch'iu Ch'u-chi, 63.
Ch'iu-ên (To seek help), 294.
Chiu-hua Shan, 109, 110, 114, 250, 285, 289, 290, 291.
Chiu-tzŭ Shan, 290.
Chi-yüan, 159.
Chorals, German, 275.
Chou Dynasty, 14.
Chou-shan Archipelago, 285.
Christ, 56, 107, 159, 163, 164, 184, 200, 309.
Christianity, 2, 4, 6, 21, 24, 64, 107, 112, 146, 148, 157, 158, 159, 163, 164, 275, 302.
Christianity, Influence of, 132, 146, 156, 158, 226.
Christian Church, 158, 275.
Christian Churches, 268.
Christian Doctrine, 303.
Christian Missions, 302.
Christian Mission to Buddhists, 56.
Christians, 303, 304, 305.
Christmas Tree, 178.
Chü (prayer rug), 242, 243, 247, 254, 273.
Chuang-tse, 130.
Chuang-yen, 209.
Chuan-lun, 83.

Chu ch'an-t'ang, 248.
Ch'u-chia-jên, 228.
Ch'u-chiang, 83.
Chüen Hsiu Chingt'u Ch'ieh-yao, 157.
Chu-fa-lan. *See* Gobharana.
Chu-hung, 157.
Chung, 215.
Chu-pa-chieh, 73 *ff.*
Ch'u shêng, 86.
Chü-shê Tsung, 307.
Chü-shih, 165, 300, 301, 304, 306.
Ch'ü T'ang Ching, 63.
Chu-t'ien, 184, 193, 253, 254.
Chu-t'u-pan-t'o-chia, 191.
Commandments, 237, 240–242.
Concentration, 152, 167.
Confession Litany, 276.
Confession of sin, 170, 224, 243, 244.
Confiscation, 23, 299, 304.
Confucian gods, 64, 66.
Confucianism, 17, 305.
Confucianists, 218, 304, 308.
Confucian Meditation, 309.
Confucian Scholars, 299, 303.
Confucius, 165, 195, 308.
Consecration of images, 173.
Consecration of laymen, 241.
Conversion, 224.
Corporal punishment, 239, 257, 279.
Cost of Masses, 99.
Couling, S., 199.
Councils, 26, 27.
Cremation, 258, 259.
Crucifix, The, 176.
Cycle, 78 *ff.*, 172, 186.
Cymbals, 272.

Daruma, 46.
Death, preparation for, 166.
Degrees, Literary, 270.
Demon worship, 4.
Devas, 162, 184, 193, 194, 195, 241, 253, 254.
Dharma (Fa), 27, 55, 106, 200, 204.
Dharmakara, 40, 141 *f.*, 217.
Dharmakaya, 200.
Dharmarakcha, 97, 114, 218.
Dhyani School, 46.
Diamond Scripture, The, "Chin-kang Ching," 195, 222.
Dice, 296.
Dipankara, 141, 178.
Disciples, The twelve, 235.

[316]

INDEX

Doctrine, The, 13, 27, 47, 102, 106, 117, 126, 165, 197, 198, 253.
Dominicans, 22.
Doré, 193.
Dove, 186.
Dragon Throne, The, 18.
Drama, 144.
Dream of Emperor Ming, 9, 11.
Drum beating, 272, 279.
Dynasties:
  Ch'en, 16.
  Chin, 14.
  Chou, 14.
  Han, 10, 15, 56.
  Manchu, 21, 22.
  Ming, 20, 146, 157, 207, 212, 213, 290, 293.
  Sui, 16.
  Sung, 14, 15.
  Tang, 16, 63, 75, 109.
  Wei, 14.
  Yüan, 207.

Eastern Buddhists, The, 159, 282, 284.
Eastern Paradise, 199.
Ecstasy, Religious, 286, 292.
Edicts, 15, 18, 22, 69.
Einstein, Professor, 86.
Ê-hun, 85.
Ê-kuei, 85.
Elephant, 188, 202, 205, 292.
Emotion, Religious, 275.
Emperors:
  Oh'ien Lung, 212.
  Chih Tê, 109.
  Hsiao Wu Ti, 14, 15.
  Hsien Tsung, 18.
  Hsüen Tsung, 17, 89.
  Hui Tsung, 19.
  Hung Wu, 212.
  Jên Tsung, 19.
  K'ang Hsi, 21, 22, 60, 61, 158.
  Kao Tsu, 17.
  Kublai Khan, 19, 63.
  Kuang Wu Ti, 61.
  Liang Wu Ti, 16.
  Ming, 9, 11.
  Ming Ti, 15.
  Su Tsung, 17.
  Tai Tsung, 17.
  Wan Li, 290, 293.
  Wu, 10.
  Wu Tsung, 17, 18, 20.

Yung Chêng, 212.
Yung Lo, 212.
Empress Shan-hsiao, 213.
Emptiness, The doctrine of, 215.
Encyclopædia Sinica, 199.
Endless Hell, 121.
Enlightened One, The, 34, 208.
Enlightened Ones, 152.
Enlightenment, The great, 110, 152, 154, 189, 280.
Enlightment, 239.
Episcopos, 108.
Essence-body, 200, 258.
Eunuchs, 17.
Expiation of sin, 293, 294.
Expositions, Daily, 270, 277.

Fa-chu, 108.
Fa-hsien, 43, 44, 45.
Fa-hua Ching. See "Lotus Scripture," The.
Faith, 2.
Fa-lo-p'o-ssŭ, 191.
Fa-lun miao chuan, 200.
Fa-mên, 204, 282.
Fan ching, 54, 214.
Fang yen-k'ou (Filling the hungry mouths), 102, 104, 105.
Fan-wang Ching, "Book of Brahma's Net," 210.
Fan-yin Tung, 289.
Farquhar, Dr., 30.
Fa-shê-lo-fu-to-lo, 191.
Fa-shên, 200.
Fa-shih, 106, 199, 234, 269, 277, 300, 302.
Fasting, 94, 290.
Fa-t'ang (Law Hall), 257.
Father in God, 235.
Fathers, Buddhist, 149, 150, 192, 193, 219, 266.
Fathers, Indian, 193.
Fa-ts'ang, 306.
Fa-yen, 308.
Fa-yüan Chu Lin, 10.
Fa-yu Ssŭ, 289.
Feast for the Wandering Souls, 90, 92 *ff.*
Feasts, Ordination, 243, 244.
Fêng-shui, 260.
Fên-shên, 124.
Ferry-boats, 221.
Festivals:

INDEX

Spirit Festival, 18, 97.
Idol, 84.
Seven times seven, 88, 99.
Wandering Spirits (Souls), 90, 92.
Kuan-yin's birthday, 180.
Great Festivals, 274.
Special Festivals, 284.
Filial piety, 118.
Finger manipulations, 95, 103, 104.
Fish ponds, 251, 253.
Forbidden City, 20.
Fortune telling, 296.
Fragrant beating boards, 257, 267, 279.
Franciscans, 22.
Freedom, Religious, 23, 299, 304, 305.
Free thinkers, 149.
Fu, 34, 35, 55, 132, 145, 155, 173, 198.
Fu-chiao hui, 304.
Fu-hi, 214.
Fu-hsüeh Tz'u-tien, 214.
Fu-hsüeh-yüan, 301.
Fujishima, L., 132.
Fukien, 287, 293, 298.
Fu-lou-na, 189.
Fu-pên-sing Ching. See "Buddha Charita Kavya."
Fu-shuo O-mi-t'o Ching, 206, 216.
Fu-ssū (assistant manager), 266.
Fu-t'o, 34.
Fu Yih, 11, 17.

Gandhara art, 30.
Ganges, 11, 27, 126.
Genku Honen, 132.
Geomancers, 260.
Gobharana, 12, 32, 205.
Gobi, 44.
God, 5, 6, 7, 21, 56, 57, 61, 64, 78, 81, 82, 107, 112, 146, 164, 199, 200, 201, 310.
Goddess of Mercy. *See* Kuan-yin.
God of Literature, 195.
God of War, 195.
Gods, 286, 296.
Golden Island, 23.
Gonshin, 132.
Gospels, The, 219, 221.
    Gospel of Mark, 226.
Gotama, 34, 38, 40, 141, 143, 174, 187, 205.

"Great Sun Religion," The, 106, 107, 108, 135, 178, 309.
Great Sun Scripture, The, "Maha Vairocana Sutra," 106, 108.
Great Vehicle (Mahayana), 1, 28, 42.
Greco-Scythian culture, 171.
Greco-Scythian people, 28.
Greece, 3.
Greek Catholicism, 30.
Greeting, One-thousand-fold, 276. *See* also under Nan-mo.
Guardians, The mighty heavenly, 168, 172.
Guest Halls (K'o-t'ang), 267, 269, 285, 286.
Guide to Buddhahood, The, 40, 225.

Haas, H., 132.
Hackmann, Herr, 199.
Hades (Hell), 68, 76, 82, 83, 85, 87, 91, 92, 95, 96, 100, 103, 104, 111, 112, 113, 114, 118, 119, 120, 121, 122, 123, 158, 161, 188, 208, 217, 290.
Hai Ch'ao Yin, 56, 263, 302.
Hall of Meditation, 152, 153, 155, 172, 248, 257, 258, 261, 267, 278, 280.
Han Dynasty, 10.
    First, 56.
    Western Han, 11.
Hangchow, 157, 161, 162, 183, 235, 254, 263, 293.
Hangmen-chiefs (Devil hangmen), 82, 83, 84, 85, 91, 92, 123, 172.
Hanlin, 75.
Han-shan-tse, 204.
Han-yu, 18.
Hardoon Edition, 212, 213.
"Heavenly Cave, Veiled with Curtains of Water," The (Happy Flower and Fruit Garden, The), 65, 68.
Heavenly Kings, The four, 194, 195, 252, 254.
Heavenly Mother Empress, 59.
Hellenistic mystical religions, 30.
Hêng Ha êrh chiang (Hêng, Ha), 195, 251.
Hêng Shan, 284.
Heresy, 157.
Hermits, 116, 286, 289.
Hinayana, 2, 4, 5, 26, 38, 42, 43, 50, 51, 55, 77, 78, 150, 190, 197, 202, 210, 223, 237, 242, 261, 282, 310.

[318]

INDEX

Hinayana School, 306.
Hinayanists, 245.
Hindu hells, 82.
Hinduism, 83, 146.
Historic documents, 286.
History of Tataghata Sakyamuni, The, 205.
Ho-chang, 276.
Hodous, Dr., 199, 200, 298, 299.
Holy Spirit, The, 135, 200, 201.
Home, The, 134.
Homes for blind and sick, 262.
Honan, 192, 284.
Honanfu, 11.
Honen, 133.
Hongwanzi, 212.
Hsan-tao, 32.
Hsia, 215.
Hsianfu, 75.
Hsiang, 201.
Hsiang-fa, 87.
Hsiang-k'o, 295.
Hsiang-pan (Beating boards), 257, 267, 279.
Hsiang-têng (waiters), 268, 279.
Hsiao Ch'êng (Hinayana), 4.
Hsiao Wu Ti, 14, 15.
Hsien (immortals), 68.
Hsien-lo, 109, 110.
Hsien-shou, 306.
Hsien-shou School, 306.
Hsien Tsung, 18.
Hsi-fang-chieh, 139, 217.
Hsi-fang Chi Lo Shih Chieh, Western Paradise, 2.
Hsi-ming, 157, 158.
Hsing-chê, 64.
Hsing-t'ang, 268.
Hsin-kuei-i (Heart at rest), 280.
Hsing-küng Tsun-t'ien, 194.
Hsin-lo or Silla, 109, 110.
Hsin Ming, 60.
Hsi-ta. *See* Siddharttha.
Hsi-tan (West party), 269, 272, 274.
Hsi-wang-mu, 70, 184.
Hsi Yu Chi, "An account of a journey to the west," 45, 63 *ff*.
Hsüan-chuang, 43, 45, 63, 72, 206.
Hsüan Fu P'u, 40, 225.
Hsüan Tsung, 17, 89.
Hsü-p'u-t'i. 67, 189, 208.
Hsü Yu-ch'i, Hsü-tao, 60.
Hua-ch'eng Ssŭ, 290.
Hua-kuang, 11.

Huang Chang-lun, 60.
Huang Hsin, 23.
Huan-yüan (Redemption of promise), 294.
Hua Shan, 284.
Hua-shên (Nirmanakaya), 200.
Huang-sui-ch'iu, 196.
Hua-yen Ching, "Buddhava-tamsaka-mahavaipulya Sutra," 37, 50, 108, 215, 307.
Hua-yen Hsüan-t'an, 215.
Hui-ko. *See* Shên-kuang.
Huei-lo (Instructor), 268.
Hui-nêng, 193.
Hui Tsung, 19.
Hui-yüan, 32, 129 *ff*., 135, 143.
Hu-chieh Lo-wang, 194.
Hunan, 16, 250, 284, 293, 298.
Hung-jên, 193.
Hupeh, 130, 298, 301.
Hung Wu, 212.
Huns, White, 11.

"I am now born for the last time," 175.
I-ch'ing, 43.
Images, 111, 112, 151, 162, Chapter VI *passim*.
Immanuel, 36.
Inana, 205.
Incarnations, 124, 125, 126, 180, 184, 185, 290.
Incense, 279 *f*., 294, 295.
India, 3, 5, 9, 10, 11, 12, 13, 14, 16, 18, 27, 28, 29, 30, 31, 32, 42, 44, 46, 48, 63, 88, 89, 171, 192, 205, 245.
Religious Literature of, 30.
Indian, an, 290.
Indian Buddhism, 2, 5, 109.
Indian deities, 11, 183, 186, 194, 195.
Indian monk, 287.
Indian religions, 197.
Indian symbol, 186.
Indiologues, 3.
Indra, 80, 82, 195, 196, 254.
Influence from the West, 3, 5, 9, 10, 11, 16, 29, 33, 132.
Inheritance, Right of, 271.
Inspector (Sêng-chih), 267, 268, 269, 272, 273.
Instructor (Wei-na), 152, 237, 239, 267, 272, 273, 276, 279, 280.
Instruments, Musical, 272, 273, 274.

[319]

INDEX

I-po (Keeper of wardrobe), 268.
Iran, 3, 4.
Isaiah, 36.
I-tu, 119.

Ja-ku-shi, 221.
Jan-têng Fu, 178.
Japan, 3, 4, 5, 24, 53, 54, 55, 109, 132, 133, 134, 144, 150, 156, 157, 159, 171, 190, 203, 212, 214, 219, 230, 277, 301, 303, 307, 309, 310.
Japanese, 286.
Japanese Buddhism, 24, 150.
Japanese Buddhists, 24, 46, 49.
Japanese Buddhist Schools, 303.
Japanese demands, 24.
Jen-tao, 80.
Jên Tsung, 19.
Jesuits, 21.
Jesus, 57, 59, 61, 163, 200.
Jewish characteristics, 193.
Jih-kung T'ien-shên, 194.
Jin-kuo, 81.
Jizo, 109.
Jodo, 132.
John, St., 163, 221.
Johnston, R. T., 110, 193.
Joseph, St., 62.
Judas, 57.
Judea, 57.
Ju-lai, 36, 37, 74, 75, 124, 127, 131, 174, 219.
Jullundur, 27.
Junan, 60.
Jupiter, 69.
Justin Martyr, 7.

K'ai-chio-wu, 152.
K'ai kuang, 173.
K'ai tan-k'ou, 263.
K'ai-yüan, 110.
K'ai-yüan mu-lu, 211.
Kahula. See Lo-hou-lo.
Kalpas (chieh), 82, 86, 118, 119, 120, 121, 122, 124, 125, 126.
K'ang Hsi, 21, 22, 60, 61, 158.
Kanishka, King, 27, 30.
Kao Tsu, 17.
Karma, 81, 186.
Karman, 205.
Kashmir, 28.
Kasyapa Matanga, 12, 32, 74, 189, 198, 254, 256.
Kempis, Thomas à, 146.

Kern, 219, 221.
Khotan, 11.
Kiangsi, 60, 129, 141, 285, 298.
Kiangsu, 161, 162, 298, 301.
Kiating, 293.
Kingdom of god, 199.
King from the West, 223.
Kitchen god, 195.
Kompendium der Religions-geschichte, 5.
Konow, Prof. Steen, 223.
Korea, 3, 49, 53, 109, 110, 144, 171, 203, 219, 230, 277.
Korean Buddhists, 46, 49.
K'o-t'ang (Guest Hall), 267, 269, 285.
Kshitigarbha, 109.
Kuang-mu T'ien-wang, 194, 195, 252.
Kuan-shên, 195.
Kuan wu-liang-shao, "Amita Yurdhyana Sutra," 53.
Kuan-yin, 2, 31, 39, 62, 71, 72, 73, 94, 104, 131, 134, 135, 161, 168, 179, 180 ff., 201, 213, 218, 223, 255, 256, 287, 288, 289, 310.
Kuan-yü, 255.
Kua-tan, 247.
Kua-tan-yüan, Yün-shui-t'ang, 248, 249, 263.
Kublai Khan, 19, 63.
Kuei Chieh (Feast of the Spirits), 18, 97.
Kuêi-tzu Mu-shên, 194.
K'u-fang, 262, 266, 269, 271, 272.
Kujo Kanezanes, Prince, 133.
Kuling, 303.
Kumarajiva, 33, 206, 210, 219.
Kung-miao, 264.
Kung-tê Tsun-shên, 194.
Ku Shan, 293.
Kutyayawa. See Chia-chan-yen.
Kwangtung, 287, 298.
Kyoto, 132, 159, 212.

Lalita Vistara, 205.
Lamaism, 19, 20, 173.
Lamas, 291, 293.
Lama society, 291.
Land of the Western Tribes, The, 56.
Lao-ho-shang, 244, 266.
Lao-tse, 71.
Law, The, 13, 34, 37, 44, 79, 106, 237.
Lay Buddhists, 40, 264, 265, 277, 301.

[320]

INDEX

Le bouldhism Japonais, 132.
Lecture courses, 277 ff.
Legalistic School, 198, 237, 255, 258, 282.
Legends, 9, 10, 284, 287, 290.
Legge, Professor, 43.
Leng-yen Ching, 80, 215.
Le-t'ai-pai, 290.
Liang Chi-chao, 31, 226.
Liang Wu Ti, 16, 46.
Li-fang, 10.
Li Li, 60.
Lin-chi, 308.
Ling Shan, 74, 190, 215.
Ling-yin Ssŭ, 161.
Lion, 188, 201, 224, 225.
Literati, 13, 15, 20, 206, 270.
Little Vehicle, Hinayana, 2.
Liu-tsu-t'an Ching, 216.
Lo-ch'a, 85, 169.
Lo-ch'ieh-hsi-na, 191.
Logos, The Eternal, 163, 164, 196, 221.
Logos Spermaticos, 7, 221.
Lo-han, 51, 81, 182, 187, 188, 190, 191, 192, 243, 245, 255.
Lo-han t'ang, 191, 255.
Lo-han, Golden, The, 76.
Lo-hou-lo, 189.
Lokaraksha, 33, 42, 206.
Lokesvararaga, 141 f.
Lo-ku-lo, 191.
Lots, Drawing of, 270.
Lotus-blossom, 59, 152, 158, 161, 175, 176, 185, 217, 251, 281
Lotus Scripture, The, 31, 52, 54, 106, 181, 218, 221, 306.
Loyang, 11, 12, 14, 46, 206, 310.
Lü, the law, 203, 210.
Lu-feng (Monastery), 130.
Lü-men ch'ih-sung, 237.
Lun (essays), 203, 210.
Lung-hu Shan, 60.
Lung-mên, 311.
Lung-shu. See Nagarjuna.
Lung-wang Shui-shên, 194.
Lü Shan, 129, 130, 192, 285.
Lu-shê, Lochana or Lu-shê-na, 106, 178, 198, 201, 255.
Luther, 133, 153.
Lü-tsung (Legalistic School), 151, 153, 282.
Lü-tsung's Law-Books, 216.

Madonna, 62, 184, 255.
Madonna of the East, 180.
Magadha, 11.
Magi, 163.
Magic arts, 68, 71, 88, 90.
Magic formulæ, 216, 225.
Mahahasthanaparapta, 186.
Maha Maudgalyayana. See Mu-lien.
Mahapragnaparamita Sutra. See Ta Pan Jo Ching.
Mahayana, 1, 2, 3, 4, 5, 6, 7, 16, 26, 27, 28, 29, 30, 31, 32, 33, 34, 35, 36, 37, 38, 41, 42, 43, 44, 45, 49, 50, 51, 52, 54, 55, 56, 63, 64, 72, 74, 77, 79, 87, 90, 109, 113, 127, 129, 131, 132, 135, 143, 145, 146, 154, 164, 171, 185, 190, 198, 200, 201, 203, 204, 210, 211, 212, 215, 216, 218, 223, 226, 243, 283, 300.
Mahayana School, 28, 306.
Maitreya, 44, 87, 125, 186 ff., 277.
Ma-ming. See Asvaghosha.
Manchu dynasty, 21, 22.
Manchuria, 144.
Mandarins, 309.
Manjusri. See Wên-shu, 119, 188, 307.
Mantras, Mystical, 45, 88, 90, 101, 102.
Marco Polo, 192.
Maria. See Virgin Mary.
Masses, 18, 77, Chapter IV passim, 130, 135, 151, 160, 161, 188, 197, 216, 217, 233, 237, 244, 246, 247, 248, 268, 272, 274, 275, 276, 277, 288, 295.
Masses for the Dead, 137 ff., 216, 223, 256, 264, 267, 276, 289.
Mass-litany, 242.
Masters (Mo-ho-sa), 197, 208, 277, 309, 310.
Mataṅga (Kasyapa Mataṅga), 12, 32, 74, 189, 205.
Maudgalyayana. See Mu-lien.
Mâyâ (Buddha's Mother), 121, 122, 184, 208.
Ma Yüan, 61.
Medicine of Life, 19.
Meditation, 16, 23, 47, 78, 110, 113, 116, 125, 142, 146, 150, 152, 153, 155, 205, 211, 216, 225, 232, 233, 248, 258, 260, 261, 265, 266, 268, 269, 278 ff., 300, 301, 307, 308.

[321]

INDEX

Meditation, Hall of, 152, 153, 155, 172, 248, 249, 257, 258, 261, 267, 278, 230.
Meditation School, The (Ch'an Tsung), 46, 47, 48, 53, 55, 151, 153, 198, 237, 282, 288.
Memoirs of Famous Monks, 43.
Merit, 170.
Messiah of Buddhism, 187.
Mesopotamia, 3.
Miao-chin, 182.
Miao-shan, 182, 183.
Miao-yin, 182.
Mi Chiao, 108.
Mi-chi Tsun-shên, 194.
Middle Kingdom, the, 12.
Millennial kingdom, 87, 187.
Mi L'o Ching, 168.
Mi-lo Fu, 87, 125, 186 *ff.*, 201, 251, 252, 255.
Mi-lo-Hsia-shêng Ching, 187.
Min, 111.
Ming dynasty, 20, 146, 157, 207, 212, 213, 290, 293.
Ming, Emperor, 9, 11.
Ming Ti, 15.
Minos, 83.
Miracles, 285.
Missionary, The Christian, 164.
Missions, Christian, 6, 302.
Missionary Motive, 7.
Missionary work, Modern, 156.
Mithras, 33.
Mithridates, 10.
Mi-tsung (Yü-chia-tsung), 108, 307, 309, 310.
Mo-fa, 87, 188.
Mohammedans, 41, 305.
Mohammedanism, 60, 146.
Mo-ho-chia-yeh. *See* Matanga.
Mo-i T'ien-shên, 194.
Mo-li Wen-wang, 194.
Monasteries:
    Ch'ang Ts'iun, 16.
    Chao-ch'ing Ssŭ, 235.
    Chiao Shan, 275.
    Heavenly River, 23.
    Hua-ch'eng Ssŭ, 290.
    Ku-lin, 235, 236.
    Ling-yin Ssŭ, 161.
    Liu Yün, 224.
    Lu-feng, 130.
    Pao-hua Shan, 198, 235.
    T'ien-ning Ssŭ, 262, 263.
    Tung-lin, 130.
    Yün-ch'i, 157.
Monasteries, Management of
    Administration department, 262 *ff.*, 269, 271.
    Guest department, 267, 269.
    Department of instruction and worship, 267, 269.
    Lax discipline, 298.
Monastery plan and layout, 248 *ff.*
Monastery and temple, Difference between, 264.
Monastic Life, Chapter VIII *passim*.
Mongolia, 3, 19, 20, 173, 291.
Mongolian, language, 34, 185.
Mongols, 13, 14.
Monk Families, 230.
Monks, Wild, 233, 286.
Moral conditions in nunneries and temples, 160.
Motives for becoming monks, 231 *ff.*
Mountains
    Ch'i-hsia Shan, 311.
    Chiu-hua Shan, 109, 110, 114, 250, 285, 289, 290, 291.
    Chiu-tzu Shan, 290.
    Heng Shan, 284.
    Hua Shan, 284.
    Ku Shan, 293.
    Lung-hu Shan, 60.
    Lü Shan, 129, 130, 192, 285.
    Nan-yü Shan, 250, 284.
    O-mei Shan, 188, 250, 285, 291, 292.
    Pao-hua Shan, 198, 235, 236, 238, 307.
    Pao Shan (Fu-yu Shan), 60.
    P'ut'o Shan, 250, 285, 287, 291.
    Sung Shan, 192, 284.
    T'ai Shan, 82, 83, 250, 284.
    T'ien T'ai Shan, 48, 55, 285, 291.
    Wei Shan, 293.
    Wu-t'ai Shan, 188, 250, 285, 288, 291, 307.
Mu-lien, Mo-ho-mu-chin-lien, 91, 92, 114 *ff.*, 189.
Mutilation, Self, 288.
Mystery School, 308, 309.
Mysticism, 40, 171, 215, 300.
Mystics, 41.

INDEX

Nagarjuna, 29, 31, 127, 128.
Names of monks and nuns, 228, 229.
Nan-hai. *See* Southern Sea.
Nan-hai chun tʻi, 184.
Nanking, 16, 46, 47, 48, 56, 192, 198, 212, 226, 235 236, 303, 304, 307, 311.
Nan-mo, 273, 274, 276.
Nan-yü Shan, 250, 284.
National Assembly, 305.
Negations, 128.
Nepal, 4, 28, 293.
Nestorian Church, 77, 88, 89, 106, 107, 108, 109, 120, 132, 134, 146, 158, 161, 162, 186, 309.
Nestorianism, 4, 41, 64.
Nestorian Monument in China, The, 77.
New Testament, The, 153.
New Testament of Higher Buddhism, The, 221.
New Year, 265.
Nieh-pʻan Ching, "Paradise Scripture," 52, 225.
Nien-fu Tʻang, 155.
Night masses, 101.
Ni-ku miao (nunnery), 236, 265.
Nimbus (Yüan-kuang), 175.
Ningpo, 183, 263, 285, 287.
Nirmanakaya, 200.
Nirvana, 52, 78, 126, 149, 175, 180, 225, 259.
No-chü-lo, 191.
Norway, 223.
Novices, 229 *ff*.
Nuns:
  Ordination of, 265.
  Number of, 298.

Obedience to parents and ancestors, 117, 118.
Offerings of food, 95, 99, 117, 118.
Officials, 270.
Official groups in Monasteries, 270.
O-hsiu-lo, 82,
O-hsiu-lo-tao, 81.
Old Testament, 164.
O-mei Shan, 188, 250, 285, 291, 292.
O-mi-tʻo Ching, 40, 53, 142, 277.
O-mi-tʻo Fu, 31, 38, 39, 40, 104, 144, 145, 151, 176, 250, 251.
Om Mani padme hum, 185.
O-na-lü, 189.
O-nan-tʻo (O-nan), 189.

O-ni Tʻi-nan, 194.
Order of daily worship, 271 *ff*.
Orders in the cycle, 78 *ff*.
Ordination, 23, 197, 210, 231, 234 *ff*., 247, 254, 262, 264, 271, 299.
Ordination:
  Instruction for, 234, 236.
  Choice of place for, 235.
  Expenses of, 236.
  Length of course of, 236.
  Instruction
  The main course, 237 *ff*.
  Severity of course, 237.
  Discipline, 238.
  Rehearsals, 239.
  Age for, 240.
  Three degrees of, 240.
  First step in, 241, 242.
  Second step, 243.
  Third step, 244.
  Final ceremony, 245.
Ordination, Certificate of, 247.
Oregon, 253.
Orphanages, 156.
O-shih-to, 191.
Ou-yang Ching-wu, 226, 303.
Oxford University, 212.

Pai-ching-shui, 196.
Pai Lien Chiao, or White Lotus Religion, 130.
Pai-ma Ssŭ, 12.
Pagodas, 14, 44, 111, 117, 119, 258, 259 *ff*., 290, 291, 293.
Pali, 3, 28, 204.
Pan-jo-tʻang (Pan-tʻang), 257, 258.
Pan Ku, 11.
Pantheism, 310.
Pʻan-tʻo-chia, 191.
Pantomimes, 102.
Pao-hua Shan, 198, 235, 236, 238, 307.
Pao Shan (Fu-yu shan), 60.
Pao-shên (Sambhogakaya), 200.
Papal bull, 22.
Paper money, 95, 119.
Paradise, 142.
Paramartha, 30, 226.
Parthia, 10, 33, 206.
Parthian Prince, 206.
Party:
  East, 269, 272, 274.
  West, 269, 272, 274.
Pataliputra, 26.

[323]

INDEX

Pa-tê-lei, 57, 62.
Patriarchs, 16, 31, 46, 47, 89, 127, 192, 193, 216, 256, 306.
Paul, St., 6, 7, 113, 153.
Pei-t'u, 290.
Peking, 20, 212, 235, 298, 303, 305.
P'ên (large dish), 118.
Penitence, 286.
Penitence, Books of, 223, 224.
Pen-lai-ti mien-mu, 281.
Perfected School, 306.
Perfected Spirits, 179.
Persecutions, 14, 17, 18, 22, 23.
Persia, 3, 30.
Persian Influence, 30.
Persiologues, 3.
Philanthropies, 156.
Pi-ch'iu, 116, 117, 125, 209, 210.
Pieh-chiao, 306.
Pien, 296.
Pi'en-chêng, 83.
Pi-kuan, 260, 261.
Pilate, 58.
Pilgrimages, 42, 43, 72, 247, 248, Chapter IX *passim*.
Pilgrim centres, 293.
Pilgrims, 30, 43, 44, 45, 111, 114, 129, 130, 206, 224, 248, 251, 268, 286, 287, 288, 290, 292, 293, 294, 295, 299.
Pilgrim's Progress, The, 63.
Pills of immortality, 71.
P'i-lu-chê-na (Vairocana), 55, 105, 178, 198, 255.
P'in, 59, 62.
Ping-hsüeh, 60.
Ping-têng, 83.
Pin-t'ou-lu, 191.
Pin-tu-lo-pa-lo-to, 191.
Pirates, 288.
P'i-tu, 196.
Piyadasi, 27.
Platform, The ordination, 235 *ff*.
Platforms, The Five, 291.
Plato, 8
Po (begging bowl), 242, 243, 247.
P'o-liao hsüeh-hu, 96.
P'o-lo-mên, 46.
Polytheism, 163, 171, 204.
Pope, The, 21, 22.
P'o-pên-ts'an, 152.
Potaloka, 289.
Po-t'o-lo, 191.
Poussin, L. de la Vallée, 132.

Praise, Hymn of, 274.
Prajna, 89.
Pratimokkhas, 210.
Pratimoksha, 242.
Prayer, mats, rug, stool, 242, 243, 247, 254, 273, 295.
Prayer Service, 270.
Prayer Tower, 100.
Prayer wheels, 291.
Preaching Halls, 302, 303, 305.
Precious Hall of the Great Hero, The, 253.
Printing, 19, 211, 213, 263.
Printing Presses, 263.
Prisoners, Work among, 156, 303.
Propitiation, 113.
Prostration, 273, 276, 289, 294, 295.
Provinces:
  Anhwei, 48, 114, 285, 289, 298.
  Chekiang, 48, 134, 141, 161, 162, 285, 298, 301.
  Chihli, 14.
  Fukien, 287, 293, 298.
  Honan, 192, 284.
  Hunan, 16, 250, 284, 293, 298.
  Hupeh, 130, 298, 301.
  Kiangsi, 60, 129, 141, 192, 285, 298.
  Kiangsu, 161, 162, 298, 301.
  Kwangtung, 287, 298.
  Shansi, 14, 32, 129, 284, 285, 291, 307.
  Shensi, 284.
  Shantung, 82, 284, 308.
  Szechwan, 182, 285, 291, 292, 298.
P'u-chi Ssǔ, 288.
P'u-hsien, 188, 201, 202, 208, 252, 292.
Pu-k'ung Chin-kang, 89.
Punjab, 30.
Pure Land, 6, 21, 31, 32, 40, 41, 53, 55, 59, 99, Chapter V *passim*, 185, 201, 216, 218, 255, 277, 282, 301, 304, 306.
Pure Land Catechism, 157.
Pure Land Hymns, 131, 134, 221.
Pure Land Prayer, 139, 277.
Pure Land Scriptures, 252, 253.
Pure Land Song, 76.
Purgatory, 102, 222.
Purna. *See* Fu-lou-na.
P'u-sa (P'u-t'i-sa-to), 51, 79, 81, 173, 179, 196, 244.
P'u-t'i Shan-nu, 194.
P'u-t'i-ta-mo, 16, 46, 192, 256.

INDEX

P'ut'o, 20, 183, 250, 254, 285, 289.
P'ut'o Shan, 250, 285, 287, 291.

Qualities of Buddha's nature, 196.
Question boxes, 278.
Quotations from the sacred books, 39, 56–59, 61, 83, 93, 116–118, 120, 121–123, 124–126, 128, 136, 137, 138, 139, 140, 141, 142, 144, 145, 152, 157, 158, 165–170, 177, 181, 182, 183, 197, 198, 200, 201, 209, 217, 219–221, 222, 224, 225, 246.

Record of Buddhistic Kingdoms, 43.
Recherches sur les superstitions, 193.
Redemption, 64, 79, 87, 96, 98, 100, 103, 113, 118, 119, 120, 126, 161, 177, 215, 221, 281.
Regeneration, 275.
Reischauer, Professor A. K., 53, 132.
Religious Speculation, 9.
Renaissance, The Chinese, 23, 24, 156, 299.
Repentance, 224.
Republic, Chinese, 23, 299, 304, 305.
Reproduction, 173.
Research work, 3.
Resurrection, The, 58.
Retribution (Compensation), 81, 83, 84, 97, 112, 121, 125.
Revealer, The, 37.
Revival, Spiritual, 305, 306.
Revolution, The, 23, 24, 299.
Ricci, Matteo, 157.
Rice Christians, 148.
Richard, Dr. Timothy, 36, 128, 181, 221, 225, 226, 304.
Ritual, Books of, 227, 273.
Roman Catholic:
    Church, 157, 158.
    Mission, 22.
    Missionaries, 20, 21, 22, 158, 164.
    Mode of Thought, 61, 62.
Rosary, 186, 309.
Ross, Dr. E. D., 212.

Sabians, 183.
Sacred Books of the East Series, The, 218.
Saeki, Professor P. Y., 77, 90.
Sacred Books:
    Amitabha Sutra. See Wu-liang-shou Ching.
    Book of the Eternal in Time (Wu-liang-shou Ching), 30, 40, 53, 141, 205, 216.
Book of the Six Patriarchs (Liu-tsu-t'an Ching), 216.
Brahma's Net (Fan-wang ching), 210, 216, 237, 244.
Buddha Charita Kavya (Life of Buddha), 12, 29, 205.
Ch'an-mên Jih-sung, 134, 227, 237.
Ch'i Hsin Lun (The Awakening of Faith), 30, 31, 127, 128, 201, 226.
Fa-hua Ching, 52, 106, 181, 218.
Fan-wang Ching, 210, 216, 237.
Fu-pên-sing Ching, 205.
Fu-shuo O-mi-t'o Ching, 206, 216.
Great Sun Scripture, The Ta-jih Ching, 106, 108.
Guide to Buddhahood (Hsüan Fu P'u), 40, 225.
History of Tataghata Sakyamuni, The, 205.
Hua-yen Ching, 30, 50, 108, 215.
Hua-yen Hsüan-t'an, 215.
Kuan-wu-liang-shou Ching (Amita Yurdhyana Sutra), 142, 218.
Lalita Vistara, 205.
Leng Yen Ching, 80, 215.
Lotus Scripture (The Fa-hua Ching), 31, 52, 54, 106, 181, 218.
Lü-mên Ch'ih-sung, 237.
Lü-tsung's Law Book, 216.
Mi-l'o Ching, 168.
Mi-lo-Hsia-shêng Ching, 187.
Nirvana Scripture (The Nieh-p'an Ching), 52, 225.
O-mi-t'o Ching, 40, 53, 142, 216.
Pure Land Catechism (The Chüen Hsiu Chingt'u Ch'ieh-yao), 157.
Pure Land Scriptures, The, 52, 53.
Scripture of the Great Physician (Yao-shih Ching), 176, 221.
Shên-hsien Kang chien, 59, 159, 184.
Sukhavati Vyuha Sutra, The great. See Wu-liang-shou Ching.
Sukhavati Vyuha Sutra, The small. See O-mi-t'o Ching.
Survey of Systems of Salvation (Wan-fa Kuei Hsin Lo), 159.
Ta-jih Ching, 106, 108.
Ta-pan-jo Ching, 52, 224.
Ti-ts'ang Pên-Yüan Ching, 118, 223.

[325]

INDEX

Wei-mo ching, 225.
Wei-shih Lun, 225.
Yü-chia Yen-k'ou, 87, 223.
Yü-lan-p'ên Ching (Ullambana Sutra), 97, 114.
Sakyamuni, 38, 39, 44, 46, 50, 55, 79, 86, 87, 91, 102, 104, 106, 151, 174, 175, 176, 198, 199, 201, 205, 208, 213, 215, 221, 222, 229, 254, 282.
Salvation, 165, 166, 169, 186, 190, 217, 221, 223, 231, 251, 282, 283.
Salvation by Faith, 2, 132, 142, 150, 151, 153, 160, 172, 226, 282.
Salvation by Works, 150, 161.
Salvation, Law of, 302.
Samantabhadra. See P'u-hsien.
Sambhogakaya, 200.
Samghapala, 206.
San-chih T'ien-shên, 194.
Sangha (Society), 27, 102, 106, 117, 126, 141, 143, 195, 197, 198, 228, 229, 231, 233, 253.
San-lun Tsung, 307.
San-pao, 117, 197, 253.
Sanskrit, 3, 19, 20, 28, 34, 36, 81, 106, 114, 119, 134, 176, 188, 197, 204, 206, 207, 209, 210, 215, 216, 218, 219, 222, 223, 229, 241, 259.
Sanskrit Scholar, 223.
San-ts'ang, 203.
San wu tao, 82.
Sariputra. See Shê-li-fu.
Saviour, 164.
Saviour from the West, The, 112.
Schools:
  Amida, 24, 132.
  Ch'êng-shih Tsung, 307.
  Chü-shê Tsung, 307.
  Dhyani, 46.
  Great Sun, 107, 178.
  Hinayana, 306.
  Hsien Shou (Fa ts'ang), 306.
  Lü-tsung or Legalistic, 151, 198, 237, 255, 258, 282, 288, 307.
  Mahayana, 28, 306.
  Meditation or Ch'an Tsung, 46, 47, 48, 53, 55, 151, 198, 221, 227, 237, 282, 288, 308 ff.
  Mi Chiao, 108.
  Mi-tsung, 108, 307, 309, 310.
  Pure Land or Chingt'u, 21, 31, 32, 40, 41, 53, 55, 62, 99, Chapter V passim, 175, 195, 201, 216, 282, 301, 306, 307.

San-lun, 307.
Shinran (Shin-Shu), 24, 132.
Special, 226, 276.
T'ien-t'ai, 49, 50, 52, 53, 54, 55, 106, 292, 306.
Tz'ŭ-ên Tsung, 307.
Vairocana, 108.
Yogacharya, 89.
Scripture of the Great Physician, 176, 221.
Sculpture, 20, 171, 191, 311.
Sea of Sorrow, The, 147.
Secret Societies, 233.
Sects, 4, 47, 218, 237. See also Schools.
Secular order, 19 ff.
Sêng, 108, 228, 255.
Sêng-chih (Inspector), 267, 268, 269, 272.
Sêng-ts'an, 193.
Sha-ho-shang ("Sand Monk"), 73 ff.
Sha-mi, or Sha-mên, 241, 243.
Sha-mi Shih-chieh, 210.
Sha-mi-t'ou, 239, 240, 244.
Shan-chiao, 306.
Shang, 215.
Shanghai, 214, 224, 263, 287.
Shang-ti, 21.
Shan-kên (Good root), 81, 113, 222.
Shansi, 14, 32, 129, 284, 285, 290, 307.
Shan-tao, 131.
Shantung, 82, 284, 308.
Shao-hsiang (Acolyte), 268.
Shê-chieh, 80.
Shên-hsien Kang-chien, 59, 159, 184.
Shê-li-fu, 189, 256.
Shê-mo-têng. See Matanga.
Shên (Gods), 78, 198.
Shêng-wên Yüan-chio, 116.
Shên-kuang, 193.
Shenpu, 65,
Shensi, 284.
Shên-t'ung, 209.
She-wei, 114, 217.
Shih-chê, 268.
Shih-fang ts'ung-lin, 262, 263.
Shih-pa lo-han, 190.
Shih ta ti-tsŭ (Ten disciples), 189.
Shining Religion, The, 107, 108, 309.
Shinran, 132, 133.
Shinran School (Shin-Shu), 24, 132.
Ship of mercy, The, 147.
Ship of salvation, 283.
Shou pi-ch'iu-chieh, 243.

INDEX

Shou p'u-sa-chieh, 244.
Shou-tso, 269.
Shou-wu-chieh-ti, 241.
Shui-lu tao-chang, 99.
Siam, 42, 109, 110.
Sian, 89.
Sianfu, 10.
Siberia, 144.
Siddattha (Hsi-ta), 174.
Silla. *See* Hsinlo.
Sinologues, 3, 34, 36, 49, 55, 102, 107, 108, 184.
Sisterhoods, 264.
Skeleton, 290
Söderblom, Archbishop, 5.
Song of the Saints, 90.
Southern Sea, 182, 183.
Soothsayer, 294.
Spirit, The, 37, 179, 180, 186.
Spirit-worship, 172.
Srosh, 109.
Ssŭ-chu, 108.
Ssu-ma Chien, 10.
State religion, The, 305.
Stone tablets, 109.
Strong men, 154.
Studies in Japanese Buddhism, 53, 132.
Subhuti. *See* Hsü-p'u-t'i.
Su-chia, 229.
Sufists, The Persian, 41, 146.
Suicide, 288, 292.
Sui dynasty, 16.
Sukhavati Vyuha Sutra, The Great. *See* "Wu-liang-shou Ching."
Sukhavati Vyuha Sutra, The Samll. *Sse* "O-mi-t'o Ching."
Sulehuti, 222.
Sumana, 183.
Sun (Sun Wu-kung), 64 *ff.*
Sunday schools, 156.
Sung Shan, 192. 284.
Sung-ti, 83.
Sung-tzŭ Niang-niang, 184.
Sung-yün, 43.
Sun Yat-sen, 23.
Su-p'in-t'o, 191.
Shu-po-chia, 191.
Sutra Pitaka, 211.
Sutras, 13, 17, 29, 33, 40, 50, 52, 53, 54, 67, 81, 95, 106, 108, 114, 118, 128, 135, 141, 204, 205, 208, 212, 213, 215, 216, 218, 222, 223, 224, 261, 274, 277, 306, 307.

Su Tsung, 17.
Swastika (sin-in), 175.
Swinging House, 54, 214.
Symbolic character of images, 174.
Syncretism, 291, 310.
Systems of salvation, Survey, 47, 159, 204, 205, 282.
Szechwan, 182, 188, 285, 291, 292, 298.

Ta Ch'êng (Mahayana), 2.
Ta-chien. *See* Hui-nêng.
Ta-fan T'ien-shên, 194.
Ta-i (Big coat), 247, 273.
T'ai-hsü, 56, 108, 301, 302, 303, 309.
Taiping rebellion, The, 285.
Taipings, The, 290.
T'ai Shan, 82, 83, 250, 284.
Tai Tsung, 17.
Ta-jih-chiao. *See* Great Sun Religion.
Ta-jih Ching. *See* Great Sun Scripture, The.
Ta-liao, 268.
Ta-lin Ssŭ, 303.
Ta-man. *See* Hung-jên.
Ta-mo. *See* P'u-t'i-ta-mo.
Tang-chia-shih-fu, 271.
T'ang-chu, 267, 278, 279.
Tang dynasty, 16, 63, 75, 109.
Tang-lai Mi-lo Fu, 187.
Tang-tu, 119.
T'ang-yao, 268.
T'an-luan, 32, 131.
Tao, The, 129, 130, 163, 196, 197, 198.
Tao-ch'ang, 93, 131.
Tao-ch'o, 32, 131.
Tao-hsin or Ta-i, 193.
Tao-jên, 268.
Taoism, 9, 14, 19, 32, 60, 131, 163.
Taoist gods (Yü-ti), 59, 64, 65, 69, 173, 184.
Taoist heaven, 74.
Taoists, 18, 19, 59, 60, 63, 129, 130, 131, 284, 305.
Tao-li T'ien, 79, 80, 124, 125, 208.
Tao-ming, 111.
Tao-shih, 10.
Tao-yüan, 310.
Ta-p'an-chiao, 152, 155.
Ta Pan Jo Ching (Mahapragnaparamita Sutra), 52, 224.

[327]

INDEX

Ta-pan Ts'ai-shên, 194.
Ta-pei-ch'an, 223.
Ta-shih-chih, 2, 39, 104, 131, 161, 185, 201, 218.
Ta-tê, 108.
Tathagata, 36, 38, 39, 124, 127, 174, 205.
Ta-tien, 253.
Ta-tso, 152.
Tat'ung, 110.
Temples:
  Pai-ma Ssŭ, 12.
  Ch'ien Ssŭ or P'u-chi Ssŭ, 254, 289.
  Fa-yu Ssŭ, 289.
  Fu-ting Shan, 289.
  Hsi Shan Chieh-t'ai Ssŭ, 235.
  Lama Temple, 20.
  Ling Wu Fu Leo, 60.
  Ling-yin Ssŭ, 254.
  Pai-sui Kung, 290.
  Ta-lin Ssŭ, 303.
  Tung-yai Ssŭ, 290.
Temple association, 264.
Temple buildings, 264 *ff*.
Temple Halls, 161, 172, 269, 272, 276, 286.
Thanksgiving, Act of, 294.
Theatrical performances, 98, 144.
Thomas, St., 193.
Three Great Values, 27, 117, 126, 137, 197, 198.
T'i, 201.
Tiao hsiang, 173.
Tibet, 3, 4, 19, 20, 28, 33, 45, 171, 173, 291, 292.
Tibetan, 185.
Tibetan Lamas, 293.
T'ieh-wei Shan, 82, 122.
T'ien (Heaven), 238.
T'ien Chu (God), 56, 61.
T'ien-chu (India), 9.
T'ien-chu huei (Catholic Church, The), 158.
T'ien-jen (Heavenly men), 78, 80.
T'ien-ning Ssŭ, 262, 263.
T'ien-t'ai (inspiring scriptures), 282.
T'ien-t'ai Shan, 48, 55, 285, 291.
T'ien-t'ai Tsung (T'ien-t'ai School), 49, 50, 52, 53, 54, 55, 106, 282, 306.
T'ien-tao (The Heavenly Way), 78.
T'ien-wang, 194, 195.
Ti-huang (district god), 84.

Ti-huang Miao, 84, 154.
Ting-ch'ih-tsai, 196.
Ting Fu-pao, Dr., 213, 214, 263.
Ti-shih, 80, 82, 194, 195.
Ti-shih Tsun-shên, 194.
Ti-ts'ang, 94, 100, 101, 105, 109, 111, 112, 113, 114, 118, 119, 120, 121, 122, 124, 188, 223, 252, 255, 289, 290.
Ti-ts'ang Pên-yüan Ching, 118, 223.
Tokyo, 212.
To-lieh, 44.
Tou-shuai, 71.
To-wên T'ien-wang, 194, 195, 252.
Trade Caravans, 10.
Translation, 12, 13.
Translation School, 306.
Transmigration, 34, 35, 77, 81, 86, 116, 120, 124, 143, 251, 281.
Travellers' guide, A, 297.
Trigram, The heavenly, 61.
Trikaya, 106, 126, 197.
Trinity, The (Christian), 37, 199.
Tripitaka, 4, 10, 17, 20, 43, 118, 143, 203 *f*., 211, 213, 256, 257, 290.
Triratna, 253.
Truth, Servants of, 164.
Tsa (Miscellaneous), 207.
Tsai-li-mên, 310.
Ts'ang-ching-lou (Ts'ang-shu-lou), 213, 256.
Ts'ao-tung, 308.
Tsêng-ch'ang T'ien-wang, 194, 195, 252.
Tsia-chia-jên, 228.
Tso Kung-fu, 282.
Tsun-chêng, 240.
Tsung. *See* Schools, 306, 307, 308.
Tsung-mên, 307.
Tsu-shih (patriarchs), 46.
Tsu-shih t'ang, 193, 256.
Tsu-t'ing Chieh T'ai, 236.
Tu-chien (manager), 266.
Tu chung-shêng t'o-li k'u-hai, 93.
T'ui-chu ho-shang, 266.
Tunes, 274, 275.
Tunes of Woe (Pei-t'iao), 274.
T'ung-chiao, 306.
Tung-lin (Monastery), 130.
T'ung-shan Shê, 310.
Tung-tan (East party), 269, 272, 274.
Tung-yü, 82, 83, 94.
Turkestan, 30, 204.
Turks, 10.

INDEX

Tu shih, 83.
Tutelary deities, See Ch'ieh Lan.
T'u-ti (local gods), 84, 94, 173.
T'u-ti miao, 84, 154.
Tz'ǔ-ên Tsung, 307.
Tzǔ-hsien, 196.
Tzǔ-sun ts'ung lin, 263.

Ullambana Sutra. See Yü-lan-p'ên Ching.
Ultra-evangelicals, 149.
Unio Mystica, 146.
Union, Cosmic, 175, 310.
United States, The, 253.
Upali. *See* Yu-p'u-li.
Upavasatha. *See* Ch'an-hui-wên.

Vagjis, 11.
Vajra Bidhi (Chin-kang Chih), 89.
Vairocana, 55, 105, 106, 107, 120, 178, 198, 200, 213, 255, 277, 309.
Vaisali, 27.
Vasubandhu, 29, 31, 128.
Vedas, 39, 78.
Vegetarianism, 13, 91, 113, 165, 167, 228.
Vegetarian food, 295.
Vegetarian groups, 141.
Vegetarian restaurants, 288.
Vehicles:
    First (Hinayana), 51.
    Great (Mahayana), 1, 28, 42.
    Little (Hinayana), 2.
Venus, 69.
Vidyama-trasiddhi. *See* "Wei-shih Lun."
Vinaya, 204.
Virgin Mary, 56, 57, 58, 59, 61, 62, 159, 184.
Vows (Oaths, promises), 14, 15, 19, 39, 40, 79, 113, 117, 118, 120, 142, 152, 177, 180, 209, 217, 221, 225, 242, 244, 245, 261, 274, 294.

Wan-fa Kuei Hsin Lu, 159.
Wan-fu T'ang, 179, 256.
Wan Li, Emperor, 290, 293.
Wan-tzǔ. *See* Swastika.
War, The Great, 24, 98.
Warriors, 172.
Wei dynasty, 14
Wei-lo, 278.

Wei-miao, 209.
Wei-mo-ching, 225.
Wei-na(Instructor), 152, 237, 267, 272.
Wei Shan, 293.
Wei-shih Lun, 225, 307.
Wei-t'o, 194, 196, 253, 254.
Wei-t'o Tien, 253.
Wei-t'o T'ien-tzǔ, 252.
Wei-t'o Tsun-shên, 194.
Wei-tu, 119.
Wei-yang, 308.
Wên-ch'ang, 195.
Wên-shu. See Manjusri, 119, 188, 201, 202, 208, 224, 252, 291.
Western Paradise, 2, 39, 73, 75, 81, 128, 139, 145, 149, 169, 176, 199, 217, 223, 288.
Western writers, 286.
West Lake (Hsi Hu), 293.
Westman, Professor K. N., 30.
Wheel of life (lun-huei), 78, 200.
White Lotus Ode, The, 135 *ff.*
Widows, 160.
Wisdom, Books of, 224, 225.
Wisdom, Hall of, 257.
Women:
    Miseries of, 177.
    Social condition of, 159 *ff.*
    Who become nuns, 234.
    Work among, 265.
Wooden blocks, 19, 211, 213, 257.
Wooden fish (mu-yü), 272.
World Conference for Buddhism, 303.
World-Honoured One, The, 208, 216.
Worlds, The ten, 225.
Worship, 1, 5, 14, 17, 232, 234, 250, 254, 259, 264, 268, 269, 284, 286, 287, 288, 295.
Worship, Daily, 272 *ff.*
Wu, Emperor, 10.
Wuchang, 56, 301, 302.
Wu-chien Ti-yü, 82.
Wu-cho, or Wu-shih, 124.
Wu-han, 301, 302.
Wu-kuan, 83.
Wu-liang, 79.
Wu-liang-shou Ching, 33, 40, 53, 141, 216.
Wu-liang-shou Kuang, 40.
Wu-shan Shê, 310.
Wu-shê-chieh, 80.
Wu-t'ai Shan, 188, 250, 285, 288, 291, 307.

[329]

INDEX

Wu Tsung, 17, 18, 20.
Wu-yü (Five sacred places), 284.

Yama, 83, 254.
Yamen, 85, 260.
Yangchow, 263.
Yang-lao-yüan, 258.
Yang, Mr., 303.
Yangtze River, 110, 275.
Yangtze Valley, 46, 192, 289, 303.
Yao-shih Ching, 176, 221.
Yao-shih Fu, 151, 176, 177, 178, 199, 201, 221, 222, 254.
Yao-shih Têng, 178.
Yeh-ch'a, 85, 169.
Yeh-ho-shang, 233, 286.
Yen-lo, 82, 83, 94, 194, 195, 254.
Yen-lo T'ien-tzǔ, 194, 195.
Yin-chieh-t'o, 191.
Yin-kuang, 189.
Ying (Incarnation), 180.
Yin-yang Ssu, 95.
Yoga, 205.
Yogacharya School, 89.
Young Men's Buddhist Association, 303.
Yüan Chiao, 306.
Yüan Chio, 162, 189.
Yüan Dynasty, 207.

Yüan-fu, 38.
Yüan-kuang. *See* Nimbus.
Yuan Shih-kai, 305.
Yüan-yin, 301.
Yü-chieh, 80.
Yü-chia-shih ti Lun, 108.
Yüeh-chih, 11.
Yü-chia yen-k'ou, 87, 223.
Yüeh-chung or Shih-chê, 267.
Yüeh-kung Tsun-t'ien, 194.
Yü Lan Hui (Land and Sea Association), 76.
Yü-lan-p'ên Ching, 90, 92, 96, 97, 114, 123.
Yu-ming Chiao-chu (Master of the Kingdom of Death), 112.
Yu-ming Chung, 100.
Yün-ch'i, 138.
Yung, 201.
Yung Chêng, 212.
Yung-kung, 248, 281, 282.
Yung Lo, 212.
Yün-mên, 308.
Yu-p'u-li, 189, 198, 256.
Yü-ti, 69, 74.
Yü-tao, 130.

Zoroaster, 33, 109.
Zoroastrians, 163.

[330]